GEORGE SCHARF

FROM THE REGENCY STREET TO THE MODERN METROPOLIS

An exhibition curated by
Jerzy J Kierkuć-Bieliński

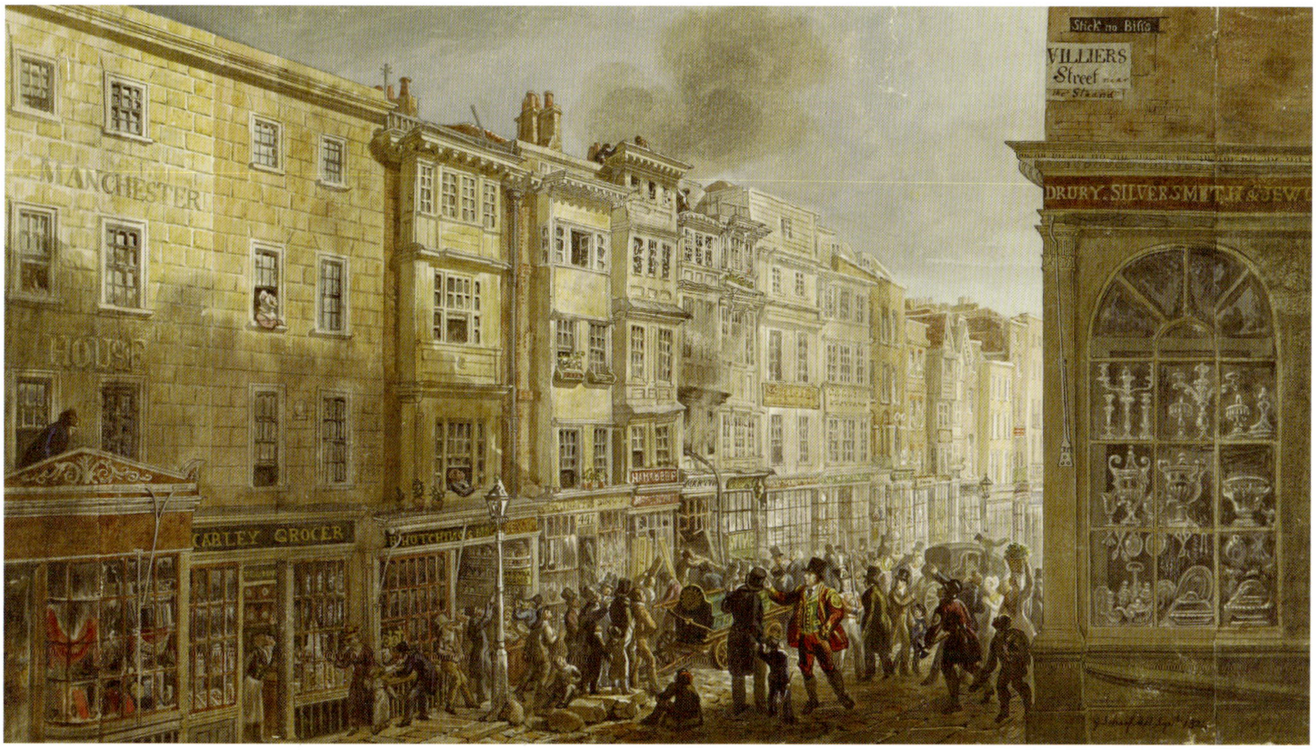

THE SOANE GALLERY 2009

Apax PARTNERS

THE BRITISH MUSEUM

This exhibition has been sponsored by Apax Partners and has been organised in partnership with the British Museum

George Scharf: From the Regency Street to the Modern Metropolis
An exhibition at Sir John Soane's Museum, London, 20 March to 6 June 2009

Published in Great Britain 2009
Reg. Charity No. 313609

ISBN 978-0-9558762-2-6

The Trustees of Sir John Soane's Museum would like to thank the benefactors, patrons and sponsors whose annual donations support the Museum's exhibitions, education and conservation programmes

Robert Adam Architects Whitney Agnew Elizabeth Angelicoussis Zeev Aram & Aram Store Catherine Armitage Philip and Pamela Baldwin Ian Barby Sir William and Lady Benyon Anton and Lisa Bilton Peter Bloxham David and Molly Borthwick Miel de Botton Aynsley Eleanor Bron Richard Broyd The Hon Mrs Buchan of Auchmacoy Peter and Sally Cadbury Dominic and Sarah Caldecott Lista M Cannon Graham Chase George Clarke Ted and Tamsin Clive David and Kay Coke Alice Coptcoat Harriet Cullen Warren Davis Mr and Mrs Bruce Dawson David Dimbleby & Belinda Giles Marina and Frank Donald Tony and Margaret Dorey Paul Doyle Peter and Marya Egerton-Warburton Ben and Rachel Elwes Giles Elwood Amelia Fawcett Gerry and Harry Fentum Muriel Fletcher Christopher Forbes The Hon. Sir Rocco Forte Mark R Franklin William Fuller Richard & Claire Gapper Christopher Gibbs Alison Gowman Veere Grenney Richard and Sheila Griffiths Karl Grossfield Lucy and Lawrence Guffey Charles and Kaaren Hale Linda and Philip Harley Katrin and Christoph Henkel Philip Hewat-Jaboor Frances and David Hickman Michael and Beatrice Hoare Niall Hobhouse Stephen and Felice Hodges Dr Carol Høgel James and Beatrice Hollond Della Howard Simon Hurst John and Rowena Jackson Lisa Jardine Mr and Mrs Konstantin Kagalovsky Donald & Jeanne Kahn Danny and Gry Katz James Kessler Mervyn King Laurence Kinney Norman A. Kurland Jacky Lambert George Laurence Victoria Legge-Bourke Diane Levene Oscar and Margaret Lewisohn Martin and Beatriz Lutyens Lulu and Charlie Lytle Sir Richard MacCormac Sir David and Lady Manning Rick Mather Christopher and Henrietta McCall Katherine McCormick Joan Meyer Richard and Rosemary Millar John W Murray Louise & Andrew Nason Sir Philip and Lady Naylor-Leyland Maureen and Francis Nicholls Adrian and Jennifer O'Carroll Amicia and Richard Oldfield Michael and Helen Palin William & Vanessa Parker James Perkins David Perry Hugh Petter Liz Philips Lord and Lady Phillimore The Hon Mrs Olga Polizzi Basil and Maria Postan Clive Potter and Harry Lee Robin and Anne Purchas Dr Lisbet Rausing and Professor Peter Baldwin Nicola Reed Janine Rensch Margaret and Tony Richardson Leopold de Rothschild Charles Rutherfoord Alex and Elinor Sainsbury The Marquess and Marchioness of Salisbury Gigi and William Salomon Ian and Wendy Sampson Mr C B Saxton Penny Shankar Mr and Mrs John Sharman Peter Shepherd and Keith Day James and Shirley Sherwood Alexandra Shulman George Saumarez Smith Shaun Springer Oliver and Sally Stocken Aidan Mortimer Alan & Ciannait Tait Mr & Mrs Jeremy Taylor Mrs A J M Teacher Andrew Templeton Susie Thomson Tony and Trish Trahar Bill and Susie Tyne Frederick and Kathryn Uhde Anthony Vernon Robin Vousden Ludovic and Camilla de Walden Mr and The Hon. Mrs Wallop Richard White Sir Christopher White Michael and Jane Wilson Rosemary Woodward Sir Peregrine and Lady Worsthorne Jonathan Zimmerman and Anne Feeley

LIFE PATRONS

Primrose Arnander Debby and James Brice The Hon.Elizabeth Cayzer Mirabel and Hugh Cecil Gisela Gledhill Dr Martin Halusa Deirdre J Hopkins John & Virginia Murray The Lord and Lady Rothschild Mrs Coral Samuel

For information on exhibition sponsorship and how to support the Museum as an individual Patron or through a company, trust or foundation please contact the Development Director: Mike Nicholson 020 7440 4241 mnicholson@soane.org.uk

Designed and typeset in Albertina by Libanus Press, Marlborough *Printed by Hampton Printing (Bristol) Ltd*
Front cover: Cat. 45. The Westminster Dairy in the Quadrant, Regent Street, near Piccadilly Circus (detail)
Back cover: Cat. 60. Group of men fitting and laying gas pipes

Sir John Soane's Museum, 13 Lincoln's Inn Fields, London WC2A 3BP Tel: 020 7405 2107 www.soane.org

CONTENTS

DIRECTOR'S FOREWORD

I have known and loved the work of George Scharf ever since being sent to the British Museum to look at a strange drawing of what looked like a heap of rocks surmounted by various dejected-looking exotic birds and animals. I was interested in menageries, and this, I later discovered, was Dr Joshua Brooke's famous *Vivarium* in Blenheim (now Ramillies) Street, just south of Oxford Street – a strange eyecatcher designed to lure people into his famous anatomical museum as well, as a 'larder' of living subjects for his experiments. This rare image of an early nineteenth-century menagerie is a good example of Scharf's sharp-eyed observation of the curiosities that abounded in the streets of Regency London. How wonderful then that it should turn out that Soane owned a copy of the lithograph that was made from the drawing and that a letter survives in Soane's archive from Brookes himself, desperately trying to sell the strange edifice – the Gibraltarian rocks, its avian residents and even the nearby 'chapel' made from whalebones – to John Soane for his Museum. What a feature it would have made in the New Court, with its vulture and trickling marble crocodile head!

How appropriate it is that an exhibition on the London drawings of George Scharf is being held at this time. Scharf came to this country from his native Bavaria in the aftermath of the Napoleonic Wars, and, in many respects, it is with the eye of an 'outsider' that he explored the city which would become his new home. The architecture, street scenes, clothes and customs that he recorded in his drawings of London all demonstrate the keenness of observation that was the result of being confronted by a foreign but nevertheless exciting metropolis. So often the outsider sees things we take for granted – witness Sir Nikolaus Pevsner's *The Buildings of England* series or Steen Eiler Rasmussen's revelatory book *London: The Unique City* (1967) – so George Scharf's recording pencil deserves to be better known and celebrated.

The London that he came to was a city of changing demographics – as it is today. The industrial revolution swelled the population of the city as it attracted those in search of employment. It was also a city whose skyline was changing dramatically. New landmark buildings, such as John Soane's Bank of England or Charles Barry and Augustus Welby Pugin's new Palace of Westminster, were all documented by Scharf. London was also a centre for scientific and technological innovation and even if it has lost this edge to other world metropoli, it is still a centre for world media and publication – fields which developed in the early nineteenth century with the development of the lithographic printing process of which Scharf was an early exponent in this country. However, the period of Scharf's arrival in London also witnessed an economic recession. This gives his records of ordinary Londoners' lives a special resonance today.

The majority of the drawings for this exhibition have been generously lent by the Department of Prints and Drawings of the British Museum. Sir John Soane's Museum prides itself on being the second oldest National Museum in the capital after the British Museum, and the opening up of the collections of both institutions to a wider, public audience fell within this era. The Soane was transformed into a public museum by an Act Parliament in 1833, while, from 1837 onwards, the British Museum began opening during public holidays in order to allow ordinary, working Londoners the opportunity to view its collections.

Scharf took advantage of this new accessibility. Very familiar with the British Museum, he drew the building and its holdings of antiquities and, as a draughtsman and printmaker, visited the Department of Prints and Drawings. A large part of his drawings entered its collection just two years after his death, the Museum showing great foresight in purchasing these works from his widow. Scharf also visited – but sadly never drew – the Soane and even tried to sell one of his paintings to Sir John Soane. It is appropriate then that the figure of Scharf and this exhibition links the two Museums.

Particular thanks are due to the staff of the Department of Prints and Drawings of the British Museum for their generous co-operation, especially Anthony Griffiths, Kim Sloan, Sheila O'Connell and Philippa Kirkham. Agata Rutkowska was hugely helpful over the photographic arrangements. Thanks too to Mrs Valerie Jackson Harris, who lent several fascinating items of ephemera from the collection of her late husband, Peter Jackson. Peter was the first historian of Scharf, and his book *George Scharf's London: Sketches and watercolours of a changing city, 1820–50* – long out of print – has up until now been the only publication devoted to his work. Our gratitude too to Simon Chaplin of the Royal College of Surgeons, and Malcolm Hay of the Palace of Westminster for lending precious and rarely-seen Scharf watercolours from their own collections. This exhibition has been curated for the Soane Museum by our Exhibitions Curator, Jerzy Kierkuć-Bieliński, with the considerable assistance of the Museum's Archivist, Sue Palmer and Caroline Arscott who both contributed essays to his catalogue. Their enthusiasm for Scharf is contagious; Helen Dorey, Lucetta Johnson, Margaret Schuelein and Jane Bush also helped in many ways.

TIM KNOX

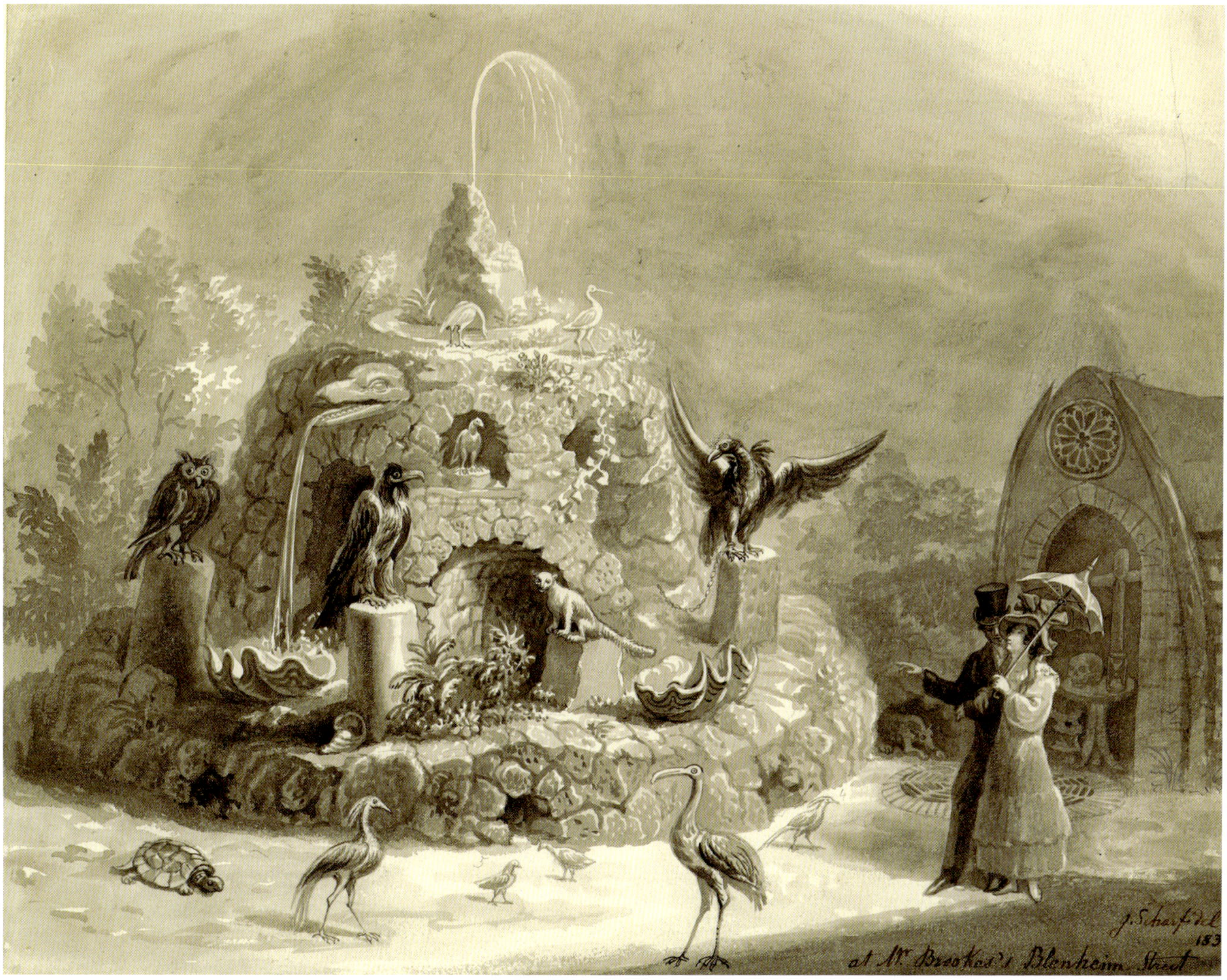

Cat. 35. A fountain of rock arches and live animals, exhibited at Joshua Brookes' Museum, Blenheim Street (now Ramillies Street)

INTRODUCTION

One of the first drawings that I saw by George Scharf was of Fleet Street showing the church of St Dunstan-in-the-West just before demolition. This has a particular immediacy for me. It was at 32 Fleet Street opposite St Dunstan's that the publishing House of John Murray was founded in 1768 and it was here, in St Dunstan's, that the Murray family worshipped. In 1812 on the success of Byron's *Childe Harold* my ancestor moved from Fleet Street to 50 Albemarle Street, just off Piccadilly in aristocratic Mayfair – and it is here that I still work. From their home in Albemarle Street my ancestors would have witnessed the great changes to London that George Scharf marvellously records. So when I look at his drawings I can imagine myself stepping out into Albemarle Street, watching the stage-coach move west down Piccadilly, just as Scharf drew it, piled high with passengers, possessions and even livestock. I might then move east to watch hundreds of squalid houses and narrow streets being swept away to make room for Regent Street that was being cut through Soho to Nash's design. Some years later, in the distance to the south, I might catch sight of smoke from the great fire that consumed the Houses of Parliament. When I started working in London I longed to discover more about this extraordinary visual chronicler of London and so during lunch hours I would follow in his footsteps as best I could. Scharf's links with my family often surprised me. His drawing of the building of the special gallery at the new British Museum to house the Lycian Marbles discovered by Charles Fellows would have been observed by my ancestor who was Fellow's publisher. Scharf also illustrated some of the works of Charles Darwin, another John Murray author, and his son George Scharf Jnr was one of Murray's important illustrators.

The publication by John Murray in 1987 of *George Scharf's London* was a revelation to all London lovers. Whereas Tallis's *London Street Views* (1838–1840) show accurate elevations and Shepherd's *Metropolitan Improvements* are static architectural illustrations, Scharf's drawings can be seen as an early ciné film with people bustling about their business, buildings being put up and pulled down, pulleys creaking, carts groaning – everything acutely observed. Mayhew's classic *London Labour and the London Poor* with its illustrations, based on daguerreotypes, of street traders and low life, lacks the immediacy of Scharf's drawings. Also the Shepherd family's views of London and London life in the first half of the century rarely come up to Scharf's standard.

George Scharf catches London during one of its great periods of transition from Regency to Imperial. He arrives on the scene at this vital moment in London's history. The Houses of Parliament are burning down, Trafalgar Square is about to be carved out clearing the west side of St Martin's Lane and across King's Mews, and Wilkins' National Gallery is about to rise up to the north. Shaftesbury Avenue, cutting a swathe through Soho, lies in the future as do the great museums of Kensington and the Albert Hall, but the remains of old London Bridge are being swept away and John Rennie's new bridge (which was sold to the USA in the twentieth century) is seen being built. The Prince Regent's eye-catching Carlton House has just been pulled down and Carlton House Terrace is in the process of construction. Scharf records all this activity in his thousands of sketches.

To me, Scharf's great contribution is the way he encourages us to use our eyes. He is one of three people who taught me the thrill of 'looking' and the riches of observation. The other two are Thomas Sharp, whose *Town and Townscape* became a classic, and John Betjeman, who took me on walks round Mayfair and Smithfield. John Betjeman then lived in Cloth Fair just beside St Bartholomew-the-Great and Scharf would certainly still have recognised this court. Even today as you wander round London, you can catch glimpses of the early nineteenth century. Behind many of the busiest thoroughfares you find courts and alleys that have changed little over the last 150 years. I often turn away from the roar of traffic at the west end of Pall Mall and step into Crown Passage. Here you immediately enter Scharf's world with the eighteenth-century houses facing each other across this narrow passage and the small shops doing good business below. It is an escape from the twenty-first century outside. However, if you have studied Scharf's drawings of the opening out of St Martin's Lane to create Trafalgar Square you will soon imagine this oasis of the eighteenth century being swept away to produce perhaps a new square. You will imagine the props (that appear in so many of his drawings) going up to support the buildings as they are dismantled with carts being filled to take away the rubble and people scurrying about.

And then again if you turn south off Brook Street just by Handel House you enter Horse Shoe Yard that runs into Lancashire Court. Although rather more polished than Crown Court, it still carries me back to Scharf. Further east in the City one of my favourite courts was Angel Court just off Throgmorton Street where there was an old apothecary's shop with a bow-fronted window that must have dated back to the eighteenth century and on the glass was etched 'Jelly for Invalids'. Sadly I got there too late to partake of it. This has now vanished.

Much of central London today is late Victorian and Edwardian and the scale is very different from Scharf's day. But if you have learnt your lesson you will find there is even more variety, that is if you keep you eyes above street level away from all the modern shop fronts. All the different styles of building are packed in together offering great riches and more often than not an eighteenth- or early nineteenth-century brick building will stand out, a gallant survivor from Scharf's days and sometimes a survivor from a Scharf drawing.

Scharf gives us such a vivid view of the buildings that existed before they were swept away in the great expansion of London and its booming prosperity that demanded prestige buildings like the Foreign Office, South Africa House and The Aldwych. This is why he is so important. But he offers us more than architecture. If you look through his drawings you will see some very familiar scenes, roads being dug up to lay gas pipes or sewers causing as much confusion as today, scaffolding blocking footpaths, people going about their normal lives. Being a romantic, the one thing I miss today are all the street vendors and entertainers. These, Scharf illustrates with humanity. I feel I am actually watching them at work when looking at his drawings. There is one other aspect of Scharf's work that particularly appeals to me. He loves all forms of gadgetry and is intrigued by engineering. You can see exactly how the stonemason shapes his blocks, how the brickwork is built for the sewers, how cobbles are shaped and laid, how gas pipes are linked one to another and how railway cuttings are braced.

Finally, there is a moral to the study of George Scharf's work – great riches come from observing one's surroundings and above all in looking up.

JOHN MURRAY

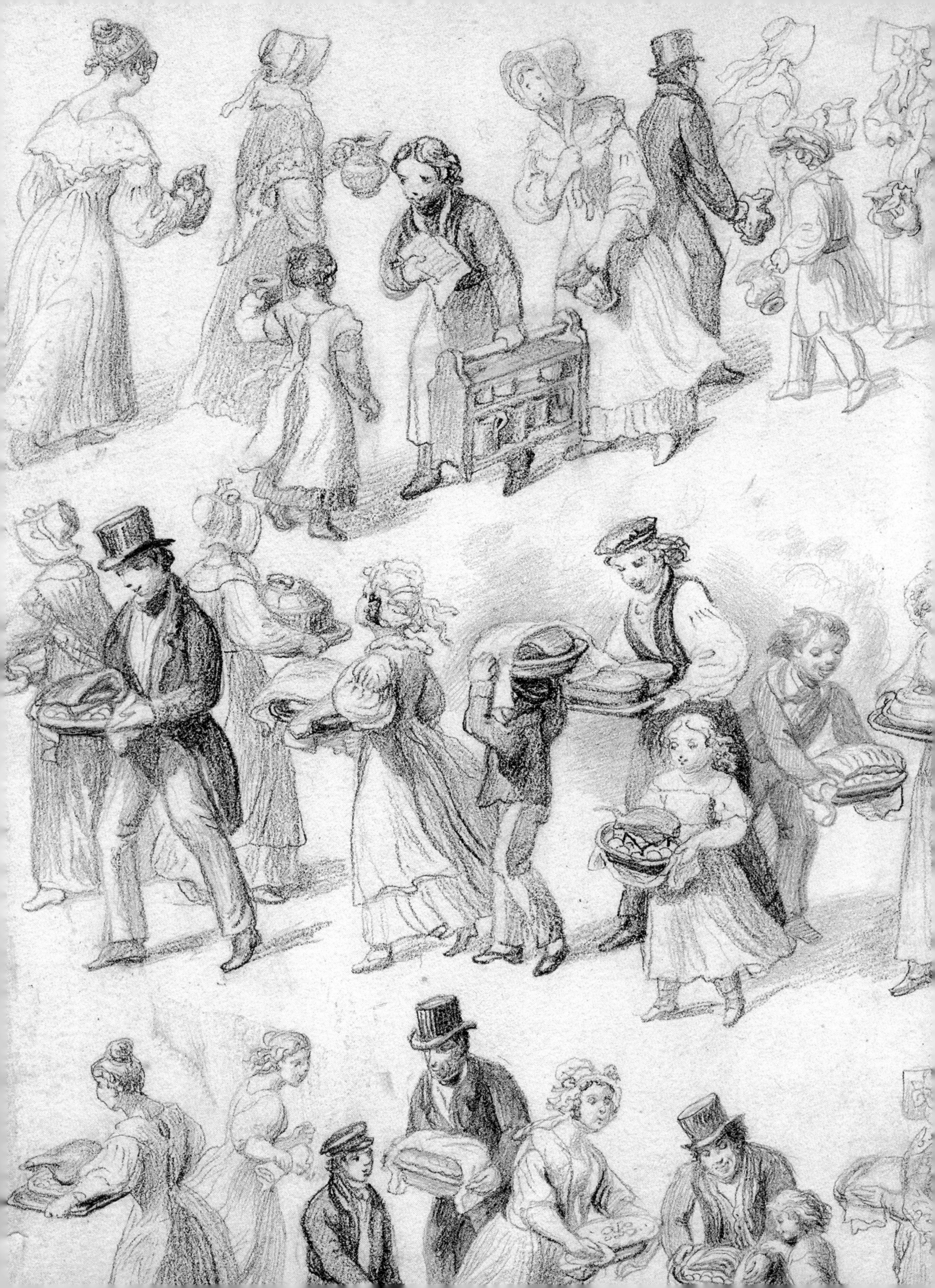

GEORGE SCHARF THE ELDER (1788–1860)

Jerzy J Kierkuć-Bieliński

His training and early years

Oh those, in whose country I have found a second home, who have let me find a living, a comfort, a happiness, ah and to crown it all, a dear little wife to share that happiness, as well as the occasional bitter [. . .] those, I say, in whose country I have found all that, and for which I am thankful, must forgive me, if I still give some preference to my native country; for not Bavaria alone, all Germany is alike the native soil of the Teutons, the ancient Saxons being part of the same race, and from whom so many English descend.[1]

These were the words George Johann Scharf the Elder wrote in his diary as he was crossing the Prussian border into his native Germany after an absence of nearly thirty years, which he had spent in London. They articulate the happiness of one who is returning to his native soil after so long a period away from his homeland, but also show some of the affection for his adopted home of England. For it was here, rather than in Germany, that he made his career as a professional lithographer, specialising in scientific subjects. However, his work as a printmaker is not primarily why Scharf is remembered today. Rather, it is for the series of drawings, watercolours and sketches of everyday London dating from the 1820s to the 1840s, for which he is distinguished. Spanning a twenty-year period, and created just as the new medium of photography was being developed, Scharf's images are of London as it changed from a late Georgian and Regency cityscape to that of the early modern Victorian city (a cityscape that still surrounds the inhabitants of London to this day). The pictures seem to bring to life the streets and inhabitants of what was the largest city on the globe. How different the London of this period must have seemed to Scharf's own small home town of Mainburg in Bavaria, just outside Munich, where he was born in 1788 on St George's Day (23 April).

Little is known with certainty of Scharf's early life and even for his later career there are few sources.[2] So much of his life will remain as anonymous as that of the countless Londoners that he sketched. It seems that his family were once prosperous; his parents were Andreas Scharf and Franziska *née* von Peffenhausen. They were described as 'trades people' whose business (what this was we do not know) had been ruined during the Napoleonic Wars, which swept Bavaria following its joining the Second Coalition in 1799.[3] However, Scharf also implies in his journals that his family at one point may have been more than just successful merchants. He claimed at least on one documented occasion that they were formerly Barons.[4] His mother's maiden name, prefixed with the German *von* would imply a status higher than that of a burgher. Whether the Scharfs at one time had been Barons is doubtful (he may have been referring to his mother's family); what is certain though is that his position in society as an artist (and one who, unfortunately, was not always successful) would always be precarious.

At the age of thirteen, in about 1801, Scharf left Mainburg and moved to the small village of Geisenfeld. It is possible that this was occasioned by the Austrian and later French occupation of the part of Bavaria where Mainburg is located. Scharf as a young boy witnessed the French blowing up the fortress of Ingolstadt in 1800 and was nearly struck by flying masonry as he recalled in later life.[5] It was at Geisenfeld that Scharf's artistic career can be seen to have begun. A year after moving to the village he is recorded as taking drawing lessons with one Herr Kiermeyer. Scharf and Herr Kiermeyer, an obscure artist who specialised in religious paintings,[6] would purchase their drawing and painting materials, such as '. . . colours, varnish and goldleaf . . .' locally in Geisenfeld.[7] Scharf was an adept pupil and in 1805 he enrolled as a student at the *Maler-und Bildhauerakademie*, in Munich, which would later become the *Königliche Akademie der Bildenden Künste München* in 1808 following the declaration of the Kingdom of Bavaria by Napoleon in 1806. At the *Akademie*, Scharf mainly studied the old master works in the *Alte Pinakhotek*, whose already impressive holdings had been swelled by the transfer of many paintings from collections in Düsseldorf, Mannheim and Zweibrücken as a result of the turmoil of the Napoleonic wars. He later claimed that amongst his fellow students were several figures who would become quite significant, in particular the noted architect Friedrich von Gärtner (1791–1847), Albrecht Adam (1786–1862), who specialised in battle scenes and became court painter to

Cat. 11. Dinner Time, Sunday, One O'Clock (detail)

Prince Eugene Beauharnais, and the lithographer Johann Nepomuk Strixner (1782–1855).[8] Although next to nothing is known of his early student work,[9] he came to the notice of Maximilian Joseph (1756–1825), proclaimed the first King of Bavaria in 1806, who purchased a copy by Scharf of a portrait of Prince Eugene Beauharnais.[10] Scharf also specialised in painting portrait miniatures.[11] More importantly, though, for our understanding of the development of Scharf's career, Munich and the circle of professors who taught him at the *Akademie* were at the forefront of the development of lithography. Lithography in part explains how Scharf later found himself in the country of the 'ancient Saxons' as he would put it.[12]

In the late 1790s the Munich-based Aloys Senefelder (1771–1834) developed a new printmaking technique, which relied on the mutually-repellent chemical properties of grease and water, which also responded to the growing demand in the late eighteenth century for prints that could be cheaply and quickly made and that readily reproduced the painterly effects that intaglio printmaking was unable to do.[13] Senefelder also saw the industrial potential of the new technique, particularly as a way of reproducing patterns or designs on textiles – especially calico.[14] And of course the leading industrial producer of cloth in Europe was Britain. In light of this, Senefelder, in the company of Philipp André (dates unknown), visited London from late 1800 to the summer of 1801 and although his attempts to apply the lithographic technique to textile production did not succeed, he did take out a patent in London in 1801. Philipp André was the brother of Johann Anton André (1775–1842), who with the help of Senefelder had set up one of the first lithographic presses.[15] In spite of the failure to apply the lithographic technique to the production of calico, the potential of setting up a lithographic press in London had been made clear to both brothers. Very shortly after Senefelder obtained his English patent, he was persuaded to sign it over to the Andrés. And shortly after that, Philipp opened a lithographic press in London – the first outside Germany.[16] What is significant is that the London press overtook, in many respects, the initiative in applying the new printing technology from the German presses. It was in the field of the artist's print that this was certainly the case where the first examples of this genre were printed in Britain.[17] Early examples of artists' lithographs include Benjamin West's 'John the Baptist' and 'Angel of the Resurrection' both of 1801 or Henry Fuseli's 1802/03 print: 'A Woman Sitting by the Window'. Thomas Barker of Bath (1769–1847) would produce early genre lithographs such as 'Rustic Figures' printed in 1802.[18] What is more, one of the first topographical lithographic albums would be published in London. In 1817 Charles Joseph Hullmandel (1789–1850), who had met Senefelder in Munich whilst on a sketching trip to Germany, produced *Twenty four views of Italy, Drawn from Nature and Engraved upon Stone*. Hullmandel would set up his own lithographic press in 1818, using equipment bought from Germany, and, as will be shown, he would become very important to Scharf (who, of course, would focus both upon lithography and topographical and genre subjects in his own work) both as a friend and a printer.[19] And Scharf was familiar with such artists' prints. He would later write in his journal of his admiration at having seen some of Fuseli's lithographs in the Library at the Royal College of Surgeons.[20]

In Munich, Scharf would have come into direct contact with the circle of Senefelder and the early lithographers through his Professor at the *Akademie* Joseph Hauber (1766–1834) who himself would teach Scharf the new printmaking techniques. Hauber contributed to the first significant collection of artists' prints to be published in Germany entitled *Lithographische Kunst Produckte*, 1805. This portfolio was published by an associate of Senefelder's and another early exponent of the medium – Joseph Mitterer. He had been taught the lithographic technique by Senefelder's brothers Theobald and Georg, who had taken over their brother's press. Thus, links between the artistic *milieu* of the *Maler-und Bildhauerakademie*, in Munich and the early lithographers in London can be discerned. It would not be too far-fetched to imagine that the young Scharf as a pupil of Hauber would be aware of the role of British printmakers in developing lithography as an artistic medium, rather than a purely reproductive and derivative one.

One other possible figure with whom Scharf may have had contact as a student and who could have had an impact upon the future development of his career, was Wilhelm von Kobell (1766–1855), a painter and printmaker who would later become Professor of landscape painting at the *Königliche Akademie der Bildenden Künste München*.[21] During the Napoleonic wars, Kobell was commissioned by Ludwig, Crown Prince of Bavaria (1786–1868), to paint large battle scenes, including those at Aspern-Essling and Wagram, which both took place in 1809. Scharf's own future work as a military artist and his interest in printmaking could be viewed in parallel with von Kobell's and, as a precocious twelve-year old lad, he had on one occasion had first-hand experience of the wars.

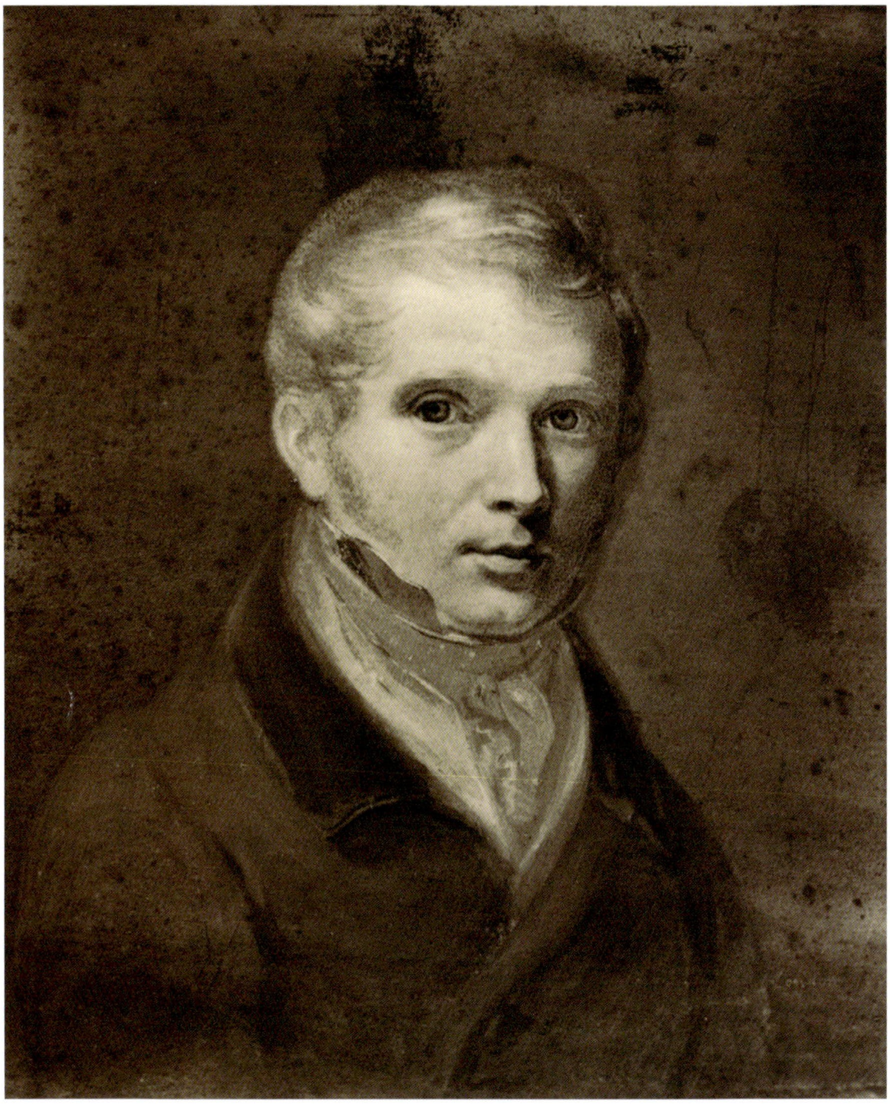

Fig. 1. George Johann Scharf,
by George Johann Scharf, miniature, *circa* 1816, RN38945, photograph National Portrait Gallery, London; unknown collection

Significantly, lithography also potentially had military applications.[22]

Scharf stayed at the *Königliche Akademie der Bildenden Künste München* until 1810, when he left Bavaria in order to pursue his work as a miniaturist. What had made him decide to leave the relative security of Munich? Perhaps his experiences of the siege of Ingolstadt had fired his young mind. Perhaps, as some academics have suggested, he had been in contact with artists such as von Kobell, who had realised the opportunities for commissions that the Wars had engendered. The Napoleonic Wars had created new patterns of patronage, particularly for a painter of small-scale portraits. The absences of many young men on the battlefields of Europe, for often lengthy periods, had resulted in the popularity of the portrait miniature as a portable and often personal way of commemorating a loved one.[23] Certainly Scharf was reaping the benefits of the conflict. But perhaps the reason is more prosaic. As he later observed in his journal, the number of artists coming out of the *Akademie* was too great for the nascent Bavarian (and German) art market. This made the pursuit of an artistic career more difficult there than in the other more economically developed countries of Europe, where art markets had long flourished, such as France or even Britain.[24] For an artist who had not made a great impact as a young man, in the way that perhaps his fellow students such as Gärtner had, leaving Munich in pursuit of lucrative commissions outside Bavaria opened up new economic possibilities.

He later recalled in his journal how he followed the armies of the French and of the Allies as they wheeled across the European continent. In 1812 he was in Cambrai, later moving possibly to Paris.[25] In 1813 he was in the Low Countries and was present at the Siege of Antwerp by the

Allies in early 1814.[26] Scharf, in a pragmatic manner, accepted commissions for portraits from officers on both sides of the conflict. Whilst at Verdun in 1811, apart from sketching the gates of the fortress, which when he visited it was full of British prisoners, he accepted commissions for several portraits including those of the interned British officers as well as members of the French garrison guarding them![27]

It was whilst Scharf was making his way to Antwerp that the course of his life changed radically. He stopped off at Michelin, which was then under Prussian occupation. Suddenly the Prussians were ordered to march on the forces of the French at Antwerp and lay siege to the town. Scharf was advised by one of the Prussian officers, a Colonel Reifs, to go to the British Headquarters.[28] There, Scharf enlisted in the British Army as a 'lieutenant of baggage' in the Engineers.[29] His experience of drawing fortifications, such as his sketches of the fortress at Verdun, has been given as one possible reason for his enlisting.[30] As a British Officer Scharf saw action at the decisive battle that would bring to a close the turmoil of the Napoleonic Wars – the Battle of Waterloo – and he joined his fellow British and Allied troops who were occupying Paris (see cat. 2).[31] Instead of returning home, as so many soldiers did after the cessation of hostilities, Scharf decided to move and settle in London. Perhaps, as one author has asserted, he had become entranced by the stories being told about London by other British officers – a metropolis far larger and affording far greater possibilities for excitement and employment than his native Mainburg or even Munich.[32] Certainly, he must have realised that, as soldiers were returning home, the market for portrait commissions was diminishing daily. However, it is equally likely that Scharf, through the connections he had made whilst a student of lithography (amongst other things) at the *Akademie*, was aware of the burgeoning market for lithography in London. As a relatively new technology and one that was totally dissimilar to the old intaglio techniques of print making, there was still a lack of experienced lithographers in Britain. What is more, there was a sizable German community in London. And so on New Year's Day 1816, he set out from Paris for London. The first thing he did when he arrived in Dover on 6 January was to take out his sketchbook and paint the white cliffs with Dover Castle standing sentinel and looking out towards the continent he had left (see cat. 4).

London

Having arrived in London, Scharf moved into a house at No. 3 St Martin's Lane in 1817. This area, just to the north-east of what would become Trafalgar Square, was associated with artists, and Scharf would have been familiar with such artists' supply shops as Allen's Colourman at No. 96 St Martin's Lane (see cat. 47). The house in which he lodged belonged to one Mary Hicks and Scharf would eventually marry her sister Elizabeth. They had two sons, George

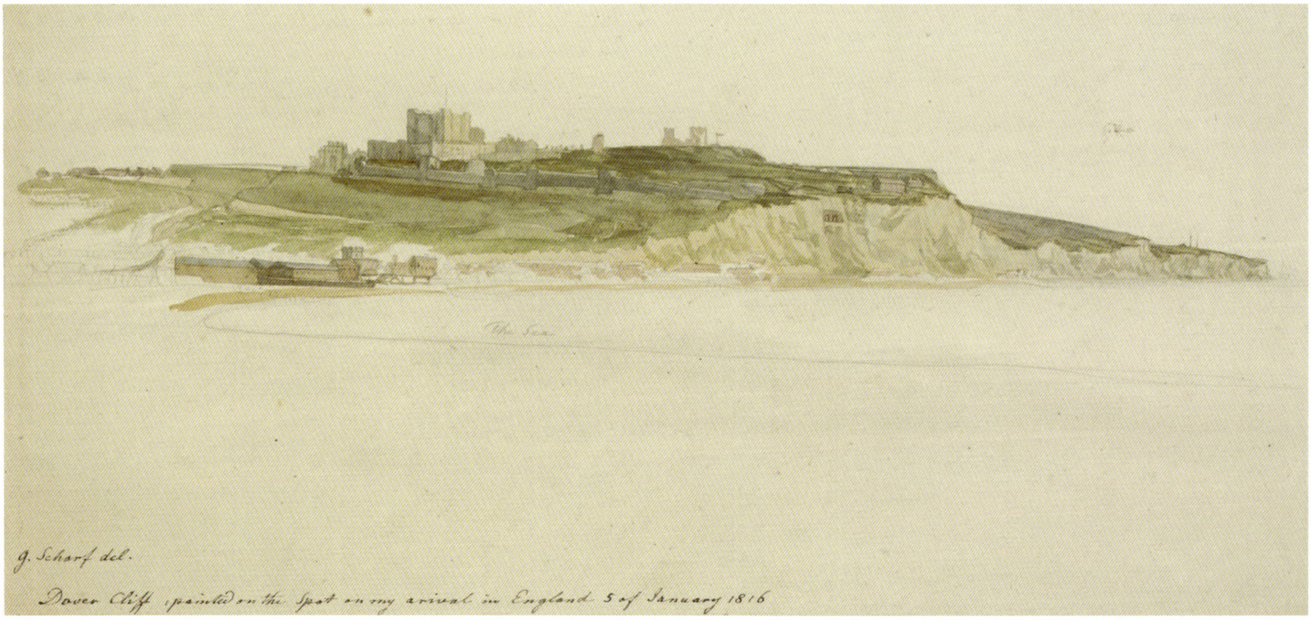

Cat. 4. Dover Castle

Scharf the Younger and Henry (see cats 6 and 8). Initially he tried to continue his work as a portrait painter, and it is possible that his self portrait, where Scharf has shown himself at the age of about twenty may have been painted in order to display his abilities (fig. 1). If so, it does not appear to have had the desired effect. Although he did exhibit three portraits at the Royal Academy in 1817 he does not appear to have received many commissions, if any, and he did not publically exhibit any other paintings until 1826.[33] After which he continued exhibiting at the Royal Academy from 1828 to 1837, then again in 1841 and finally from 1848 to 1850, similarly without great success.[34] His involvement with the New Watercolour Society, from 1833, proved slightly more fruitful – at least on a critical level. His large painting showing the 'The Ruins of the Late Houses of Parliament', 1835, (see cat. 56), was described in a review published in *The Atlas* as: '. . . most remarkable . . .', '. . . powerful and spirited . . .' and '. . . in all its bearings, perfect'.[35]

In the other aspect of his work – printmaking – he was more successful. After the initial burst of interest in lithography in Britain, following the establishment of a press in London by André and the development of the artist's lithographic print as a specific genre, lithography underwent a second flourishing in the period just when Scharf decided to move to London in 1816. Several new lithographic presses were established, including Moser and Harris. It was at the latter where the aforementioned Hullmandel published his *Twenty four Views of Italy*. Scharf would later work with Hullmandel as well as with Ackermann. Of these it would be Hullmandel who would forge the longest association with Scharf.[36] Amongst Scharf's lithographs printed by Hullmandel were: 'A View of the City of Bahia in the Brazils, South America', 1826, (BM 1862,1108.609); 'A Silver Table Service Presented to Major General Sir Lionel Smith . . .', 1830, (BM 1862,1108.620); 'Procession of Electors . . . from Blagdon and the North Marsh, District of East Somerset to the Polling Place at Axbridge . . .', 1832, (BM 1862,1108.559); 'University College School, London', 1833, (BM 1862,0614.748); 'View of the Great Chasm of the Axmouth Landslip, looking Westward, Reaping the Wheat', 1840, (BM 1862,1108.602) and 'A View of the Vivarium . . . in the Garden of Joshua Brookes Esq' (see cat. 36), 1830, (Sir John Soane's Museum 57/11/10).

Scharf and Politics

The London to which Scharf came in 1816 was a crucible for radical politics. In the past, writers have asserted that a political reading of Scharf's work or life would be problematical.[37] They have stated that there are no indications that he was in contact with any of the radical politicians or groups in London, particularly during the period 1816 to 1825 when the radicalisation of London politics was at its greatest. In fact, one writer states that he '. . . did not have any sympathies with their cause . . .', citing his lithograph of the coronation of George IV (see cat. 15) as evidence of his acquiescence with the political *status quo*.[38] The political subject matter of his drawings and printmaking has also been down played in the past. However, from 1816 to 1820 Scharf's early drawing and printmaking responded to particular aspects of London's political context.

Although it would lose this status to the burgeoning industrial cities of the north in the later part of the nineteenth century, the first quarter of that century would see London don the mantle of the centre of reformist politics in England. London was one of Britain's largest parliamentary constituencies in the first quarter of the nineteenth century with four MPs representing some 1,600,000 inhabitants in the period 1818 to 1820. The Boroughs of Westminster and of Southwark elected their own two MPs respectively.[39] In addition, London was the seat of British *national* politics, of the banking system and of the British press – and a highly politicised press at that.[40] This ensured that, in the first quarter of the nineteenth century at least, the average Londoner was more politically aware than the inhabitants of other parts of the country. The period 1816 to 1821 also saw a marked decline in the British economy following the end of the Napoleonic Wars. The period of conflict had seen London's artisan community heavily taxed to help the war effort. In addition, the raising of European tariffs closed the continental market to British goods (London being the main port for this maritime trade). With the cessation of hostilities, tax reform was directed in favour of the upper classes, and the lower-middle and artisan classes still bore the brunt of taxation. These were just the people who formed the subject matter of so many of Scharf's sketches and of whose class he was also seen as a member (see cats 26–32). However, this system of tax reform resulted in a further economic recession that lasted until the early 1820s.[41] Consequently, demand for political and economic reform began to grow. In 1817 Jeremy Bentham's 'Plan for Parliamentary Reform', which espoused a utilitarian approach to parliamentary reform and called for democratic representation based upon the judgements of the individual, became public.[42] Some MPs who represented London constituencies, such as Sir Francis Burdett, the MP for Westminster from 1807 to 1810 and again from 1818 to 1837, were early supporters of universal male suffrage. Burdett was described on one occasion as '. . . an implicit follower of Robespierre . . .', and his election to the House of Commons transformed Westminster into the centre of radical politics throughout Britain (see cat. 14).[43] Others organised themselves on what one would now term a 'grass-roots level'. Under the influence of the radical Robert Owen (1771–1858), who championed the idea of using small, self-supporting communities as a response to the challenges of urban industrialisation and the economic depression, a co-operative community, made up in large part of printers, was set up in Spa Fields, Islington (see cat. 53). It functioned from 1821 to 1824.

This call for reform also encompassed the question of religion and religious equality. Apart from his calls for universal suffrage, Burdett also championed Roman Catholic emancipation. The Test and Corporation Acts, which dated back to the seventeenth century, excluded Roman Catholics, non-conformists and non-Christians from holding public office. In 1828, through the campaigning of people like Burdett, these Acts were repealed. This was followed, in 1829, by the Catholic Relief Act which granted Catholics voting rights. Bentham also questioned religious authority as he saw this as being complicit with political and social authoritarianism and as curtailing free thinking. One of the most notorious cases of extreme anti-clericalism involved the setting fire to York Minster in 1829. Although probably mentally unstable, Jonathan Martin (1782–1838), the brother of the artist John Martin, was inspired in a dream to set fire to the building:

> I was told by the Lord that I was to destroy the Cathedral, an account of the clergy going to plays and balls, playing at cards, and drinking wine . . . the Lord showed me the vision of a dark and thick cloud to point out the propriety of setting the Cathedral on fire . . . I found the Lord determined to have me show this people a warning.[44]

Scharf was a Roman Catholic and attended the Bavarian Roman Catholic Chapel on Warwick Street.[45] However, just how orthodox he was in his faith is unclear. He sent his sons George and Henry to the non-denominational University College School, which had been opened in 1830

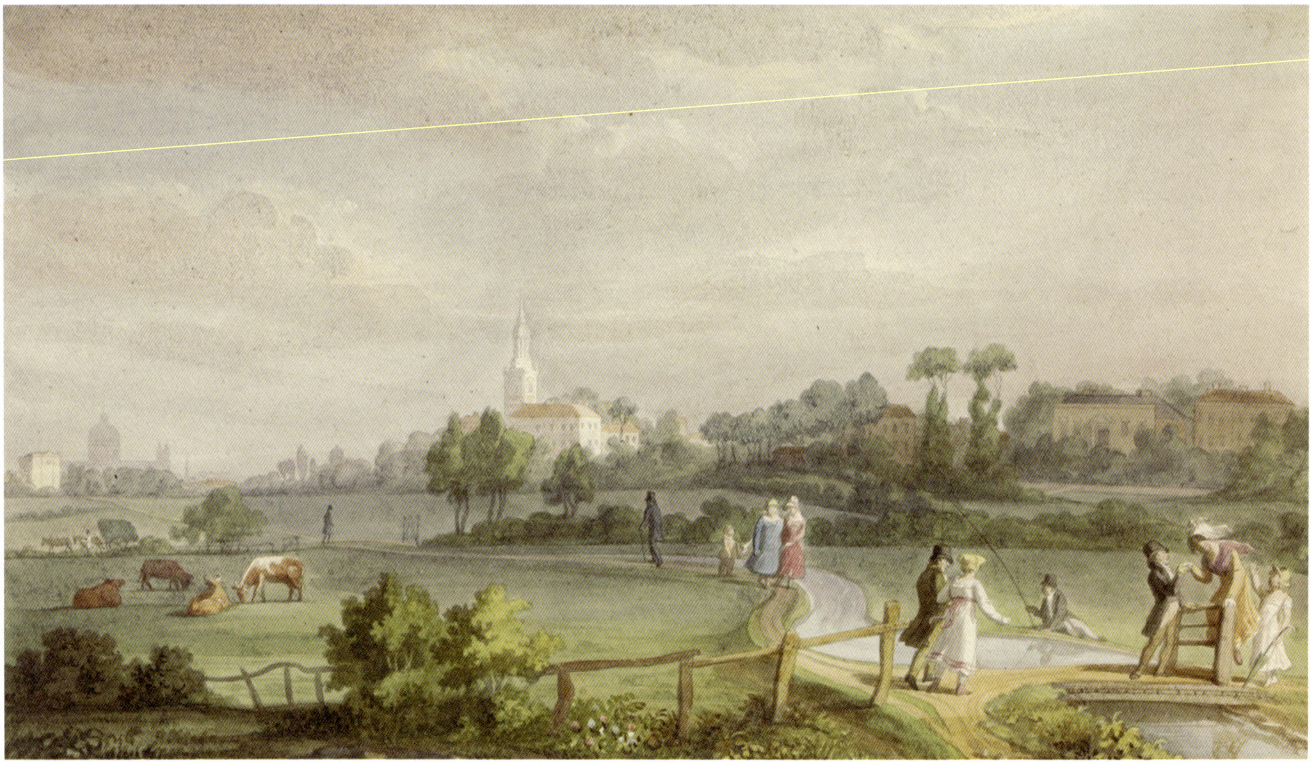

Cat. 53. View from the New River, Islington, London

with a liberal ethos to provide an education to those who had previously encountered barriers due to their religious or ethnic backgrounds. Scharf records with interest in his journal an article that mentions the inauguration of '. . . the New Christian or German Catholic Church by Herr Ronge of Preslau . . .' that appeared in the *Illustrated London News*, 20 September 1845.[46] The German Catholics were a schismatic sect that was organised along democratic principles. Formed under the leadership of Johannes von Ronge, a former Roman Catholic priest, many members were involved in politics and espoused a rational interpretation of Biblical texts.

Amongst Scharf's earliest known works several have a clearly political theme. These include a sketch of the prison reformer Elizabeth Fry (1780–1845) (see cat. 7) and his four portrait studies (BM 1900,0725.1-4) of the leaders of the ultra-radical 'Society of Spencean Philanthropists', which for a brief period in late 1816 led the parliamentary reform movement. These four men – Arthur Thistlewood, (bap.1774, d.1820), Thomas Preston (1774–1850), John Hooper and James Watson (1766–1838) – espoused the radical ideas of Thomas Spence (1750–1814), who argued for the equal redistribution of all land amongst the British population arguing: 'The land is the People's farm!' Following Spence's death the Society continued his aims. On 6 December 1816 Thistlewood and Watson organized a mass meeting at Spa Fields, which they used to agitate a riot. Their intention was to spark a nationwide uprising. The failure of the Spa Fields riot eventually led to Thistlewood, Watson, Preston and Hopper being arrested in 1817, although charges were dropped against the rioters following the acquittal of Thistlewood.[47] On the basis of Scharf's four portraits, a print engraved by William Holl the Elder (1771–1838) showing the four accused was published (fig. 2). This print slightly altered Scharf's original studies by showing the four sitters ranged together and in profile. In 1820, Thistlewood, along with Preston, was involved in the Cato Street conspiracy – an attempt to assassinate the members of the British cabinet. During the struggle that ensued following the discovery of the plotters in a loft on Cato Street, Marylebone, Thistlewood killed a Bow Street Runner. He was found guilty of high treason and in 1820 was executed by hanging followed by public decapitation.[48] Thistlewood's notoriety resulted in a second demand for his printed image and once again Scharf's 1817 sketch was used. This time though the printmaker, George Humphrey, based the composition of his engraving, published in 1820 by Moser and Harris, directly on Scharf's study of Thistlewood (fig. 3).[49] This print somewhat 'brutalises' Thistlewood's features: Scharf's original sketch depicted the sitter with greater sympathy.

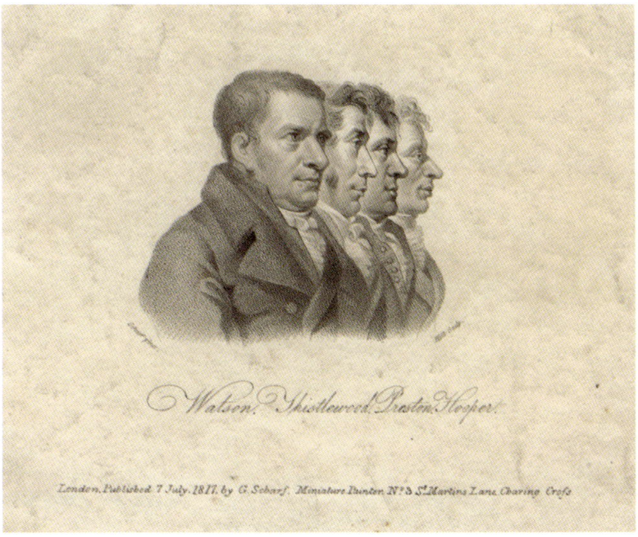

Fig. 2. *James Watson; Arthur Thistlewood; Thomas Preston; John Hooper* by William Holl Sr, after George Scharf, stipple engraving, published 1817, NPG D18602, National Portrait Gallery, London

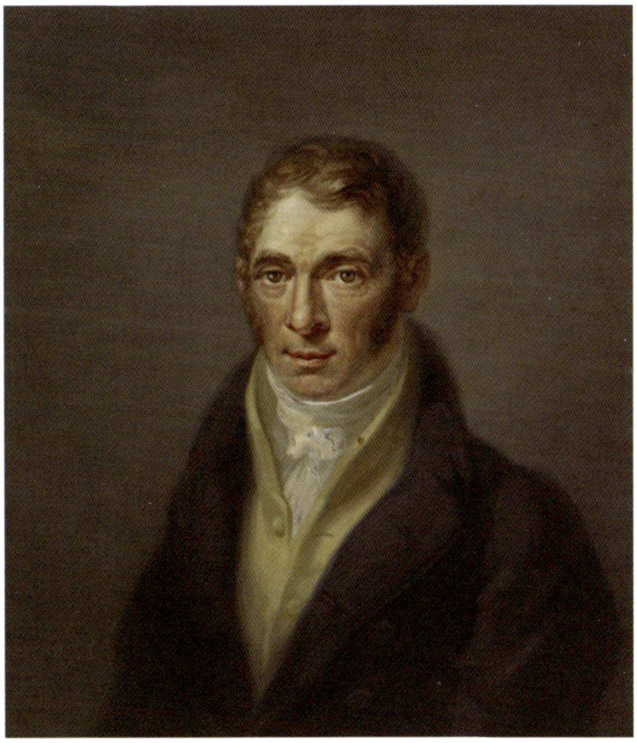

Fig. 3. *Arthur Thistlewood*, George Scharf, watercolour and bodycolour on vellum, 1817, the British Museum 1900,0725.1

Two other political prints followed. Thomas Preston was also a supporter of the aforementioned radical MP for Westminster, Sir Francis Burdett, and Scharf commemorated Burdett's election as MP for Westminster on two occasions in prints dating to 1818 and 1820 (see cat. 14).

It could be argued that Scharf was merely seeking work where he could find it and that these political subjects did not reflect his personal convictions. After all he was happy to draw both captured British officers at Verdun and their French guards. And Scharf later abandoned this type of early work in favour of the scientific drawing which would become the mainstay of his career (see below). Nevertheless, an awareness of and interest in liberal politics is also backed up by references in his journal (albeit these are often laconic in nature). Whilst making preparatory drawings for his 1837 lithograph of the Anniversary Banquet for the City of London Conservative Association, Scharf witnessed the speech given by Sir George Palmer. He described it as: '. . . painfully ill liberal against the reformed party, accusing them unjustly of every wrong possible, alluding particularly to the church income reform, and which, he called, mistakenly Popisme [sic].'[50] He was aware of the Chartist demonstration that was held in Kennington in 1839 (the first of three), organised with the intention of '. . . sending a memorial to the Queen concerning the supposed awful state of the country and for pardoning some of their party who were tried . . .'. Scharf records that the demonstration '. . . behaved otherwise very quiatly [sic]'.[51]

His interest in liberal politics also extended to what was happening on the continent and, of course, in his native Germany. Apart from expressing his interest in the German Catholic Church he also recorded, on 27 September 1845, that: 'Mr. Ruge and Mr. Martz clever German authors, who made free observation of European Governments, were unjustly expelled from France in 1844.'[52] More politically telling though are his journal entries dating to his return visit to Bavaria in 1845 to 1847. In particular he praised the deceased King Maximilian Joseph (1756–1825) on having granted Bavaria a new, liberal constitution, which was in contrast to his more repressive successor Ludwig I (1786–1868) whose regime was marked by censorship and a ban on the discussion of internal politics within Bavaria – censorship which Scharf notes.[53] Whilst in Munich, he visited the House of Representatives of the Bavarian Parliament: '. . . I have now the pleasure of hearing occasionally very fine speeches there, indeed, there are such bold and liberal members here as would do credit to an English Parliament; a great pity only, that the censorship does not allow of those speeches to be published as they were spoken . . .'[54]

Even works that were not overtly political in content also had the potential to be understood in those terms. This was particularly the case with his sketches of the Bank of England and those produced in response to the fire at the Old Palace of Westminster (cats 50–52 and 55–58). Scharf's lithograph of the Bank and related sketches were produced following Cockerell's first modification of certain parts of the building. In 1848, following the Chartist troubles, Cockerell further modified Soane's building by adding a semi-fortified walkway at parapet level around the exterior of the building changing Soane's original attic storey. Scharf's sketch records the Bank as it was before this modification. The fire at the Old Palace of Westminster and its subsequent rebuilding had an even more charged political symbolism. Occurring at a time when the question of political reform was acute, the destruction of the old building and its rebuilding was seen by some as a potent symbol of the extinction of the old modes of British government in the flames of the blaze and the hope for a new, reformed political future for the country the physical form of which would be a new 'modern' parliamentary building. In particular, the radical MP Joseph Hume (1777–1855) argued not only that the new building should be designed with the practical aspects of governmental business in mind; he even went so far as to suggest relocating the building away from Westminster to a more convenient area of the city that would allow greater access by the populous and greater circulation of light and air. Such considerations would, Hume argued, reflect Parliament's more progressive tendencies as well as instilling a greater trust of the government in the people by being '. . . a visual statement of its ability to maintain the well-being of its citizens'.[55]

Scharf and the Sciences

Scharf's arrival in London also coincided with a formative period in the development of the various branches of the sciences.[56] London, in the first quarter of the nineteenth century, became a world-leading centre in the study of geology, naturalism, biology, electromagnetism, astronomy and anatomy, and this would have an impact on Scharf's work.[57] Having failed to secure himself a place as a portraitist in London and following his early forays into lithographs showing topical subjects – such as the Spa Fields Rioters or the coronation of George the IV – Scharf's professional attention turned towards scientific lithography. From about 1825 he started working for the Geological Society, founded in 1807, which was one of a number of such scientific institutions that flourished in London. Scharf would work for them throughout the 1830s and they would become one of his principal employers. It appears that Scharf had already undertaken a lithograph of a mammoth, published by Moser, in about 1819.[58] He now developed this part of his *oeuvre*, producing finely detailed drawings for the Society of fossils to illustrate the *Transactions of the Geological Society*. His journals for the period constantly refer to the various commissions that he undertook for them and the names of the various extinct animals he was paid to sketch. On one occasion Scharf even took one of the Society's fossil specimens to the studio of the sculptor Sir Francis Chantrey (1781–1841) in order for some of the stone, in which the creature was embedded, to be removed.[59] As part of this work, he also attended lectures given by the Society, on occasion taking his two sons, as well as those given by the Zoological Society.[60]

Scharf's scientific drawings were proving successful and he gained a number of prominent clients. Amongst these was Charles Darwin, whom he met through the Geological Society.[61] Amongst the work he undertook for Darwin, Scharf mentions drawings of dinosaurs.[62] Scharf also worked for Darwin's great rival Sir Richard Owen (1804–1892), who was one of the pioneers of comparative anatomy and palaeontology and who, from 1827 to 1832, was the Conservator of the Hunterian Collection at the Royal College of Surgeons (see cats 61 and 62).[63] The Royal College of Surgeons had strong historical links with the Geological Society, having at one point shared the same building on Lincoln's Inn Fields. By the early 1830s, through his scientific drawings and lithographs, Scharf had developed the reputation of '. . . a most useful artist . . . a draftsman of great talent and ability: he is principally known as a delineator of anatomical and geological subjects, in which he is not surpassed'.[64] Amongst the other institutions where he undertook scientific commissions he worked for the British Museum, colouring casts of the fossils that at that stage formed part of its collections.[65] He also mentions some work undertaken for the Linnean Society, although it is unclear from his journal whether this came to fruition.[66]

Scharf's interest in new discoveries also extended to antiquity. He had previously undertaken a few drawings after the antique, such as a sketch (produced for a lithograph?) showing the Temple of Jupiter at Pozzuoli, near Naples,[67] and had drawn the interior of the Townley

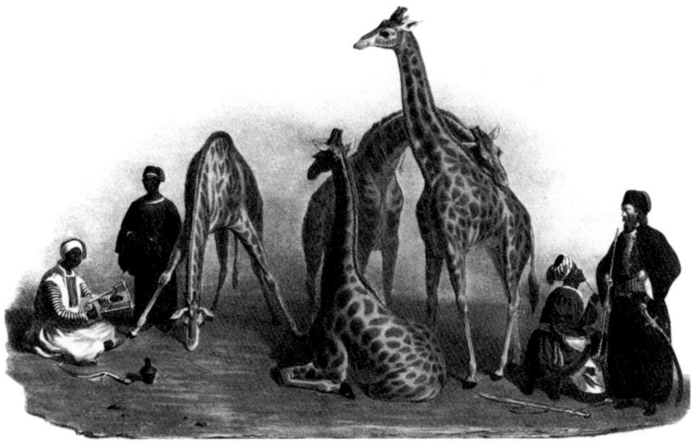

Fig. 4. The Giraffes with the Arabs who Brought them over to this Country, George Scharf, lithograph, 1836, private collection

Gallery at the British Museum in 1827, including several of the antiquities displayed there such as a bust of the Emperor Lucius Verus and statues of Thalia and also of Bacchus (BM 1862,0614.632). It was whilst drawing antiquities in 1835 that he met the sculptor and Egyptologist Joseph Bonomi (1796–1878).[68] Bonomi remembered Scharf when, two years later, he commissioned him to produce some lithographic prints showing Egyptian and Mexican antiquities, possibly for the Royal Society of Literature.[69] The result was not a success: Bonomi, who had sketched the Egyptian antiquities *in situ*, criticised Scharf for not reproducing them accurately enough.[70]

Possibly through his work for Owen, who was also a member of the Zoological Society, Scharf undertook one of his most successful commissions – a set of lithographic views of their newly opened Gardens in Regent's Park published in 1836. These included a print of the first giraffes to be seen in London (fig. 4). Queen Adelaide (1792–1843), the wife of William IV (1765–1837), visited the Gardens and, having seen Scharf's prints, ordered three sets. Scharf personally delivered his lithograph of the giraffes to Buckingham Palace. The images proved so successful that he was summoned to the Bavarian Embassy in London where, Scharf related with some pride:

> Baron Cetto [*vel* Zetto], the Bavarian Ambassador, having sent for me told me the agreeable news that the Queen of Bavaria ordered him to pay one hundred Florins, £9"17"7 for the seven coloured views of the Zoological garden which I had sent through Mr. Drinkel the summer before, which was in fact a very generous and a magnificent payment for coloured prints, and showed a comparatively poor Bavarian

> Queen so much more liberal, as the rich Queen of England only gave 14 schillings for the same sort of prints.[71]

Another Royal patron was the King of Prussia who, whilst on a state visit to London, ordered a set of these views.[72] The lithographs proved so popular with the general public (500 prints were sold in two days) that Scharf was approached by Ridgway of Staffordshire who wanted to reproduce his images of giraffes on their pottery.[73] Scharf's lithograph 'The Giraffes with the Arabs who Brought them over to this Country' was reproduced on plates, teapots and tureens and sold across the country.

London was also the capital of the nation that had taken the lead in the Industrial Revolution, and Scharf was keenly aware of new technological developments. Machines of all sorts fascinated him and would often take machinery as his subject matter (see cats 40 and 42). He produced at least one technical lithograph illustrating a 'Blast Furnace of Clausthal', printed by Hullmandel, (BM 1862,1108.601). This interest may have sprung from his time as an officer in the Engineer corps of the British Army, and lithography in itself was a scientifically and technologically advanced process. Even Hullmandel consulted Farraday in order to learn more about chemical processes.[74] Scharf would likewise attend lectures on 'chimistry', as his idosyncratic use of written English put it, at the National Gallery of Practical Science on Adelaide Street where the latest technological advances of the first quarter of the nineteenth century were displayed to the public.[75] The Gallery at Adelaide Street would become one of his favourite haunts; his journals, particularly those dating to the 1830s, often record one or two visits per week. These visits, of course, were for professional as much as leisure reasons.[76] However, Scharf's scientific curiosity was far-ranging and he also attended lectures on subjects that did not necessarily have any practical applications to his commissioned work; he used drawing as an extension of an intellectual exploration of unfamiliar fields of study.[77] Scharf would also exhibit one of his paintings at the National Gallery of Practical Science (see cat. 55).

Tantalisingly, for an artist who is seen as being an objective recorder of everyday London life, Scharf was aware of that other scientific development that, in certain ways, would make his topographical sketches obsolete – namely photography. He demonstrates this awareness of the new method of capturing the everyday in his journals, writing in 1839: 'The members of the British Association are now assembled at Birmingham. The Revd. W.V. Harcourt President, Mr. Murchison Secretary and Monsieur Arago from the French Institute is to disclose Daguére's secret of the photographic process which last was done by Mr. Talbot.'[78] Scharf witnessed this new process at the Adelaide Street Gallery and declared the daguerreotypes he saw there to be '. . . very beautiful . . .'.[79]

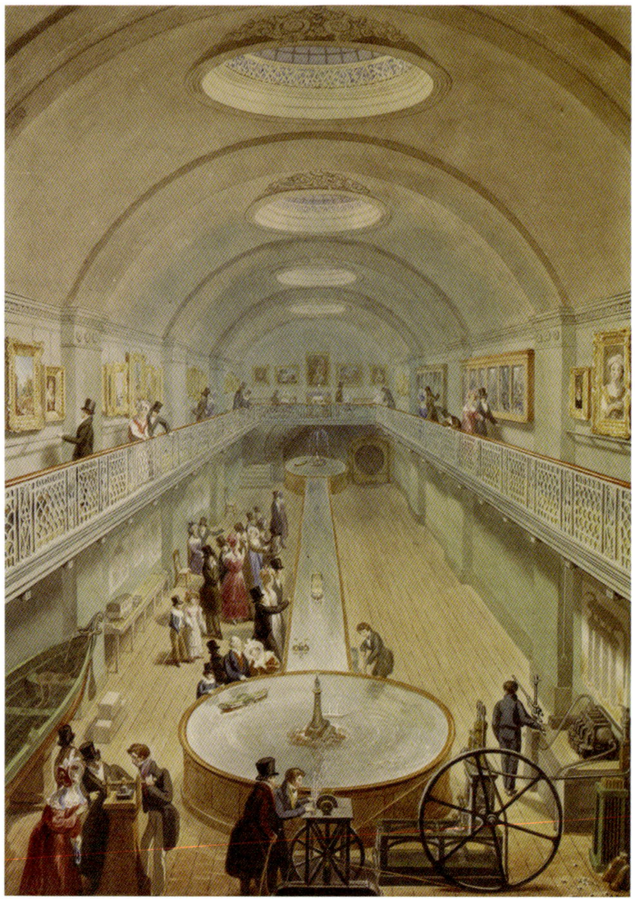

Cat. 38. Interior of the National Gallery of Practical Science, Adelaide Street

Scharf and Architecture

Although architecture did not form the primary subject of his everyday work, Scharf is primarily remembered today for his sketches of London's streets and buildings. Unlike the architectural draughtsman, whose renderings are often devoid of human presence, Scharf chose to depict everyday Londoners interacting with their built environment. His drawings then are not just a 'picturesque' record of how London looked in the 1820s and 1830s but often show how buildings were used. Frustratingly, we have surprisingly little documentary evidence for this aspect of Scharf's work. We do not know who trained him in architectural or topographical draughtsmanship whilst he was a student in Munich, if he was formerly taught in this field at all (he may have been self-taught). His journals record, in often repetitive detail, the many commissions for drawings or lithographs of fossils or anatomical specimens for the Zoological Society, the British Museum or the Geological Society. In comparison, he mentions his architectural undertakings or the everyday sketches, which so often included close studies of London's buildings and that make up the bulk of his surviving *oeuvre*, less frequently. When he does mention architectural subjects at length, these drawings of buildings are related to ambitious projects that seem to have preoccupied him. Scharf did, though, have a good grasp of architectural draughtsmanship, as evidenced by his sketches and in fact he was employed on a few occasions as a tutor in this.[80]

As early as 1822 he produced thirteen lithographs of buildings for John Parton's publication *Some Account of the Hospital and Parish of St Giles-in-the Fields*. These prints, in comparison with his later work, are somewhat conventionalised renderings. His first major architectural commission, which showed the full range of his draughtsmanship in integrating the anecdotal with the monumentality of the London vista, was for the London Bridge Committee who engaged him to record the building of the new London Bridge in 1830. Scharf had been documenting the building work on the bridge, together with its associated demolition work, since it started in 1824. He utilised these sketches to produce two large watercolours, each five foot long that showed the Bridge from either end of its two new approach roads using a highly foreshortened viewpoint.[81] In addition, the architect of the Bridge, Sir John Rennie (1794–1874), commissioned three drawings of the project. By acting as records of the building work, the two large watercolours can be compared to the type of architect's renderings that were used to record or explain the building process, most notably those produced by Sir John Soane's office showing the building of Dulwich Picture Gallery or the construction work for the Infirmary of the Royal Hospital, Chelsea (figs 5 and 6). Scharf's images showing the rebuilding of the Royal College of Surgeons or of the British Museum can also be compared with his watercolours of the Bridge as records of a construction process, although they were not commissioned work (see cats 61 and 62). The two watercolours were reproduced by Scharf as five-foot-long lithographs (fig. 8), though unfortunately they took a long time to produce.[82] Scharf was forced to use two individual stones for each print in order to accommodate

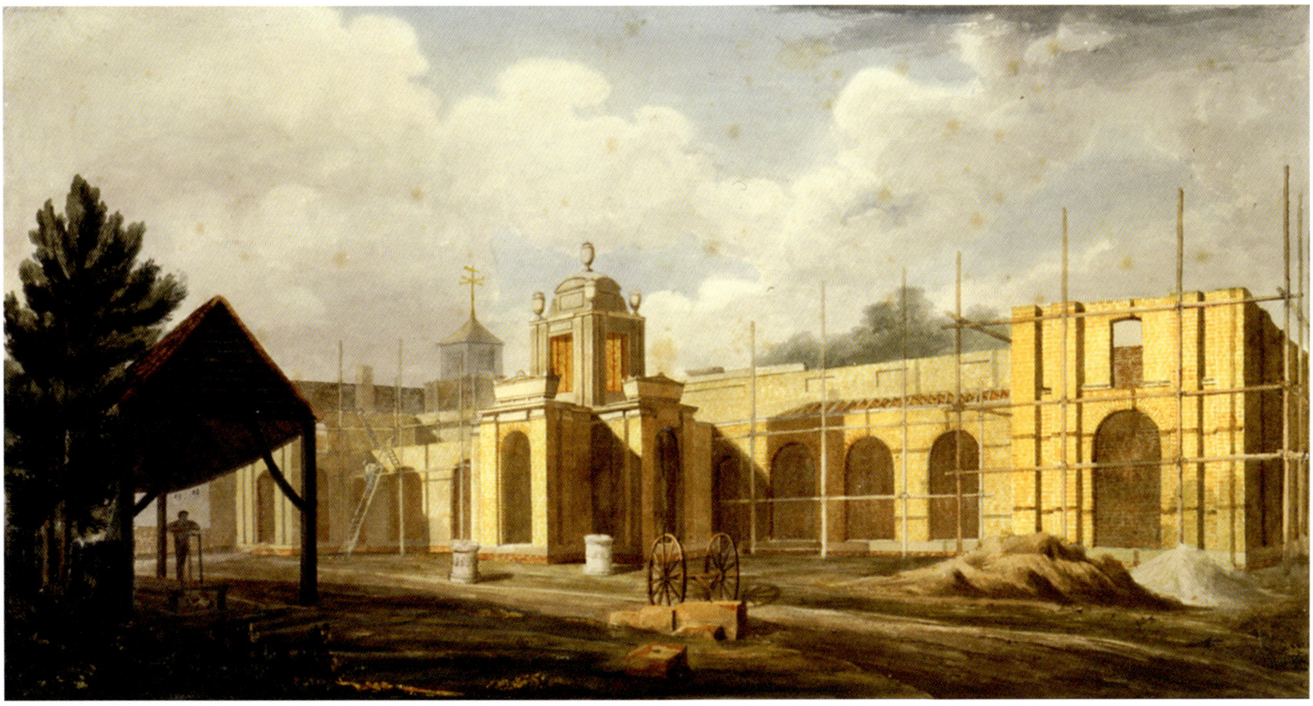

Fig. 5. Royal Academy Lecture drawing showing a progress view of the west front of Dulwich Picture Gallery, pen and watercolour, *c.* 1815, The Trustees of Sir John Soane's Museum, SM 15/2/10

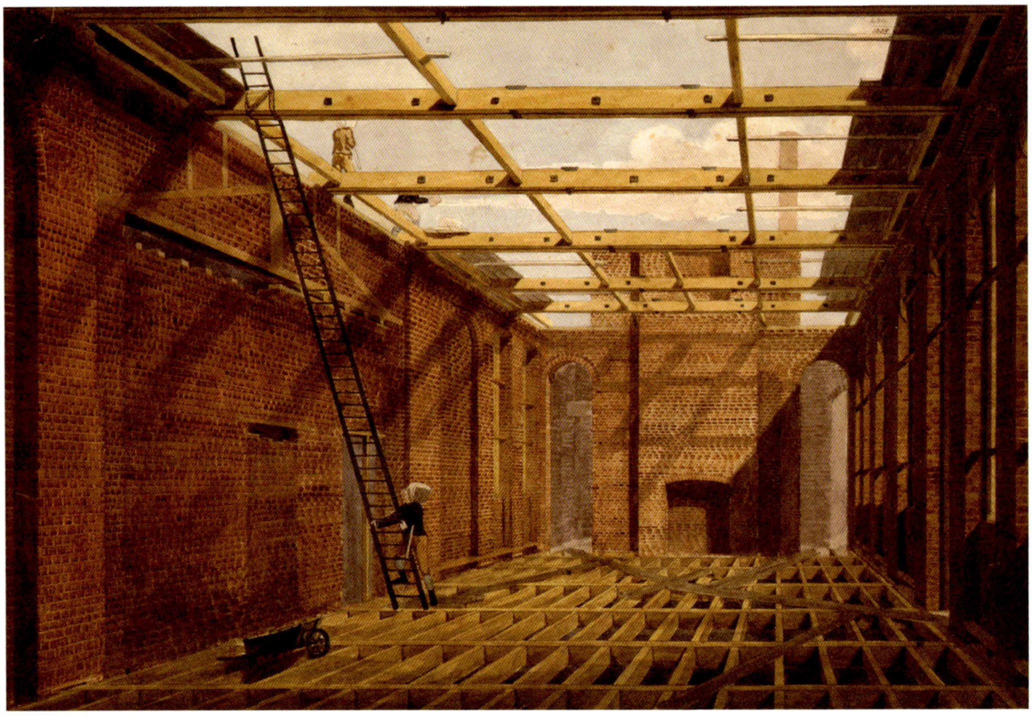

Fig. 6. Royal Academy Lecture drawing showing a progress view of construction work in the long ward of the Infirmary, Chelsea Hospital, pen and watercolour, *c.* 1814, The Trustees of Sir John Soane's Museum, SM 14/7/2

the ambitious scale of the originals. He had very carefully to ensure that the highly detailed views aligned correctly on each stone. To compound his difficulties he realised that he had considerably undercharged his clients, particularly when considering the complication of the print commission, and tried, unsuccessfully, to appeal to the Committee for more money.[83]

Scharf also worked for the architect Charles Robert Cockerell (1788–1863), and in 1831 produced the architect's rendering of Cockerell's design for the Westminster Life and British Fire Office, that was proposed for the Strand. On the strength of this project, Cockerell was appointed architect to the Bank of England in 1833. In this new role Cockerell commissioned Scharf, in 1835, to produce a lithograph of the New Dividend Pay Office of the Bank of England (see cat. 51).[84] Much later, when his son George Scharf the Younger was employed to produce lecture drawings for Cockerell, Scharf the Elder assisted him in completing the commissions.[85] Of his other architectural work of the 1830s, the most important items were the series of sketches documenting the ruins of the Old Palace of Westminster after the fire of 1834. These were preparatory studies for his paintings 'The Ruins of the Late Houses of Parliament', and 'The Ruins of St Stephen's Chapel', the former forming the basis for a proposed lithograph of the same subject (see cats 55–58). Other smaller projects included a commission in 1834 to lithograph the proposed designs for a monument to Sir Isaac Newton, to be set up near Leicester Square[86] and the drawing of plans of some buildings on the Downshire estates, Ireland, for the Marchioness of Downshire.[87]

Unlike his frequent attendance at lectures at the Royal Geological Society, which he carefully recorded in his journals, Scharf rarely attended lectures given on architectural subjects. However, he does mention two notable occasions. The first was one of Sir John Soane's lectures at the Royal Academy.[88] The second was one given by Cockerell, who had replaced Soane as Architect to the Bank of England.[89]

Scharf and Germany

Having settled in London, married an English woman and raising two sons who, he hoped, would become English 'gentlemen', Scharf was nevertheless attached to the country of his birth. He was friendly with the German ex-patriot community in London, notably through his work as a lithographer – a field that was dominated by Germans or those of German descent such as Hullmandel – and he attended a German church. His journals record his contacts with the Bavarian Embassy[90] and he witnessed the opening, in the presence of the Prussian Ambassador, of the New German Hospital in Dalston.[91]

He was in contact with his family in '. . . our dear home of Bavaria . . .'[92] – his brother Joseph, who was the Burgomaster of Mainburg, and his wife and children – although the postal service between Germany and London could be unreliable and he sometimes had to rely on news from Bavarian visitors to London.[93] Scharf kept abreast of German current affairs, such as political developments (see p. 16), and took pride in German achievements. He notes in a long journal entry the opening of the Danube-Main canal as a significant Bavarian achievement: '. . . a work attempted by Charlemagne renewed and completed by Louis the First King of Bavaria!'[94] Other monuments that glorified Bavaria were also noted by Scharf, such as the colossal personification of Bavaria, some 84 feet high, with a head cast in bronze that was erected at the Grand National October Festival held in Munich in 1850.[95] At the back of the colossus was a temple containing busts of celebrated Bavarians along similar lines to the 'Walhalla' German Hall of Fame, Regensburg, built from 1830 to 1842, which contained the busts of celebrated German-speaking artists, writers, scientists and philosophers. Amongst Scharf's prized possessions was a large oil painting showing the 'Walhalla'.[96]

Although his career was London-based, Scharf cultivated German clients to a certain extent (see below) and sent examples of his work to Munich (see cats 18 and 51). How successful he was at asserting his presence back in Germany is debatable. He certainly considered his work to be known there: 'Mr. Kamp from Darmstadt, came to the British Museum where, he seeing me draw on stone, he said he knew my name must be Scharf, from having seen my name to similar drawings'.[97] A German audience's familiarity with Scharf's work could also have arisen from the only return trip Scharf made to Bavaria in 1845.

It was whilst he was sketching figures from the Parthenon in the British Museum that news came that his brother was seriously ill:

> George came down to me about the middle of the day saying, that a letter was sent me from Mr. Francis, then travelling in Bavaria, and who had been to see my brother Joseph in passing through Mainburg on his way to Ratisbon [Regensburg] and the Walhalla, and that he found him dangerously ill with the complaint of cancer, wishing anxiously to see me before dying, which news, of course afflicted me much, as well as

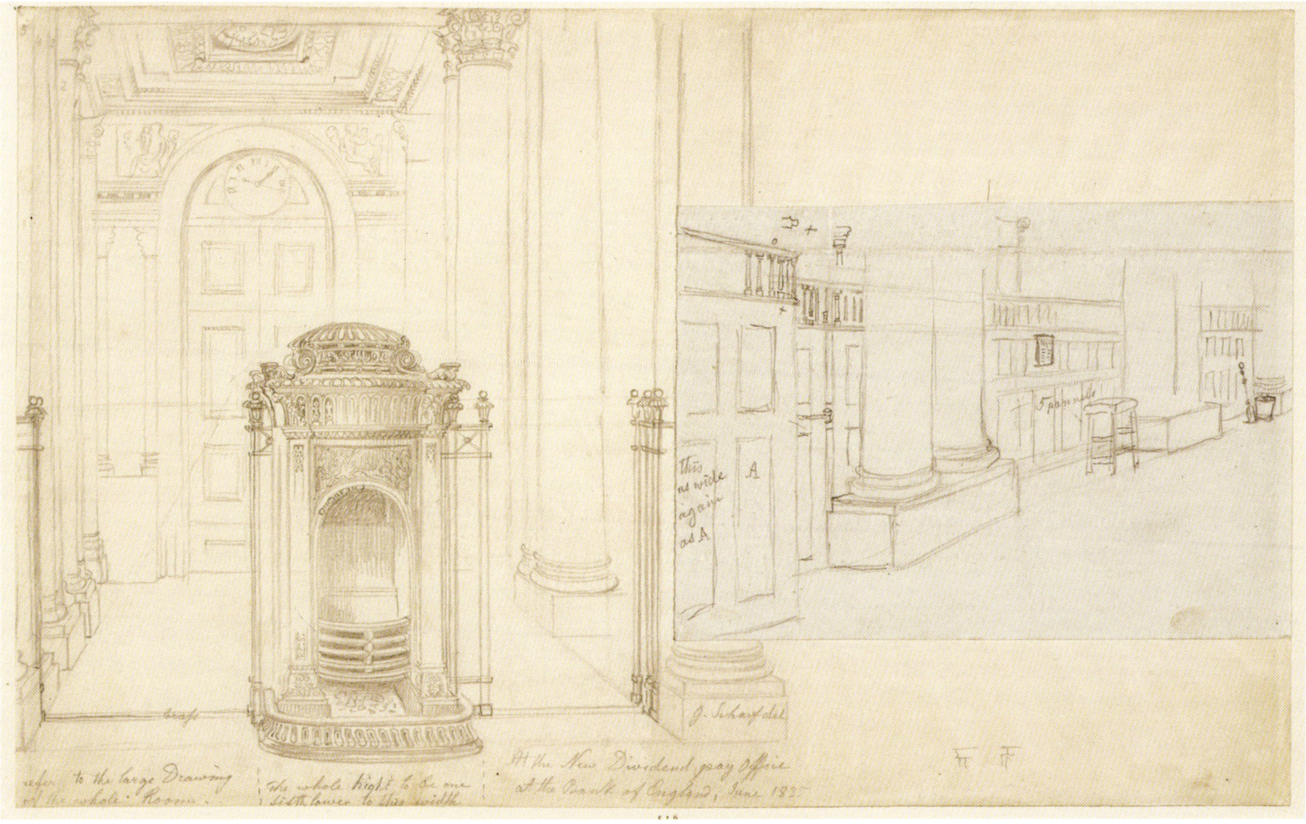

Cat. 51. The New Dividend Warrant and Pay Office, at the Bank of England 1835

excited my whole family, who all very kindly participated in my feeling, and there was of course no other way but to prepare for departure at once, which was a serious and difficult thing; Good God![98]

Scharf retraced his 1816 journey to Britain on his way back to his dying brother, passing through many of the towns he had first seen when following the armies engaged in the battles of the Napoleonic Wars.[99] On 22 October he crossed the border into Prussia at Aix-la-Chappelle: 'I was up at sunrise it was a beautiful morning and sketched at the open window where I breathed with pleasure the fresh air of Germany once more, after so long an absence.'[100] From there, Scharf made his way south along the Rhine, stopping off at Cologne to sketch the great medieval cathedral.[101] He was too late though: by the time he reached Mainburg his brother had died. In spite of this, Scharf took the opportunity to extend his stay in Germany. He was able to do so due to the legacy left to him by his late brother. As in England, Scharf both drew and made prints and attempted to cultivate a Bavarian circle of patrons.

Following his brother's death, he left Mainburg and moved to Munich, where he tried to engage in the city's artistic life. He produced a number of works such as a lithograph of Mainburg (BM 1900,0725.132) and also took the opportunity to revisit familiar places such as the *Pinakhotheke*[102] and also some of the newly built monuments of the city. In particular he was impressed by the historical wall paintings in the *Schlachtensaal* or 'Hall of Battles' that formed part of the new additions to the *Munich Residenz*, seat of the Bavarian Kings, by Peter von Hess (1792–1871).[103] These showed episodes from the Napoleonic Wars in which the Bavarian Army participated.[104] He was joined in these explorations by George the Younger, who visited his father whilst he was in Germany. For the first time, at the age of sixty, as he noted, he had work exhibited publicly in Germany – at the Munich Art Union – where some of his watercolours were shown.[105] Scharf even attempted to become a member of the Union.[106] He also attended the Artists' Masked Ball but, not knowing anyone, stood to one side hardly talking to any the other guests.[107] The sense of estrangement that he experienced at the Ball characterised his stay in Munich as a whole. He had been out of Bavaria for too long and many of his former colleagues at the *Akademie* were now dead. Scharf left Munich for Ratisbon (Regensburg) where he produced, amongst other things, a large panorama of the town from a tower of the inn in which he was staying. He was also taken under the wing of one of the noble families who kept a town house there and was introduced to the Prince and Princess von Thurn und Taxis, a family of great patrons, sketching their Christmas celebrations.[108] In spite of all his attempts, Scharf found that his work was not selling in sufficient quantities in Germany.[109] His brother's legacy was also dwindling, forcing Scharf to move into smaller and cheaper accommodation. In 1847 he retraced his steps across the former battlefields of Europe and returned to England.

Scharf's decline

In spite of his professional successes, Scharf was far from secure financially. Throughout the period of the 1830s he had been undercharging clients for his work.[110] It would also appear that he was beginning to suffer ill health, with his eyes giving him concern.[111] Even successful projects such as the lithograph of the Zoological Society's giraffes, which held the promise of a lucrative franchise with Ridgway for the use of his design, proved to be a disappointment. The manufactory offered payment in kind – a tea service with his giraffe design; Scharf needed money.[112] Much to his regret, he had to leave the New Watercolour Society as he could not keep up with the payments for his subscription.[113] To remedy this he raised his hourly rate. Unfortunately, this move did not sit well with certain clients and was the cause of an argument with one of his distinguished ones. In 1838 Darwin asked Scharf to produce a lithograph of the large fossilised skull of a *toxodon*; the lithograph did not print well as Scharf had used a poor quality lithographic stone and he was forced to redo the print free of charge. However, the episode had incurred Darwin's displeasure, as Scharf noted: 'Mr. Darwin called and surprised me by complaining of my charging too much, my reckoning only two schillings per hour; in drawing his fossil bones from South America.'[114] To make matters worse, Darwin had just been made Secretary of the Geological Society. Relations between his major employer – the Society – and himself reached a low point in 1841. Having undertaken some work for the Society, Scharf fell behind with the agreed delivery date. He was visited by a Mr Lonsdale of the Society who berated him for his lateness. Scharf was incandescent at being treated in a less than dignified manner, as his journal records: 'Consideration ought to be made . . . that artists ought not to be treated or spoken to like to a common mechanic or a servant, as he then did, and has done before I did not like to be used in that way, at which he left offended and said that he should take good care that I should never draw for the Geological Society any more.' Mr Lonsdale ensured that this would be the case.[115] It also seems that he was owed money by clients, as his journal mentions that he was owed twenty-four pounds by a Mr Bloxham, a member of the Medical and Chirurgical Society. Bloxman had been declared bankrupt and in desperation Scharf appealed to the Council of the Society in order to secure payment of his debt. They, however, refused to be held responsible for the arrears of one of their members.[116] In total for the period 1840 to the end of July 1845, Scharf calculated, he was owed £185 – over a year's salary.[117] His extended stay in Bavaria allowed a little respite from these concerns. The promise of a substantial legacy from his dead brother Joseph also proved illusive. Although he had been left the sum of four thousand florins, half payable immediately and half following his sister-in-law's death, the money just covered his two-year stay in Germany. Scharf complained bitterly in a letter addressed to his sister-in-law that she and his late brother, who was said to have left a fortune of some twenty to forty thousand florins, had not ensured him a greater legacy: 'I was very sorry that they should not have considered my situation more, such as my uncertain profession, the great expense of living in England, the want of more money for continuing to work . . . .'[118] Scharf had been aggravated by the fact that his sister-in-law had 'adopted' a young woman – 'Nany' or Ann Birringer to whom she had given a substantial sum upon the occasion of her marriage, money that Scharf felt should have come his way.[119]

Upon his return from Bavaria in 1847, Scharf attempted to continue his former work. Clients, however, were now few.[120] In addition, his great friend Hullmandel, who had worked with Scharf on so many lithographic commissions, died in 1850 – from apoplexy.[121] Of the projects undertaken during his final decade a number can be mentioned. In late 1848 he started work on a large panoramic view of London, but it remained unfinished.[122] He also produced a lithograph showing Sir Richard Westmacott lecturing at the Royal Academy, Somerset House, in 1850 based upon earlier drawings of the same subject from 1830 (BM 1862,0614.179 and 1862,0164.184).[123] In 1851 he sketched the rotunda at University College London for a lithographic illustration for a catalogue of the works by John Flaxman (1755–1826) that were displayed there (University College Art Collections, Strang Print Room, G2849).[124]

He placed his hope in the ability of George Scharf the Younger to support his father and mother: 'The eldest [son] expresses his grateful feelings towards his parents in holding out a hope to me of having to live more comfortable and independent of troublesome scientific work . . . and to have the happiness I long wished for, of finishing up my begun sketches . . . to what a happy ending of my partially troublesome life, have I to look forward, through the grateful acting of my sons . . .'.[125] Unfortunately this was not to be. Relations between George Scharf the Elder and his oldest son had deteriorated, as the father complained: '. . . [George] is not friendly with me . . .'.[126] George Scharf the Younger records in his own journal that: 'My father seems broken and discontented'.[127] In spite of this Scharf continued assisting his son with his drawings.[128]

Following the end of their lease of No. 1 Torrington Square, where the family had lived since 1848, it was decided that George Scharf the Younger, his mother and her sister Mary would move to Camden. His father found single-room lodgings in Preston Street not far from the rest of his family.[129] In spite of the tension between Scharf and his eldest son, relations with Elizabeth were cordial. Amongst the final entries in his surviving journals Scharf notes a pleasant excursion they enjoyed together in the company of Elizabeth's sister to the Great Exhibition of 1851. Scharf described it as '. . . a wonderful assemblage of all kinds of objects, which astonishes one, but could only take a hasty glance of it generally having to return to it several times'.[130] Strangely, for one who was so interested in technology and mechanics in his younger years, Scharf does not seem to have made any sketches of the Exhibition. Perhaps at the age of sixty-three his desire for new subjects had left him – Scharf certainly seems to have turned towards his stock of images of an earlier London and reworked some of those at this time.

Scharf's finances must have been dire at this stage as he attempted to sell by public auction some of his own work, including his panorama of the 'Ruins of the Late Houses of Parliament' and of 'St Stephen's Chapel' (see cats 55 and 56), as well as his prized large oil of the Walhalla, Regensburg. He also attempted to sell some of the drawings and sketches he had made of London since his arrival in 1816 to the City Corporation, without success. They declined '. . . for want of interest and want of money . . .' as the Corporation's representative explained.[131] Finally, in 1857, he appealed to the Prince von Thurn und Taxis, requesting a pension in exchange for the entire collection of his work. His petition did not reach the Prince as his representative considered it '. . . so strange to ask anyone for a Pension on whom one has no claim'.[132] One small respite was provided by his former employer Owen, who was now Superintendent of the Natural History Department of the British Museum. He commissioned Scharf to draw whatever took his fancy in the collections for the salary of one pound per week.[133] Amongst these drawings was one showing the famous relief of the Lion Hunt discovered at Nineveh.[134]

The final blow came in April 1859, when it was discovered that the family's old servant had been stealing money that had been intended to pay tradespeople. Scharf was held liable for the debt. His health finally broke down and he developed severe bronchitis in the winter of 1859 – although this did mean that he now received a small pension.[135] In spite of his doctor's recommendation that he stay indoors, he was forced to leave the house to get his doctor's signature for his health certificate. Having walked all the way from Camden to Manchester Square in freezing weather his condition worsened again: 'Father very ill, confined to his bed, severe coughing' as George the Younger noted in his diary. The illness lingered. George Scharf the Elder finally died on 11 November 1860. He is buried at Brompton Cemetery.

Following his death, in 1862, the British Museum purchased some 1,225 drawings by Scharf from his wife Elizabeth. This was followed, in 1900, by Sir George Scharf the Younger's bequest to the Museum of some 200 drawings and sketches by his father. The present exhibition is drawn mainly from these holdings.

1 Journal entry 22 October 1845, pp. 14–15
2 His surviving Journals, donated to the archives of the National Portrait Gallery, London, by his son Sir George Scharf the Younger, cover the years 1833 to 1852 and 1860. There is as yet no definitive *catalogue raisonné* of either his paintings, drawings or prints and this exhibition catalogue does not attempt to act as one
3 Schwarzbach, F S, 'George Scharf and Early Victorian London', in *Victorian Artists and the City: A Collection of Critical Essays*, Nadel, Ira Bruce and Schwarzbach, F S, Eds, Pergamon Press: Elmford, New York, 1979, p. 94
4 Journal entry 17 March 1846, p. 32. In a note appended to journal entry dated 29 March 1846 he again implies that the family was once of some consequence, claiming: '... a name [Scharf] quite strange now, but known to many 95 years ago'. In addition, his journal for 1846 contains a slip of paper with two impressions of a coat of arms, taken, as a note explains, from Scharf's brother's signet ring. The coat of arms, whose charge displays an arm emerging from a cloud, bound at the elbow by a sash, the hand clasping a circlet, does incorporate a coronet in the crest with points terminating in three strawberry leaves and two pearls. It is not similar to the coronets used by Barons of the Holy Roman Empire or of the later Kingdom of Bavaria – it could have been an heirloom of his mother's family
5 Journal entry 22 October 1845, pp. 22–23
6 Jackson, Peter, *George Scharf's London: Sketches and Watercolours of a Changing City, 1820–50*, John Murray: London, 1987, p. 4
7 Journal entry 22 October 1845, pp. 22–23
8 Journal entry 31 December 1846, p. 43. Scharf seems to have been in contact with Gärtner on at least one occasion after he left the *Akademie*. See journal entry 1 October 1836 and cat. 18
9 Only one identified work of this period survives – a watercolour copy of a portrait of Augusta Emilia, Queen of Italy, by the painter Kellerhofen. It is in the collection of the Staatliche Graphische Sammlung, Munich. See Schwarzbach, F S, 1979, op. cit., p. 94
10 Jackson, P, 1987, op. cit., p. 1
11 Ibid., p. 4
12 It is also interesting to note that the limestone quarries of Solnhofen, Bavaria, were located not too far from Mainburg. The quality of this limestone was ideal for the production of lithographic plates and also, significantly in light of the development of Scharf's career, contained many well-preserved fossil specimens, including the *Archeopteryx Lithographica*. I am grateful to Tim Knox for drawing my attention to this
13 Twyman, Michael, *Lithography 1800–1850, The Techniques of Drawing on Stone in England and France and Their Application in Works of Topography*, London: Oxford University Press, 1970, p. 4
14 Ibid.
15 Twyman, Michael, *The Panizzi lectures: Breaking the Mould: The First Hundred Years of Lithography*, The British Library: London, 2000, p. 16
16 Ibid.
17 It was only in 1810 that the first significant German artist's lithograph was published – Karl Friedrich Schinkel's 'Gothic Church behind an Oak Tree'
18 Published by Redman of Bath
19 For full descriptions of the development of lithography and its adoption in Britain see Man, Felix H, 'Lithography in England (1801–1810)' in: Zigrosser, Carl, Ed. *Prints: Thirteen Illustrated Essays on the Art of the Print Selected for the Print Council of America by Carl Zigrosser*, Holt, Rinehard and Winston: New York, Chicago and San Francisco, 1962 and Twyman, Michael, 1970, op. cit.
20 Journal entry 15 January 1840. Scharf comments that alongside the work of Fusseli he also viewed other prints that were, in his opinion, '... the most beautiful lithographs of anatomical subjects I ever saw ...'. Alongside these he also admired the work of '... Jacob of Paris – whose talented works I knew for sometime past, those by F. Wagner of Zurich and Dr. Frideric Arnold'
21 Jackson, P, 1987, op. cit., p. 4
22 There is a reference in *The Philosophical Magazine*, Vol. 49, 1817 that suggests lithography was used by the Duke of Wellington to duplicate dispatches with drawings of troop positions. See Schwarzbach, F S, 1971, op. cit. p.104. Scharf would, much later, also make lithographs of military maps. He was commissioned in 1839 by Sir Thomas Mitchell to produce lithographs showing Spain during the period of the Peninsular War. See Journal entry 29(?) November 1839
23 See Sumner, Ann and Walker, Richard, *Secret Passion to Noble Fashion: The World of the Portrait Miniature*, Exh. Cat., The Holburne Museum of Art, Bath, 1999
24 Journal entry 31 Dec 1846, p.43
25 Schwarzbach, F S, 1979, op. cit., p. 94
26 Ibid.
27 Journal entry 15 June 1839
28 Journal entry 21 October 1845
29 The presence of a native German amongst British ranks was not unusual. The King's German Legion was a British regiment formed of German volunteers. As it did not fight as a unit, officers were seconded to other regiments, including the Royal Engineers. Curiously, Scharf's name does not appear in the Army Lists for 1814–16 either under the Royal Engineers or under the King's German Legion, nor under any other regiment. He is not listed on the roll calls of the Royal Engineers Regiment, 1600–1898, or on that of the Waterloo Medal
30 Schwarzbach, F S, 1979, op. cit.
31 See footnote 29 above
32 Jackson, P, 1987, op. cit., p. 4
33 Schwarzbach, F S, 1979, op. cit., p. 95
34 He tried to exhibit once more in 1852, but the painting he submitted had already been rejected twice See Jackson, P, 1987, op. cit., p. 15
35 Reprinted in: Jackson, P, 1987, op. cit., p. 11
36 It is interesting to note that these publishers of lithographs were all of German descent, as their surnames indicate
37 Schwarzbach, F S, 1979, op. cit., p. 95
38 This view may be clouded by the fact that we only

possess a complete run of his journals from 1833 to 1852. The period when the London political scene, in particular the radical and reformist tendencies, was at it most vibrant falls outside the period covered by his surviving journals. See Schwarzbach, F S, 1979, op. cit.

39 Dickinson, H T, 'Radical Culture', in *London: World City 1800–1840*, Fox, Celina Ed., Exh. Cat., The Museum of London, London, 1992, p. 209

40 Londoners had the highest levels of literacy in the UK at this period. See ibid., p. 209

41 Ibid., p. 211

42 Ibid., p. 215

43 Marc Baer, 'Burdett, Sir Francis, fifth baronet (1770–1844)', *Oxford Dictionary of National Biography*, Oxford University Press, 2004 [http://www.oxforddnb.com/view/article/3962, accessed 28 Nov 2008]

44 *The Apocalypse and the Shape of Things to Come*, Carey, Frances Ed., Exh. Cat., The British Museum, London, 1999, p. 226

45 See journal entries for 30 March 1834 and 17 May 1837 and Leigh, Samuel, *Picture of London*, 1818, p. 446. When Scharf arrived in London this was one of the thirteen Roman Catholic Chapels that operated in the city at the time

46 Journal entry 21 September 1845

47 Charges were dropped against Hooper, Watson and Preston after the acquittal of Thistlewood upon the exposure of the Crown's chief witness – John Castles – as a perjurer, pimp and *agent provocateur* in the affair

48 Preston was not prosecuted for his role in the conspiracy

49 This engraving is reproduced in: Priestley, J B, *The Prince of Pleasure and his Regency 1811–20*, Sphere Books Ltd: London, 1971, p. 259. Not much is known of the publishers of this print – Moser and Harris lithographers – although Scharf and Hullmandel both worked with them

50 Journal entry 14 June 1837

51 Journal entry 11 August 1839

52 Journal entry 27 September 1845

53 Journal entry 10 May 1846, p.16

54 Journal entry 11 April 1846, p.46

55 Fredericksen, Andrea, 'Parliament's Genius Loci: The Politics of Place after the 1834 Fire', in *The Houses of Parliament: History, Art, Architecture*, Riding, Christine and Riding, Jacqueline Eds., Merrell Publishers Ltd: London, 2000, p. 108

56 For a detailed account of Scharf's relationship with the sciences see Caroline Arscott's essay in this catalogue

57 For an account of this see Morus, Iwan, Schaffer, Simon and Secord, Jim, 'Scientific London' in Fox, Celina Ed., 1992, op. cit., pp. 129–142

58 Journal entry 20 January 1836

59 Journal entry 8 December 1837

60 Journal entry 22 November 1833

61 Journal entry 22 March 1837

62 Journal entry 23 May 1837

63 Jacob W Gruber, 'Owen, Sir Richard (1804–1892)', *Oxford Dictionary of National Biography*, Oxford University Press, Sept 2004; online edn, Jan 2006 [http://www.oxforddnb.com/view/article/21026, accessed 25 Nov 2008]. Owen would teach Henry Scharf anatomical drawing at the College of Surgeons

64 *The Library of Fine Arts*, 1831, reprinted in Schwarzbach, F S, 1979, op. cit., p. 96

65 See journal entries for 22 November 1837 and 16 January 1838

66 Journal entry 1 June 1834

67 Journal entry 11 March 1834

68 Journal entry 25 June 1835. Bonomi became the Curator of Sir John Soane's Museum in 1861

69 Journal entry 14 January 1837

70 Journal entry 27 January 1837

71 Journal entry 13 November 1837

72 Journal entry 31 January 1842

73 Journal entry 9 September 1836

74 Twyman, Michael, 1970, op. cit., pp. 133-4

75 On another occasion, Scharf records drawing an 'electricity apparatus', possibly an early type of generator, which was being displayed to the public in Charing Cross. See journal entry 9 December 1837

76 Such as on 14 August 1833, where he records in his journal: 'Painted a circular plate with seven colours for the steel cutting engine at the Exhibition of Practical Science, Adelaide St'

77 For example, on 22 November 1833 he attended a lecture given at Adelaide Street on magnetism. The next day, he records, he drew magnets

78 Journal entry 28 August 1839

79 Journal entry 10 February 1842

80 See journal entries 11 July 1835 and 16 November 1841, where he states he is teaching 'architectural lithography'

81 These paintings were destroyed during the Blitz

82 Scharf sent an example of each of these lithographs to Munich in order to be presented to the *Akademie*. Journal entry 2 July 1844

83 Jackson, P, 1987, op. cit., pp. 8–10 and pp. 110–115. Scharf also took an extremely long time with the drawings for Rennie. They were finally ready in 1835 by which time Rennie had forgotten that he had commissioned them. Scharf offered them to the London Bridge Committee

84 Journal entry 9 May 1835

85 Journal entry 16 November 1841. On this occasion Scharf the Elder helped his son complete a lecture drawing '. . . of a room in the Palace at Mantua painted by Giulio Romano . . .' that Cockerell would use at the Royal Academy

86 Journal entry 26 June 1834

87 Journal entry 9 May 1840

88 Journal entry 6 February 1834

89 Journal entry 3 February 1842

90 See Journal entries for 26 August 1833 and 13 December 1837

91 Journal entry 15 October 1845

92 Journal entry 9 May 1844

93 Journal entry 25 February 1836

94 Journal entry 13 September 1845. He also describes the iconographic programme of the sculptures by Leo von Klenze that decorated the monument set up to commemorate the opening of the canal

95 Journal entry October 1850. Scharf had sketched a model of this

96 Jackson, P, 1987, op. cit., p. 15

97 Journal entry 23 July 1845

98 Journal entry 20 October 1845

99 See footnote 29 above

100 Journal entry 22 October 1845

101 The completion of this great medieval cathedral, which had stalled in the sixteenth century, was resumed once more in 1842 becoming a symbol of German resurgence, under the aegis of Prussia, following the Napoleonic wars

102 Journal entry 22 March 1846, p. 35

103 Journal entry 12 February 1846

104 Von Hess' wall paintings in the Hall of Battles included the 'Encounter at Wörgel, 1809', the 'Encounter at Bar sur Aube, 1814' and the 'Battle of Aras sur Aube, 1814'. In addition wall paintings by William von Kobell, by whom it has been suggested Scharf was possibly influenced in his early career, also decorated this room in the *Residenz*

105 Journal entry 29 March 1846

106 Journal entry 27 February 1846

107 Journal entry 19 February 1846

108 Journal entry 31 December 1846, p. 43

109 Journal entry 31 December 1846, p. 43

110 Hullmandel wrote to Scharf on this subject: 'I know your prices are very moderate – often too much so, I therefore think it better to let you know that you may ask a price which may pay you as they expect it will come high'. Reprinted in: Jackson, P, 1987, op. cit., p. 7

111 As early as 1833 he complains that he suffered difficulty whilst drawing an *ichthiosaurus platyoton* [sic] due to the weakness of his eyes. In a note appended to the back of his journal for 1839 he notes that he has seen five doctors regarding his eyes. They prescribed respectively the following treatments which certainly would not have helped: '. . . a solution of sugar of lead [lead acetate], rosewater, a teaspoonful of laudanum in a tumbler of water, Singleton's golden ointment mixed with lard, cold water and laudanum alone', Journal 1839

112 Jackson, P, 1987, op. cit., pp. 12–13

113 Journal entry 21 July 1836

114 Journal entry 28 April 1838

115 He resumed work for the Society in 1842, but received far fewer commissions than before

116 Journal entry 22 October 1841

117 Note at the back of Scharf's journal for 1840–1845

118 Journal entry 31 December 1846, p. 53

119 Journal entry 31 December 1846, pp. 51–52

120 One of these infrequent commissions was a view of Belvoir Castle, Rutland painted for the Prince von Thurn und Taxis in 1856

121 Journal entry 19 November 1850

122 Schwarzbach, F S, 1979, op. cit., p. 97

123 Journal entry 12 November 1850

124 Journal entry 23 January 1851

125 Journal entry 17 March 1847, p.97

126 Schwarzbach, F S, 1979, op. cit., p. 97

127 Jackson, P, 1987, op. cit., p. 15

128 In his journal entry for 20 January 1851 he records producing a lecture drawing of the Parthenon for George after Cockerell's restoration of the monument plus figures from the 'Harpy' tomb that George had helped discover in 1838

129 Henry had left to pursue his acting career

130 Journal entry 24 January 1851

131 Jackson, P, 1987, op. cit., p. 17

132 Ibid.

133 Schwarzbach, F S, 1979, op. cit., p. 97

134 Journal entry 25 January 1851

135 This was now provided by the Artists Amicable Fund, which he had joined in 1839, as he was no longer able to work

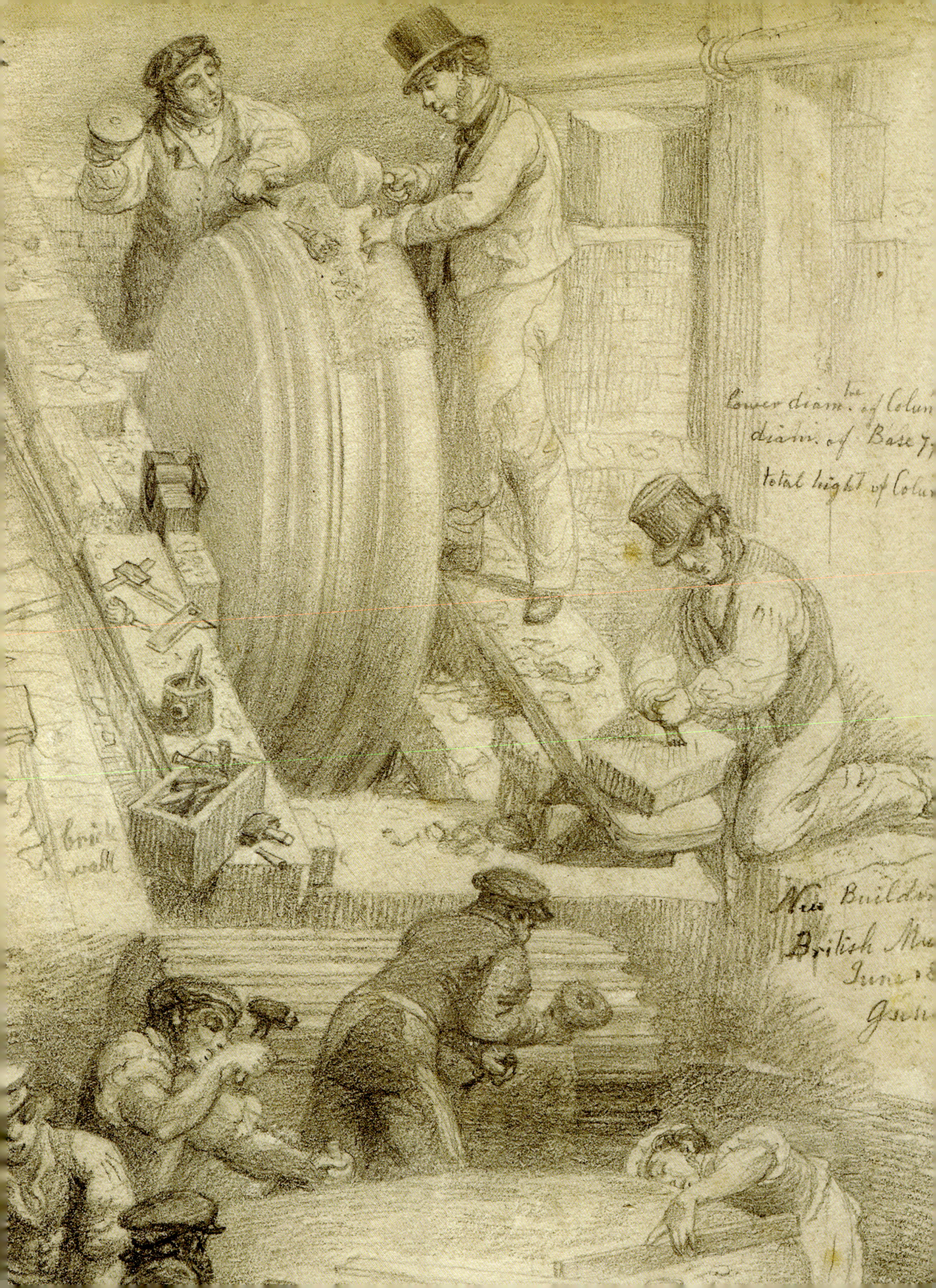
Lower diam.ter of Colun
diam. of Base 7
total hight of Colun
brick wall
New Buildi
British Mu
June 18

GEORGE SCHARF AND THE ARCHAEOLOGY OF THE MODERN

Caroline Arscott

Within nineteenth-century discourses on urban development and sanitary reform it is possible to identify an ideal of free circulation in the social body. Blockages were understood to cause disease and putrefaction.[1] Putrefaction would manifest itself in the form of dangerous fluids and gases. Where free circulation was not allowed miasmatic gas were liable to collect in an opaque pall. In such situations shadow takes on substance and threatens visibility itself.[2]

We can link the entertainment phenomenon of the panorama, enormously popular in the early to mid-nineteenth century, to the fantasy of a world where circulation was perfect. The delightfully vivid panoramic installations held out the fantasy of entirely unimpeded vision.[3] Panoramas encompassed many subjects and *topoi* but a number of key representations depicted London to its own inhabitants (and of course to visitors to the metropolis). The schemes of nineteenth-century urban planners were, by and large, concerned with unblocking the systems of the city, whether of air, sewage or traffic, and projects concerned with the abolition of random twists and turns and ancient impediments reinforced an aesthetic which was based on a modern commanding vision – immense in its scope, comprehensive in its detail. We see in the panoramas depicting the British metropolis a new-age confidence which could at its most bullish equate the viewing of London with the command of the entire globe. There is a readiness to emphasise open route-ways leading the eye through the built-up environment. In the panoramas depicting London from one central point there is an orchestration of vistas radiating outwards for the viewer to enjoy, empty paths amid the crowd of information.[4] The mass circulation panoramas of the 1840s, notably the strip panoramas offered by the illustrated papers, link the totalising capabilities of wrap-around vision with the ideological claims of bourgeois ideology, which asserts that opportunities and access to standardised truth are available to all subjects, without distinction.

Foucault's disciplinary society is very often invoked in discussions of the rendering visible of swathes of the nineteenth-century city. When back alleys as well as grand façades find their way into representation: in illustration, in reportage and in increasingly sophisticated kinds of mapping, and when street folk and the dispossessed are represented as well as the denizens of fashionable society, it seems that the viewer is being offered an opportunity for surveillance, or the pleasures and reassurance deriving from the power to see, and the opportunity to exercise the distinctions of category vital for control.[5] I would argue that the operations of surveillance are not necessarily congruent with that promise of social equality associated with the democratised panorama. Surveillance depends on one-way looking, carried out across a power differential. The forms of depiction associated with social exploration of the 1840s and 1850s (for instance illustrated reportage relating to impoverished areas of the city) emphasised the hard-won nature of those insights that were made available to readers and viewers. Texts and images dramatised those moments where the viewer was granted partial access to the previously unknown, but also dwelt on the murk or barriers that continued to hide further elements. One way of differentiating the visual regime of social exploration from the rhetoric of the panorama is to say that in social exploration the limits and thresholds of visibility are being tested. The pleasure offered to consumers of 1840s and 1850s images of slums and back courts was not that of omnipotence deriving from an idea that the world was complete and indivisible, rather these representational practices involved a fearful examination of difference.

This essay examines the topographical watercolours, prints and pencil drawings of George Scharf the Elder (1788–1860), father of Sir George Scharf (1820–95) the first Director of the National Portrait Gallery. Scharf's tireless sketching of the streets and sites of London, evidenced by a mass of loose and mounted drawings most of which are now in the British Museum, formed the basis for a number of quite ambitious projects: highly finished watercolours for the Royal Academy and other fine art exhibitions, and elaborate lithographs based on these that he published privately on a speculative basis, or very occasionally as commissions. He had most success with his hand-coloured lithographs of the Regent's Park Zoological Gardens (see fig. 4). In examining the characteristics of this work I will consider the ideological implications of Scharf's mode of

Cat. 29. Stonemasons at work on the columns in the British Museum (detail)

vision. It becomes apparent that Scharf's aesthetic does not rely on the rationalisation of space and guarantee of access in the panoramic mode nor does it depend on wresting insights in circumscribed forays into alien territory. My analysis of Scharf's topographic work invokes not the most obvious state institutions of the disciplinary society: the prisons, the workhouse, the police, but another set of voluntary and state institutions: the Geological Society of London, the Zoological Society, the College of Surgeons and the geological and medical departments of the universities. I want to suggest that the panopticon is not the only visual paradigm for the nineteenth century and to attend to modes of looking which characterised early nineteenth-century palaeontology. Too great a reliance on the panopticon makes us conceive of classification as a synchronic activity: identify, divide and rule. The classificatory activities of the palaeontologists, by contrast, have to do with diachronic systems. The arguments of Foucault's work on science, *The Order of Things* (1966), are perhaps more useful in this respect than his later work on prisons, *Discipline and Punish* (1972). Foucault asserted that the nineteenth century is marked by the incursion of time into previously fixed classificatory systems. Strata and species are distinguished in order to recombine them, eventually, in evolutionary syntheses. 2009 is the bicentenary of Charles Darwin's birth and the 150th anniversary of the publication of *On The Origin of Species* and, at this juncture more than ever before, it seems important to situate Darwin as one of the key thinkers allowing us to theorise modernity. It has been pointed out that Walter Benjamin invoked the fossil in his discussion of modernity in the *Passagen-Werk*.[6] To see fossils in the modern city: ladies' perms as fossilised curls, the glass-topped arcades as aquariums of primitive sea-life, is to emphasise the movement of history, as modernity leaves its earlier forms behind. It is also to suggest through fashion, through retail development, through technological change, the way that a material remnant (whether fossil or 'trace') can act as historical evidence, focusing historical forces as Benjamin's dialectical images attempt to do. If the modern is conceived of as prehistory then it is possible to conceive of a further social transformation, of a transition into actual history. Modernity might be thought of as an epoch subject to transformation rather than as an achieved end point.

Within Benjamin's fragmentary remarks on this matter, the homogenising effects of the panorama come to stand for an elision of disjuncture; this he sees as a misreading of Darwinian development, a refusal of the potential for morphology to express the doubleness of the dialectical image. The case I want to make for Scharf is that his idiosyncratic version of panoramic vision recognises morphology and perhaps leaves space for transmutation – that bothering and all-important cross-species jump. The contest in nineteenth-century science between Cuvier, on one hand, and the Lamarckians such as Geoffroy and Oken, on the other, split opinion into functionalist and evolutionary camps.[7] For the functionalists form followed function, as they considered different organisms to be tailored by God to occupy different niches. The proponents of evolution saw form developing throughout animal creation from one single fundamental type. In terms of geology as well as palaeontology a key debate was that between Cuvier, on one hand, as a proponent of catastrophism, and scientists such as Charles Lyell, on the other hand, who were arguing for uniformitarianism in the shape and phenomena of the earth. This essay asks whether we can position Scharf in the camp of the proponents of evolution and with the uniformitarians, assessing his social and professional contacts, his own views on the scientific debates insofar as the archival sources reveal them, and the motifs and formal characteristics of his topographical work. It does not arrive at a definitive answer to this question though, acknowledging the contradictory tropes in play.

Scharf's topographical views are most unusual in the number of working figures that are included.[8] He presents a city that teems with activity from knife grinding and chair mending to large scale construction work for roads bridges and railways. I would suggest, however, that Scharf's major preoccupation is not labour as such but the transformations brought about by labour. He attends to the controlled exertion of force on particular substances, very often with the interposition of mechanical devices (fig. 7). Without the effort at panorama it might be hard to discern anything in the fragmentary sketches that escapes the category of genre. However, it is important to realise that his sketches were produced as elements to be worked up and combined in various ways. His panoramic effects total up the dispersed activities and give us not just a fresh and amusing array of busy urban types but a sense of place and an inkling of an urban project. We might hesitate to attach the label 'progress' to their sum, because these scenes do not carry the usual markers of progress. We do not see finished environments for the modern bourgeoisie to inhabit: stable spatial systems that guarantee their safety

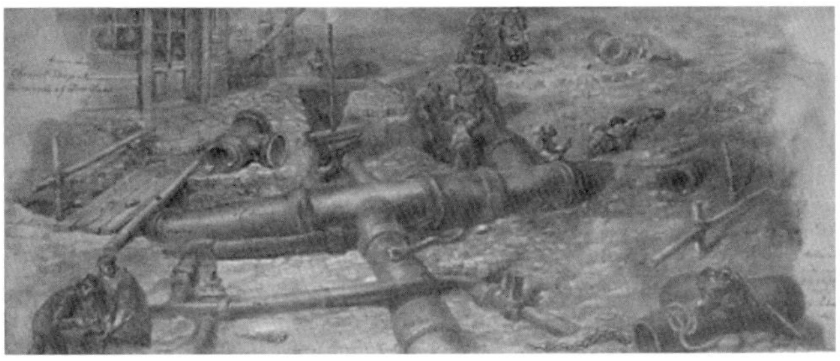

Fig. 7. Building common sewers in London: men laying pipes at the corner of Drury lane, George Scharf, graphite, 1845, the British Museum, 1862,0614.226

and yet include sufficient dynamic elements to bring to mind their ability to accumulate. What we see instead is the city in process: the dynamic elements have overtaken the markers of stability.

Scharf offers us a particular kind of urban landscape in which the visual organisation speaks of modernity in quite a different way from contemporary topographers such as Shepherd or Boys. The views in Shepherd's *Metropolitan Improvements* of 1829 or Thomas Shotter Boys's *London As It Is* of 1842 offer regular spaces, foursquare monuments and open paths for celebratory viewing. In one coloured lithograph in the Boys volume an air balloon in the sky serves as a focus of attention for the figures depicted. The inclusion of this modern spectacle alludes to the ideal of visual access within the improved metropolis. Even the sewer workers shown in this plate pause from their labour to view the balloon. An overview is given of all and the implication is that this clarity of vision is available for all. At ground level hollow pipes (elements of the sewer to be put in place) serve as eye glasses since the viewer of the print can look through them. Turning the pages of the volume the viewer is given a series of clearly set up perspectival schemes. If we consider the characteristics of Scharf's visual logic, in contrast, we find that geometric, single-point perspective does not dominate, and that vision is thematised in a different way. My argument is that his work suggests analogies with the investigations and records produced within the scientific community of the day. It is possible to develop a notion of scientific vision, proper to modernity, that is nonetheless at some distance from correct perspectival systems, with their associations of rationality, which are usually described as scientific.

Scharf did undertake a number of panoramic representations of London sites. His panoramic views represent his attempts at a synthesis of the urban scene for public consumption. His large-scale lithographs of the works for the new London Bridge, commissioned by the London Bridge Committee of the City Corporation date from 1830. These prints were produced by Scharf from the two large-scale watercolours he painted for the Committee, each five feet in length (subsequently destroyed). The view of the southern approach road to the new bridge falls into three zones: the new road and bridge, Southwark High Street (to be demolished) and the ancient buildings around the church that became Southwark Cathedral. In one hand-coloured version of the lithograph the working forge in this medieval section on the far right stands out with a red glow against the darkness, linking the most ancient to the technological processes of the modern.[9] This immediately alerts us to the way Scharf's views escape the binary alternatives of dark/light, dirty/clean, or ancient/modern.

It is always hard to get a secure footing in Scharf's views, but, in the spirit of the excited and intrepid family groups he depicts, viewers can pick through the disruption and rubble of the bridge works and find much to fascinate and entertain them. A group in the middle ground of the view of the northern approach road gazes over at Thames Street (fig. 8). The improvements bring, as a consequence, the ability to survey the surrounding city, but this is only part of the visual experience here, because the building activity itself creates so much to look at. The image's emphasis is on the interest and ingenuity of labour rather than on the sublimity of disciplined cohorts: industry is conceived of as episodic. In this it contrasts with other representations of industrial projects from this time period, for example, J C Bourne's views of railway works. In Scharf's scenes time discipline is not observed: strenuous work coexists with meal breaks and workers knocking on or knocking off. The operations are particularised. Individual craftsmen dress stone with plain and decorative finishes: some blocks scattered about the site, others already in position on the walls of the approach steps to the bridge. A massive joist serves as platform on one side while a rope and timber cantilevered platform provides more orthodox support on the other. Elsewhere workmen form teams to shift the gigantic slabs. On the left a winch and rope and wooden rollers are employed, on the right another group is busy with levers and wedges. In the centre of this view a temporary railway makes it possible to shift a block on a trolley so that it can be hauled into the depth of the picture. There is a remarkably democratic, unstructured mix, in a single arena, of labourers, overseers, engineers and sightseers. We are not given variety of character but variety of means and variety of engagement with the materials and substance of the urban environment.

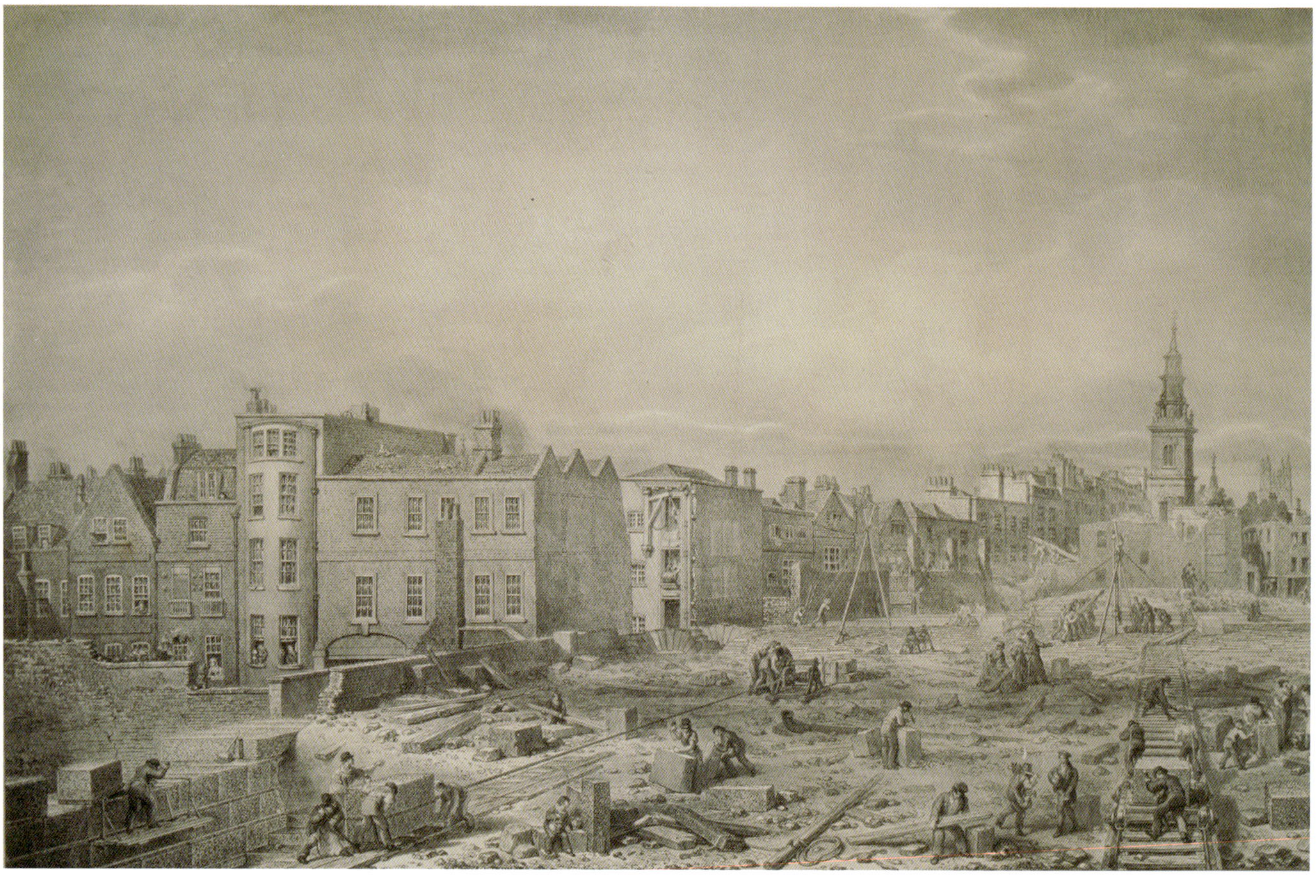

Fig. 8. Northern approach to London Bridge, George Scharf, lithograph, 1830 (detail) © City of London

The size of the images and the level of detail mean that the viewer is obliged physically to move along while viewing the scene, picking out interesting items, whether the prints are laid out on a table or hung on a wall. This progressive, rather than integrated, viewing was in fact characteristic both of the full-size panoramas installed at London's Colosseum in Regent's Park and elsewhere and the fold-out panoramas that were a side product of such installations. In other respects Scharf departs from the conventions of the panorama. He does not give us a disembodied viewpoint, and, rather than adopting the standard ploy of de-emphasising the embarrassingly stretched foreground of a panorama to create the illusion of scanning an actual distance, he makes a virtue of opening up the foreground. The opening up almost seems to operate at the level of the opening up of the ground itself as we are faced with earth and rubble and piles of building stone.

The central feature of the bridge approach road in each of these images opens up the view as a prospect to some extent, though the odd plunging perspective, produced by the exaggerated width of the foreground, moderates this effect. Furthermore the view through is blocked by not-yet-demolished buildings, notably the brick buildings immediately in front of the centrally placed church of St Michael, Crooked Lane, in the view of the northern approach. The images are in transition between panorama and vista but the transition cannot be made without the physical dismantling of obstacles and construction of the road. It is absolutely characteristic of Scharf that these processes should be twinned. In this way Scharf's departure from an authoritative overview depends on excavation that is both literal and pictorial.

We can see many of these characteristics in less formal work on a domestic scale. Scharf made drawings of the view from the back of his house for instance. In the 1844 pencil drawing of the back of the house in Francis Street (cat. 12) which shows painters at work two doors away, he shows us the way in which the solids and voids of the architectural structure are subject to interchange as hinged openings on coal shute and brick privy are liable to open, as do the hinged and sash windows; the empty space of the back court further down is transformed by the mass of scaffolding animated by busy painters. The environment is full of quirks and surprises including the geraniums on a first-floor windowsill, the maidservant leaning out of a window at second-floor level next door, and the little heart cut into the privy door, just visible at it swings open. Another drawing from a back window dating from 1850 employs a peculiarly elastic viewpoint. The view takes us across roof tops and along the row of houses, glancing through into Woburn Square on the left and up to the chimney stacks on the right. Along the way we look through windows and doorways, peer down into yards and note a range of activities: sand being dug into a wagon, a coach being driven away. In one house milk is being delivered at the door downstairs while clothes are being pegged out from an upper window on to a line that can be

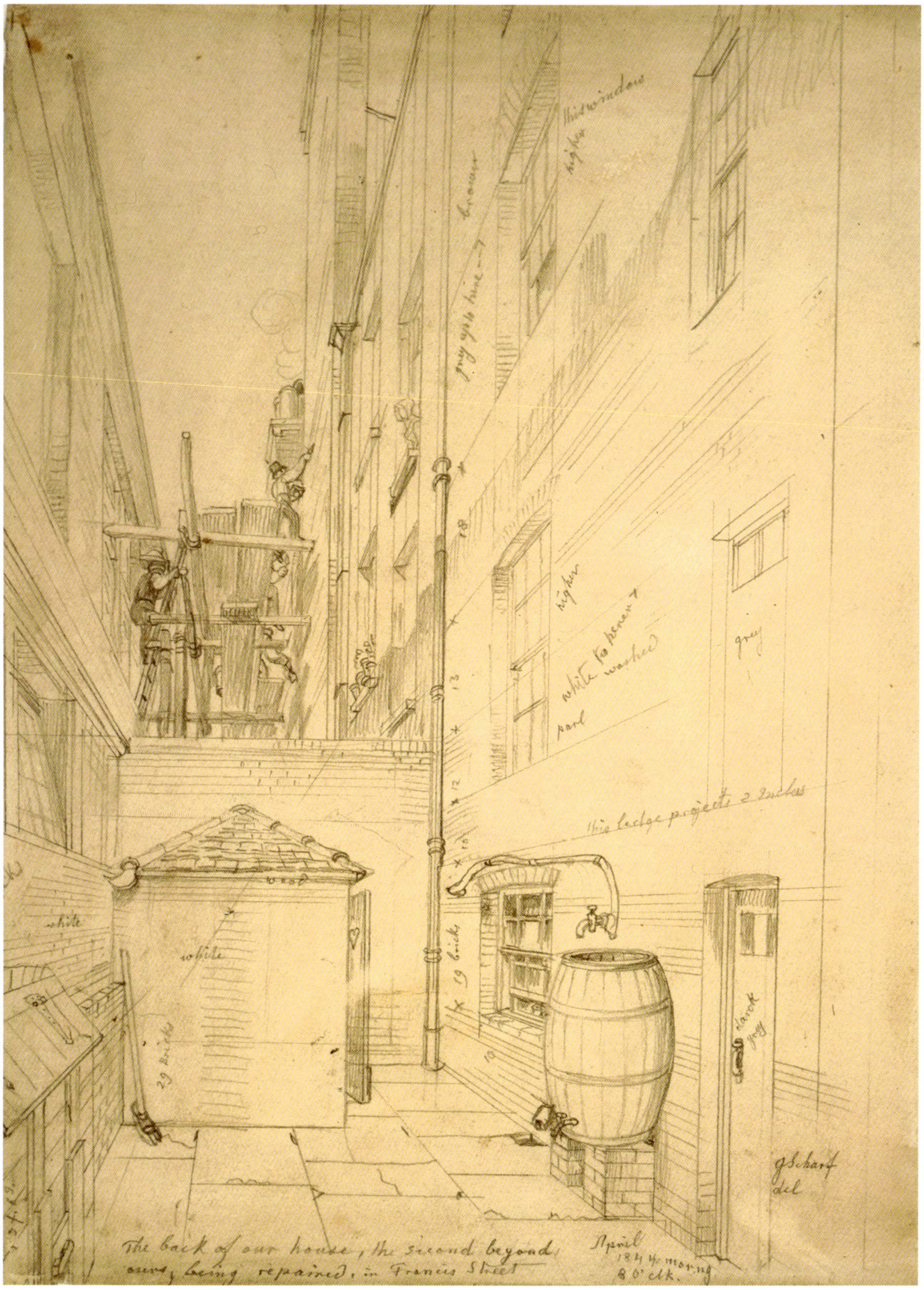

Cat. 12. The back of Scharf's house in Francis Street

moved between the buildings on a pulley. One level further back we can see a housemaid inside cleaning a third-floor window, while outside a man climbs a ladder past the fourth-floor window and, above her, roofers hoist up planks with ropes. This is the registration of accidental detail, a scrutiny that takes no account of finished façades, but directs its curiosity to the obverse and the inside – red geraniums put out in pots on sills, plants glimpsed through the raised side section of a conservatory extension, a carriage pulled out from an open mews for its wheel to be repaired. It is a world that constantly entails activity. Figures work in and on an open structure that is conceived of as being in process.

On the building site labour demolishes the past and lays foundations for the future, whereas in the archaeological excavation it unearths the past. Digging on either kind of site might uncover fossils. The excavation is the contingent form of the intersection between the industrialising present and the prehistoric past – crucial in the link between the mining industries and the burgeoning science of geology. As a skilled lithographer specialising in scientific subjects Scharf was professionally employed in drawing antiquities, fossils, maps and sections, skeletons and organs of creatures, and dissections of the human body. He had close contact with the leading scientists of the day, and as a regular attender at learned society meetings saw geologists, zoologists, surgeons and naturalists presenting and debating their work in the field that came to be known as palaeontology: the study of fossil remains. I would suggest that the intellectual issues of the day, concerning the differentiation of species and the history of the earth's structure are relevant to the whole range of Scharf's work.[10] We can point to a level of intellectual engagement on Scharf's part, drawing on the evidence in his journals. He worked for competing figures: for Buckland as well as for Lyell, for the young Darwin, for Mantell and for Murchison.[11]

Among the scientific fraternity the only man who was a close friend of Scharf was the geologist Thomas Webster who was appointed Professor of Geology at University College, London in 1842.[12] Webster brought him a copy of Buckland's Bridgewater Treatise to look at, in 1836, which Scharf described as 'a curious book' on natural theology and geological subjects.[13] Buckland was one of the main proponents of a reconciliation of geology with scripture, and stressed the role of the Biblical flood in the extinction of species. Catastrophism linked Buckland's work to the position established by Cuvier. Scharf had done drawings for Buckland on a regular basis at least since 1833 (fig. 9) and

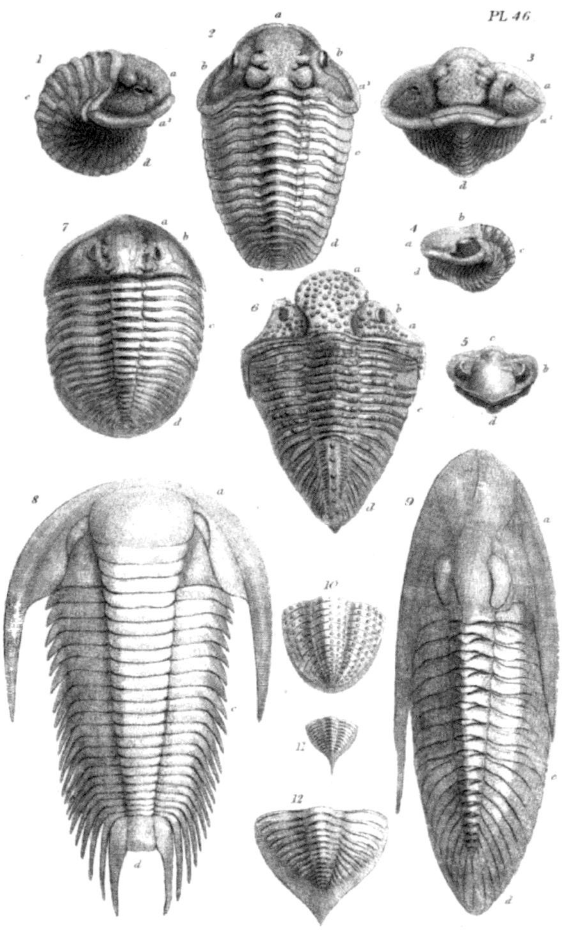

Fig. 9. Trilobites, George Scharf, plate 46, in Revd William Buckland, *Geology and Mineralogy*, 1837, vol. II

in recognition of this work, and in particular for redrawing a view of the Axemouth landslip, Buckland himself made a present of the volume to Scharf in 1840 (21 April) – 'a very handsome present', noted Scharf. He was quite taken with Buckland's comments on the fusing of shells into crystalline matter and with this sixth Bridgewater Treatise generally. The class and educational difference meant that Scharf was, by and large, perceived as a valued ancillary rather than an equal in this elite scientific circle of London, but he was a particularly privileged onlooker with unique access to the newest work of a range of writers and investigators. Despite the lively controversy between competing theoretical positions in this area, Scharf remained, as far as we can work out from his journals, unpartisan. His association with these scientists exposed him to a range of predominantly Tory or Peelite, Church of England positions. The energetic, radical, dissenting position represented by Grant, Ryan and the London medical schools remained marginal to the centre of power and institutional recognition. The most explicit proponents of a developmental history of the world were these radicals – and they were unequivocal in their support of Geffroyan notions of transmutation.[14]

Within the elite circle, one great opponent of Buckland was Lyell who rejected an explanation of change in terms of a cataclysmic event, and conceived of change as taking place gradually over very long periods. For him the earth was a steady state system where rising land masses were compensated for by sinking ones and new species replace those extinguished, in a system of dynamic stability. Scharf did work for Lyell, and enjoyed his interesting papers, for instance on 2 June 1841, and also prepared drawings for Lyell's ally Mantell who worked primarily on fossils. He also drew fossils for Murchison whose major intervention in the field rested on his identification in the 1830s of a Silurian system below carboniferous levels in the mountains of Wales, where there was no land vegetation, and limited and fairly uniform fauna. This system, which seemed to be world-wide, from evidence elsewhere, lent weight to opponents of Buckland, and supported the notion of, at the lowest level, a layer without life, (not, according to Murchison to be explained by metamorphosis or the fusing of organic matter) with subsequent layers of increasingly complex life forms. Murchison proposed a model that, unlike Lyell's, was progressive and directional. Scharf's enthusiasm for the papers presented at the Geological Society was constant. Whether the papers were by the glacier-mad Louis Agassiz, the astronomer Sir John Herschel or a lesser known name logging flint finds, Scharf was equally appreciative, finding the talks 'interesting' or 'very interesting', and often giving a brief indication in his journal of the topic.[15] But his greatest enthusiasm was undoubtedly reserved for Richard Owen the anatomist. His papers were always marked as 'very interesting', whether at the Geological Society: on Saurian teeth for example, or in his annual series on comparative anatomy at the Royal College of Surgeons, for example a lecture on the digestive organs in insects or the comparative anatomy of the recent and extinct animals.[16] In 1837 Scharf said of the introductory lecture in this series '[it was] one of the best delivered and most interesting I ever heard'.[17] On another occasion he was moved to call Owen's lectures 'beautiful'.[18]

Richard Owen was Hunterian Professor of Anatomy at the Royal College of Surgeons. In a portrait of 1845 by Pickersgill (National Portrait Gallery) he is shown at the age of 41 years, at a time when he held a prestigious position, highly respected in his field, not yet locked into damaging disputes with Darwin and, especially, Huxley over evolutionary theory.[19] These disputes emerged post 1859 in the wake of Darwin's publication of *The Origin of Species*. Pickersgill shows Owen with a nautilus shell and the portrait nicely sums up his twin interest in living and extinct organisms: the nautilus was a living version of the ammonites that regularly turned up as fossils. On the left of the portrait is the internal part of the creature, preserved in a jar.

Owen's fame in the 1840s was based on his work in comparative anatomy. He had published important work on teeth, on the extinct, ostrich-like Moa and on the prehistoric giant sloth, the Mylodon. His monograph, *Memoir on the Pearly Nautilus*, was published in 1832. The nautilus is a cephalopod. In his 1860 volume *Palaeontology* Owen notes that there are 1,400 extinct species of lower cephalopods while there are only three equivalent modern species.[20] The fossil varieties sometimes reached great size, some ammonites three foot in diameter and some of the straight shelled species six foot in length, equivalent to the height of a man. Owen as anatomist is concerned with insides as well as outsides, with the fact that the shell itself is made of two layers, 'the outer porcellanous the inner pearly', and with the organisation of the soft inner portion which can be linked with the less ancient cephalopods represented by the modern cuttlefish and octopus, which are 'more active and intelligent', and have an interior or endogenous skeletal structure, rather than an external or exogenous one.[21] The study of fossils is predicated on an interest in the insides and outsides of structures, as the process of replacement of organic matter by mineral matter depends on the differential decay of soft and hard portions. Pickersgill's portrait alludes to these matters through the analogy it offers between the figure of Owen and the nautilus. Most clearly we see a visual parallel between the broad forehead of Owen and the shape of the shell. We might be led to describe the quality of shine on his forehead as porcellenous, and the even brighter highlight on teeth and gum as pearly. We are led to wonder what is inside this smooth surfaced man, indeed the very idea of comparative anatomy permits such speculation. The rather extraordinary ridged furry outline of his arm, half hidden in the shadows on the side of the preserved internal organs, suggests there is something other than a somewhat blank exterior. But Owen's ideas offer an additional, less visceral, way of thinking about inside and outside in this case. He proposed a Platonic explanation of development in which successive stages of creation are understood as the embodiment of God's ideal plan. By 1849 in *On the Nature of Limbs* he had formulated this, in the case of vertebrates, as an archetype: a schematised blueprint for fish, reptiles, birds and mammals, including man. The ideal diagrammatic vertebra has bony extrusions forming channels for the nerve and blood supply. These extrusions can become displaced and develop further appendages. Careful comparison, Owen argued, could demonstrate the homology between bones in early or primitive vertebrate forms and those in more recent or higher species such as man. The polarity of surface and interior can then be reframed as idea and embodiment, God's mind and earthly matter. The natural world appears very generally as the word made flesh, and this depiction of a scholar in his robes takes on the quality of an ecclesiastical portrait. The divine does not just offer an item from mundane existence, rather he is offering the glowing and shining elements of the Eucharist in which the word is made flesh.[22] Pickersgill's portrait might be said to indicate the mental energy and sense of divine mission that could move Scharf to describe Owen's lectures as beautiful.

In terms of scientific investigation and visual perception, I want to investigate a number of themes: this question of interior/exterior, and other themes such as homology and fusion. The incisions of anatomical study offer a ready analogy to the cutting of railway or road routes, or the opening up of underground systems to lay gas or sewage pipes. Some of Scharf's views of roadworks look very much like diagrams of dissections or operations. In his large watercolour of the New Fleet Sewer (fig. 10) the neat oblong shape of the cavity suggests first of all a recumbent figure and then the controlled and limited opening of a surgical procedure. The notion of surgical procedure being controlled or investigative was quite a new one in the

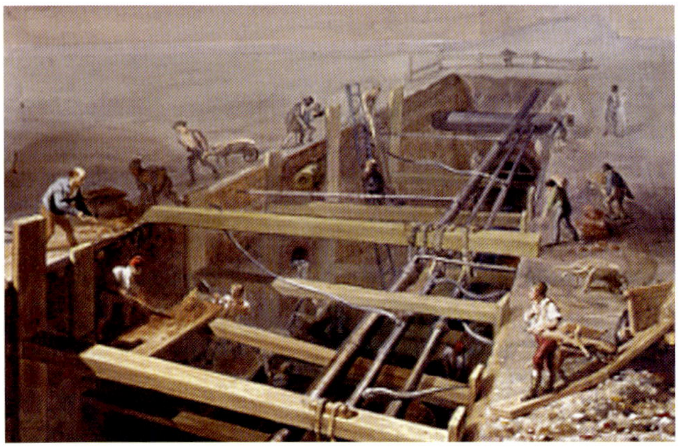

Fig. 10. Building the New Fleet Sewer, George Scharf, watercolour over graphite, 1825, the British Museum, 1862,0614.416

early nineteenth century as the discovery of anaesthetic had transformed the possibilities of surgery; in this respect Scharf's metaphor includes an additional connotation of modernity. Earth and rubble is being moved out of the pit, but there seems to be very little sense of the earth being dirty or in any way contaminating. It has to be cleared to give access to the sewers and service pipes, and the digging has rendered visible the many different pipes and channels that exist underground. If we bear in mind the surgical parallel we can think in terms of the fluids and tissues of the body that do not constitute dirt for the surgeon – dirt comes from outside the body – but fluids and tissues may have to be swabbed or cut away to reveal the inner workings. The dull gleam picked out by the highlighting on the top of the gas and water pipes that run the length of the opening, the brighter shine indicated on the snaking supply lines running from these pipes and the light catching the water that falls from the arched sewer on the left imparts a sense of wonder to this picture of a muddy hole. This is marvellous first of all because it is so large that a huge ladder is needed to provide access the base of the sewer, fifteen feet down: it is a pit on an immense scale that dwarfs workers and spectators. Secondly it is marvellous because it is so complicated. The viewer of the image is not swept away with awe but is permitted to get a grip. This is a scientific viewing that, we might argue, precludes an experience of the sublime. Ten or twenty years later Ruskin's project was to use natural theology to wed science to the sublime but in the 1830s and 1840s it seems that the visual experience and mental operations required by science could stand aside from the sublime. This was not the standard mode of perceiving the city in the pre-Victorian and early Victorian period. Emerging out of a fantasy of unimpeded vision and clear streets was the evocation of a filthy city of miasmatic back courts. Owen himself contributed to the literature of social investigation and it is interesting to look at his text of 1845 on urban conditions.

A report on Lancaster was prepared by Owen for the Second Health of Towns Enquiry, and Owen was sufficiently invested in the findings to issue it separately as a pamphlet. He starts with an ironic vision of a sparklingly clean Lancaster framed in an eighteenth-century tradition of cityscape. His description is taken from a guidebook of 1807:

> Lancaster . . . being built on rising ground is remarkable for cleanness; this and its proximity to the coast, render its air pure and salubrious . . . The cleanly aspect of the

town is heightened by the effect of white and variegated sandstone of which the houses of the principal streets are mostly built.[23]

He then goes on to detail the horrors of the backcourts of modern Lancaster, a town of 2,260 acres, not including the prison and the lunatic asylum. Sugar-house-alley is just one foul example.

> In Sugar-house-alley . . . the backs of the houses open upon an inclosed area, along the bottom of which flows the old mill-race. The approach to this area is by a narrow covered passage, on entering which I was met by an indescribable kind of damp, sub-foetid emanation; at the end of the passage was a privy: the midden-heap being partly concealed in a vault or cellar, beneath the ground-floor of the house, perforated by the passage. Emerging thence, I stood upon a steep bank leading from the backs of the houses to the bed of the mill-stream; on the opposite side was a lofty wall, at each end a low arch, through which the black filthy stream was sluggishly flowing. Each arch supported houses, completing the inclosure of the area. The stream was confined to the mid-channel; at the sides it formed stagnant pools, receiving the drainings from ash and midden heaps and the out-castings from the overhanging windows. The foetid solution soaks through the foundations of the houses. When the tide flows, the mill-race, receiving the main sewage of the town, is driven back towards its source, traversing the area in its progress, and again slowly returns at the ebb. Thus the inclosed area, about forty yards in length, is ventilated chiefly by impure atmosphere, which escapes from beneath the arches at the end of every flux and reflux of the stream. A more typical source of miasmata can scarcely be conceived.[24]

The concern with circulation and blockages is evident and the miasmatic pall is vividly evoked. Owen's piece ends with a contrast between the awful state of the town he has just described and the sanitary system of Lancaster prison, which had been explicitly excluded from the area assessed. The prison with its flushing toilets and its ceramic pipes for waterborne sewage stands on a hill like an ideal industrialised version of that gleaming guidebook town that opened the report. He concludes by hoping that 'that which has been done on principles of economy for the sanitary condition of the inmates of the jail, will be attempted, its equal economy and efficiency being made manifest to the authorities, in behoof of the health, the cleanliness, the domestic comfort and the morals of the honest and industrious poor'.[25] Owen's text reproduces the ideal and the infernal city familiar from nineteenth-century literary and investigative texts. It is intriguing to see the prison being proposed as the paradigmatic technological solution to the aesthetic and moral problems of modernity.

A further examination of Scharf's drawings reveals some of the scientific aspects of his vision. In a drawing of 1834 (cat. 60) we see a junction section of pipe being put into place. This is part of the process of inserting a side supply off the mains gas. To do so the labourers have to incise a section for a T-junction, and we see further T-junctions, in various diameters, lying on the ground. The surface of cobble stones gives way to earth beneath and existing layers of sewage pipes in various diameters, distinguishable from gas pipes by their sweeping curves (necessary to prevent blockages) running alongside and

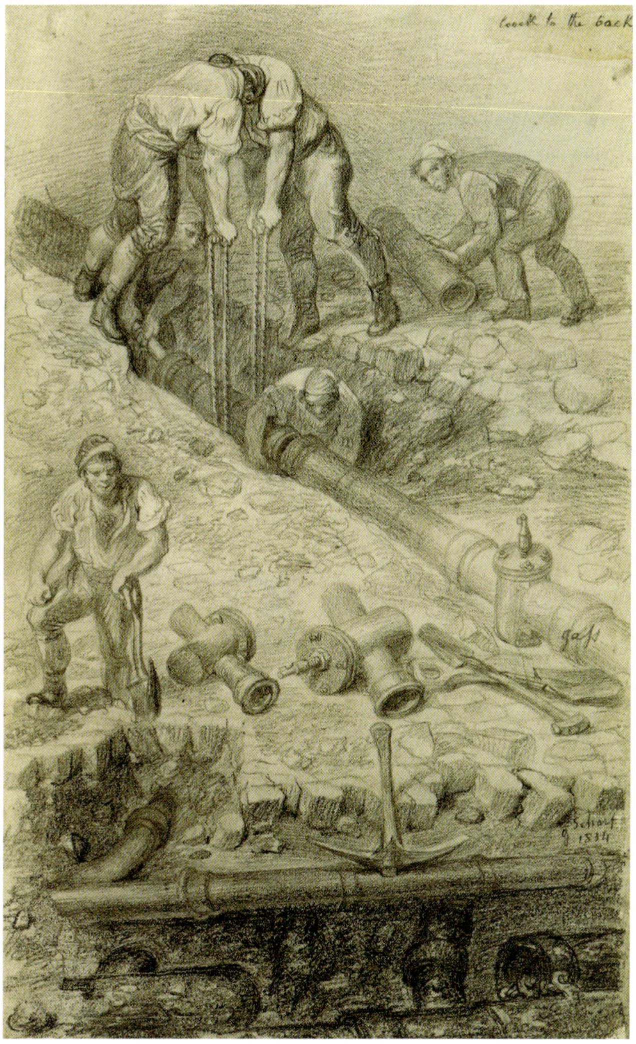

Cat. 60. Group of men fitting and laying gas pipes

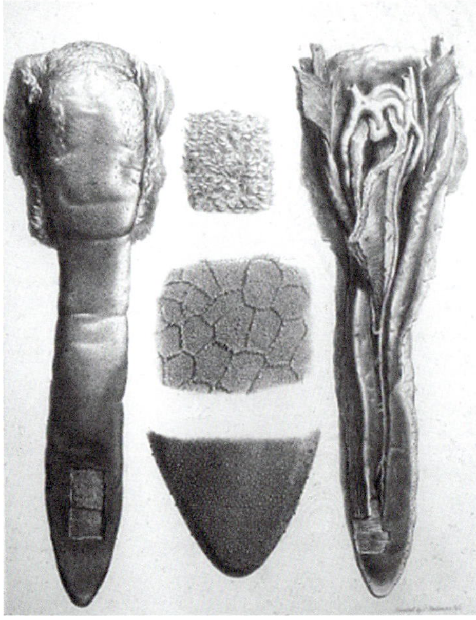

Fig. 11. Giraffe's Tongue, George Scharf, in *Transactions of the Zoological Society*, vol. 2, 1841, pl. 41

underneath each other. The city itself is seen to be a multi-layered system of immense complexity, where the features to be noticed are both structural and have differentiated functions. Here the image seems to offer us both a view from above and an archaeological cross-section. Scharf is always quite precise about the materials and structure of different elements, and his notes to the drawings indicate that this was linked to an awareness of their function. A note in the margin of the Fleet Sewer watercolour notes that the thick pipe is 'Gass' [sic] and the two smaller ones 'water'. The gas pipe lies nearer the surface and is thicker and heavier, consequently it is lashed to its support with a heavy iron chain. This is juxtaposed to the bindings for the water pipes which have to be longer, but for which stout rope suffices. As in the anatomical drawing of a giraffe's tongue (fig. 11), done for Owen in the *Transactions of the Zoological Society*, Scharf is not just interested in what a surface looks like, but in the organisation of different surfaces, and the underlying elements. So we can compare the attention to the cutting and laying of hexagonal and diamond shaped wooden paving blocks on sand, in Scharf's drawing of workmen laying a pavement in London in 1840 (fig. 12), to the differentiated surfaces of the giraffe's tongue. Owen's text on the tongue is concerned with how the tongue works. He explained:

> The giraffe being endowed with an organ so exquisitely formed for prehension, instinctively puts it to use in a variety of ways while in a state of confinement . . . In our own menagerie many a fair lady has been robbed of the artificial flower which adorned her bonnet by the nimble filching tongue of the object of her admiration.

He sought to demonstrate that the tongue does not become erect by being charged with blood, that it works with the same muscles, nerves and blood vessels, as tongues of other herbivores. Clearly there are issues of gender and sexuality involved in this discourse. Owen demonstrates, in this case, that the giraffe's long tongue does not erect like a penis, but his work deals so often with the enlargement or shrinking of comparable organs in the species under consideration that the phallic analogy never seems far away. Owen is preoccupied with the relationship between the small horns of the giraffe and its long neck, compared to the huge horns and short neck of the elk, and surmised that the vital force of a creature could only be stretched so far. The uterus of the giraffe was studied along with other parts (fig. 13). The preoccupation with life force carried over into his concept of the relationship between higher and lower life forms, the using up of vital force creating a break between species. This kept his morphology from straying into the dangerously radical territory of a continuous evolutionary chain. We might speculate as to whether the gender implications of Owenite comparative anatomy can be discerned in the vision of the city that emerges in Scharf's work. At first sight the motifs of excavation and investigation might lead us to assume that the city is being subjected to the punishing medical investigation reserved especially for female bodies and that the city, consequently, is identified as female. But Scharf's city seems to be an organism or system that pulses with life, and the gendering of this pulse is ambivalent. A link is often made between heat and growth in these works. If the earth itself is volcanic then city-dwellers access this fire for their transformative endeavours: one connection

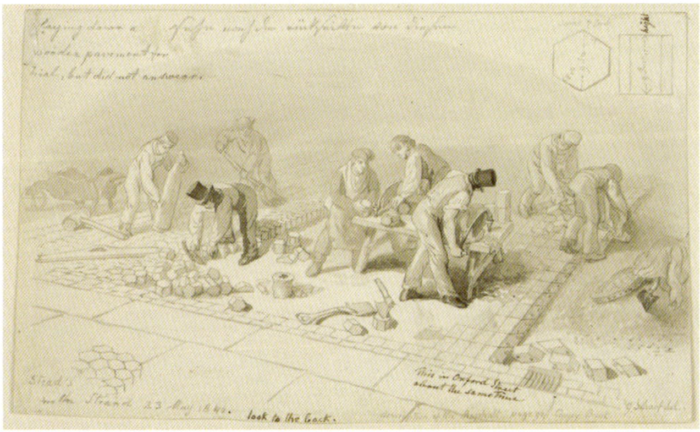

Fig. 12. Labourers using a guillotine(?) on a bench while others lay a wooden pavement as a trial piece in the Strand, George Scharf, graphite, 1840, the British Museum, 1862,0614.1132

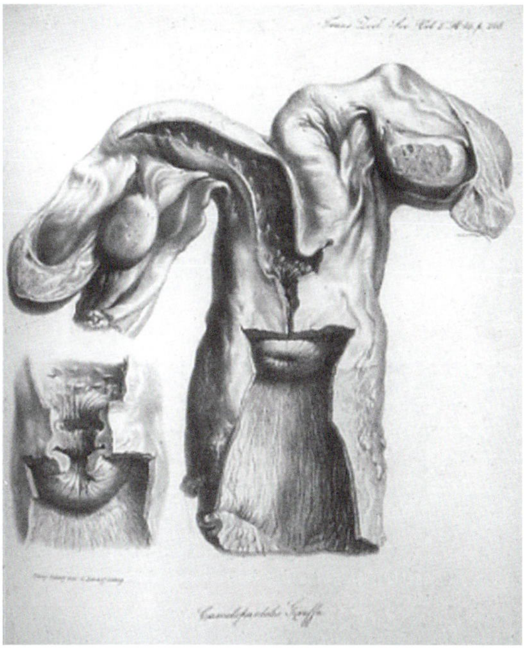

Fig. 13. Giraffe's Uterus, George Scharf, in *Transactions of the Zoological Society,* vol.2, 1841, pl. 45

being made is between vitality and virility. The defining characteristics of modernity, for Scharf, include a gigantisation of form. Once again it is possible to unearth or bury massive elements comparable to the remains of creatures of prehistory.

The skeleton of the city can be seen round and seen through in Scharf. Passages take us in and round structures, figures are seen to disappear down little alleys and people occupy and look through the shop elements in scenes that do not settle as vistas. We lose a sense of the clearly inside or outside. Frameworks are usually collapsible and reconfigurable, like the umbrellas and folding bedsteads he details. Hats can be transposed and glued on boards inner side showing or on heads. The quality of material substance is never lost sight of. The boots in one advertising display that he draws are impermeable and dipping them in a portable water tank will prove it. The hydraulic systems that fascinate Scharf, whether in ingenious coffee pots or mighty engineering works, depend upon impermeable pipework, but these pipes move between street and dwelling upsetting a barrier of inside and outside, and any breach can have the fluid contents dripping (fig. 14). For all his interest in machines and industrial technology Scharf's city is an organic system in which transformations can take place equivalent to the mystery of an exogenous organism giving way to an endogenous one. The biological processes involved when the vascular pulp of teeth is transformed to dentine, and the chemical processes when organic dentine changes to stone as a fossil is formed are both relevant.

Owen's anatomical investigations are always concerned with the comparison of organs and features of different creatures. This brings me on to the question of homology and analogy: the same things, different in size, like a giant ammonite and a modern pearly nautilus, or similar in shape but different in kind, as in the giraffe that was thought from its neck to be a kind of camel, but is shown by Owen not to be, and things where the shape has changed but the functional structure is identical, as in an uncoiled ammonite. This seems to me an important organising feature of Scharf's city views, where much of the humour consists in puns between forms. As just one example we can take the craning necks of spectators and the curve of skirt and frock coat which is humorously compared to the stuffed giraffes on the landing in the British Museum (cat. 34). The question of scale was a crucial part of Scharf's practice of scientific drawing; he took lithography to its limits, producing life-size renderings of huge fossils, as in his depictions of the Giant Sloth produced for Owen, which were produced as plates that folded out (fig. 15), and he was frequently engaged in reproducing scientific drawings on a huge scale for lectures. We can start to see enormous building elements in the modern city as

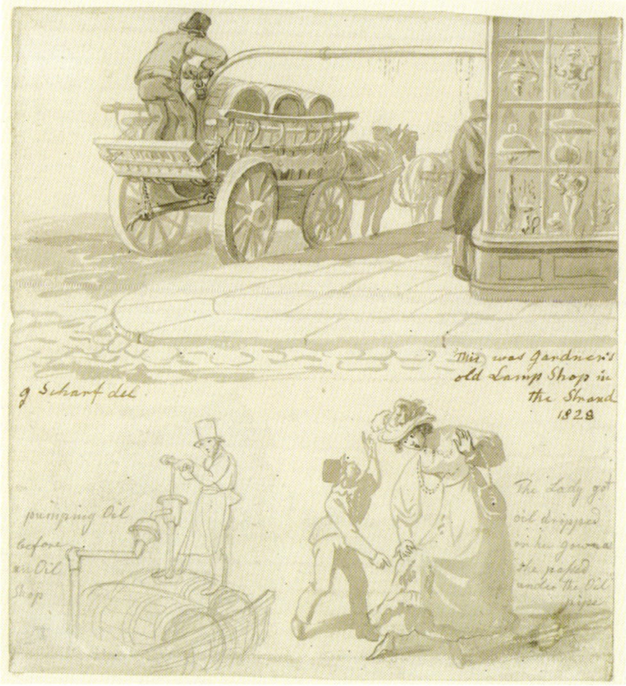

Fig. 14. Cart carrying oil barrels making delivery, George Scharf, watercolour with graphite 1828, the British Museum, 1862,0614.1042

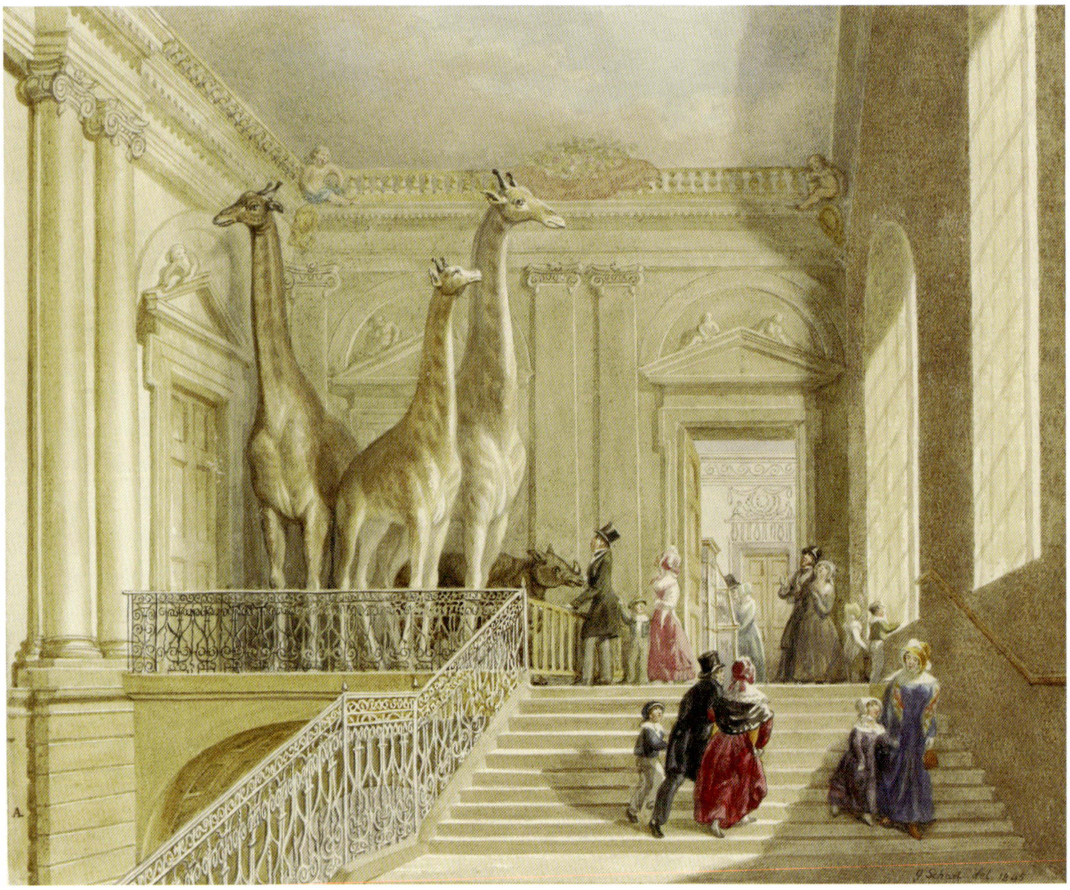

Cat. 34. Staircase of the old British Museum in Montagu House

homologous to the gigantic creatures of pre-history – a girder for the British Museum or for the Royal College of Surgeons as a rib or jaw bone.

My final point concerns fusion. If the transformation of soft organic matter into stone is a fundamental concept in palaeontology then so is the notion of the melting of rock and the movement of the earth. Scharf presents us with a number of cases where solid substances are liquidised, and liquids turn to gas. Gas in turn seems to be so thick it is almost solid. In his watercolour of the steamboat landing jetty at London Bridge there is a play on these themes as the solid land and the rocking boats form a common path, as the thick black obscuring smoke from the steamship is contrasted with the illuminating gas. The light renders transparent veils, which on the darker side seem opaque. In the watercolour of the laying of a gas main a workman cooks up lead to seal the joint, while the main is being cut with a drill clutch (cat. 28). Thick black smoke belches out,

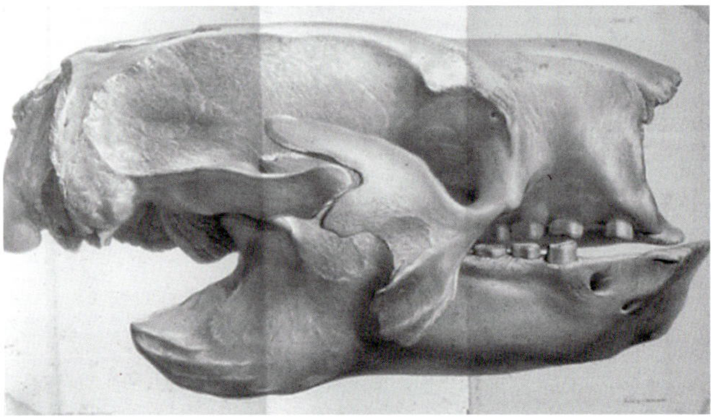

Fig. 15. Skull of the Giant Sloth, George Scharf, in R Owen, *Description of the Skeleton of an Extinct Gigantic Sloth Mylodon Robustus,* London, 1842, Plate II

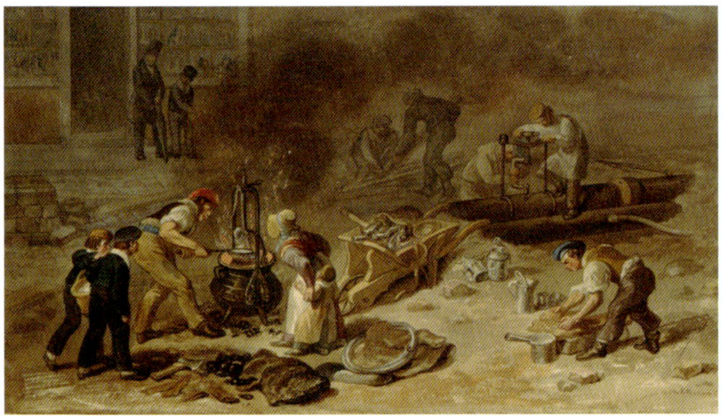

Cat. 28. Men repairing the gas pipes in Tottenham Court Road

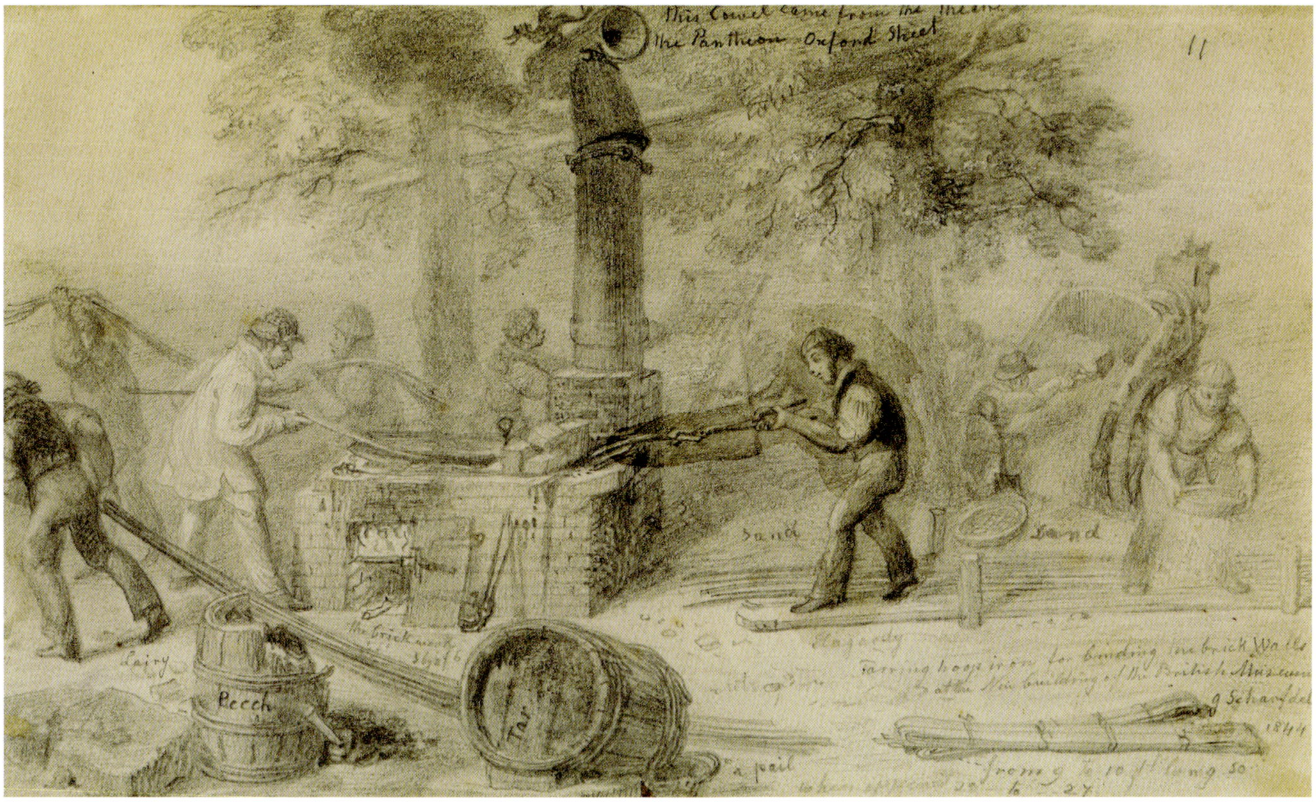

Cat. 30. Tarring the iron hooping used for binding the brickwork at the New Building of the British Museum

again raising the question of the transformation of inert substance. In the drawing of buildings for the British Museum Scharf shows us iron rods (labelled hoop iron) being heated and coated with tar, and then with sand to stop corrosion, to be used to make cramp fixings to reinforce walls, tying brick and stone structures together (cat. 30). The theme of cycles of substance in this drawing is first indicated by the recycled architectural feature, used as the chimney, and then in the zigzag progress of rods from bundles, bottom right, to iron passed across the stove, from left to right, through the sand, again to the right, and then taken away as treated rods, from right to left. Then we are given a tar barrel in the foreground which is itself made with iron hoops. There is a circularity here which is taken up in a larger, finished watercolour view of the scene, which includes a horse-driven machine in the centre, a huge circular pit where the mechanical paddle mixes lime mortar (fig. 16). Slaked lime is known as quick lime, and this instance of life in stone, and the building process of liquefaction and solidification, as the cement paste is made and then sets, offers a parallel to the processes of the emergence and extinction of life.

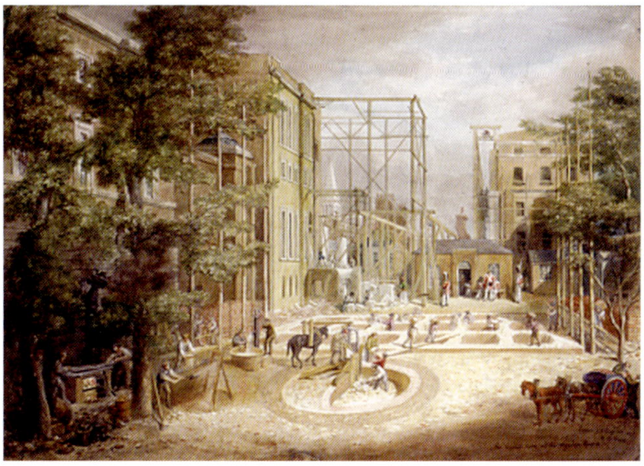

Fig. 16. Laying the Foundations of the Lycian Room, the British Museum, George Scharf, watercolour over graphite, 1845, the British Museum, 1862,0614.617

The pattern of visual attention in Scharf's topographical work tempts us to make general thematic points. The simultaneous raising and demolition processes in Scharf's views might make us see Lyellian themes, the motifs of measurement, set squares and the unrolling of plans; Owenite ones, the fusion of substance, could be linked to Buckland's notion of transformed diluvial layers. I am not arguing anything so specific. Given the fierce controversy in scientific circles in the period 1820–50 there is some difficulty in conceiving of such specific references and

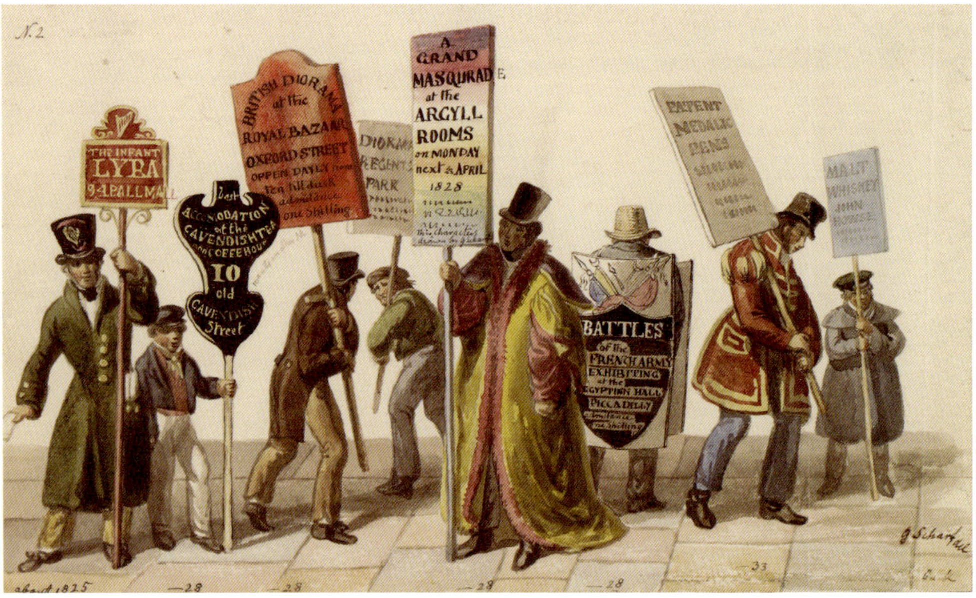

Cat. 22. *Men and boys with advertising boards*

paradigms as coexisting in a single *oeuvre*. However Scharf seemed able to take on a range of perhaps contradictory tropes; for all the potential for contradiction I would argue that they are recognisable as tropes in his topographical work.

I have looked at 'some motifs in' Scharf, and hope to have indicated the importance of time and process within his representations of the modern city. This constant relabelling and retouching of his sketches, the addition of sections of paper to existing views, the rearrangement of sketches in groups and series, clearly seen in the chronological sequence of street sign carriers (cats 22 and 23), indicate that his work, too, was a series of historical remnants that he hoped to render meaningful by an act of

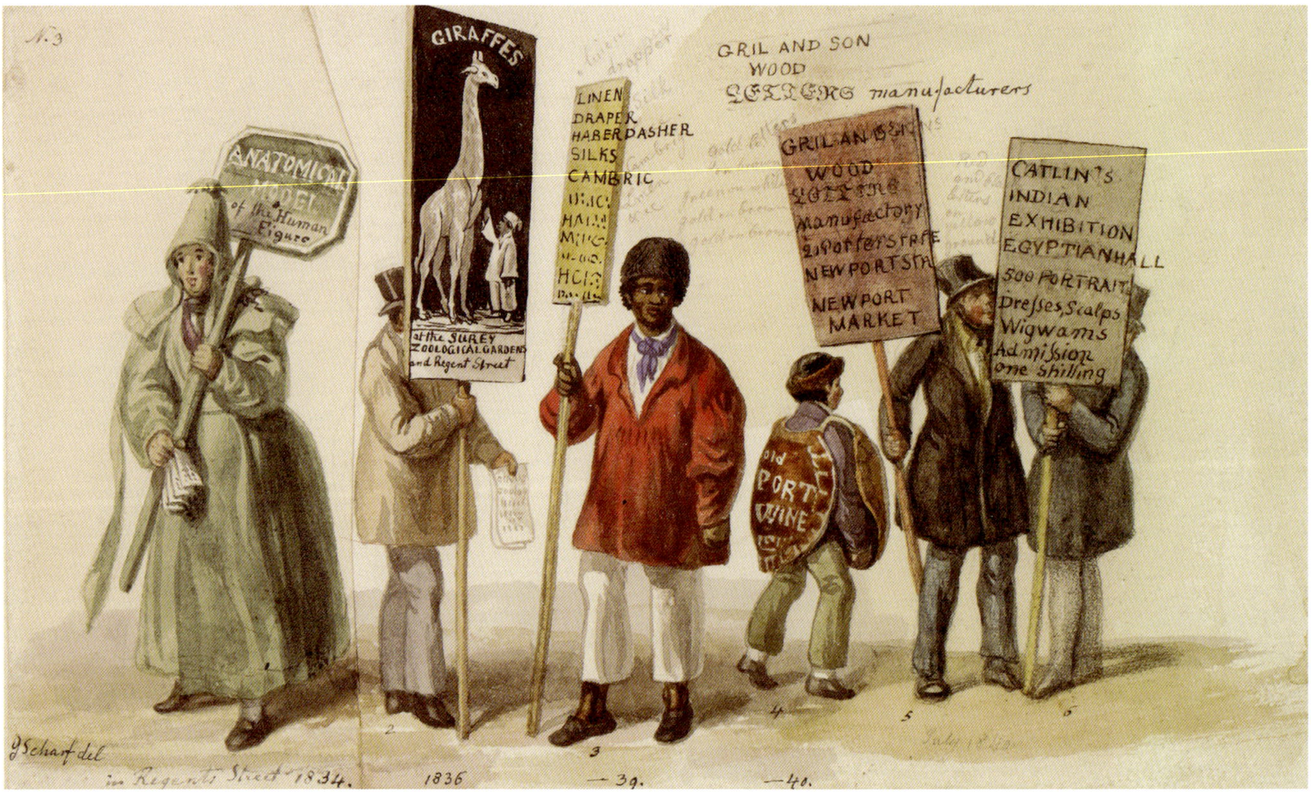

Cat. 23. *Men and boys with advertising boards*

historical explanation and organisation. The many lithographic stones that he drew, each bearing a trace of the modern city, may be thought of as a discontinuous fossil record. Maybe the disarticulated sketchbooks participate in this too. It is a record that does not quite yield an explanation of the mechanisms of historical transformation.

Scharf was no Frankfurt School historical materialist but he inhabited an intellectual environment where history, on a grand scale, was intertwined with science. His work stands as evidence that there were visual means of engaging with modernity that acknowledged materiality, and allowed for the possibility of social mutation.

This essay was first developed as a paper for the British Watercolours Symposium held at the Royal Academy, London in March 1993. I subsequently presented this material to the Department of History of Art, University of California, Berkeley in May 1995. Many thanks to the audiences on these two occasions for their interesting comments. I am grateful to David Solkin for encouraging me to work on this material, to Steve Edwards, Briony Fer, Mary-Lou Arscott and Ricky Rooney for help and advice in researching the topic. I would also like to thank generations of BA and MA students at the Courtauld Institute of Art who chose to work on the Victorian city and contributed to my thoughts on Scharf.

1 Poovey, Mary, 'Anatomical realism and social investigation in early nineteenth-century Manchester', *Differences*, vol. 5, no. 3, Fall 1993, pp. 1–30; Gallagher, Catherine, 'The Body Versus the Social Body in the Works of Thomas Malthus and Henry Mayhew', in Gallagher, C, and Laqueur, T, Eds, *The Making of the Modern Body: Sexuality and Society in the Nineteenth Century*, University of California Press, Berkeley: Los Angeles and London, 1987, pp. 83–106; Trotter, David, *Circulation: Defoe, Dickens and the Economies of the Novel*, Macmillan: Basingstoke, 1988

2 Arscott, Caroline, 'Luke Fildes: from Graphic to Academic' in Trodd, Colin and Cardoso Denis, Rafael, Eds, *Art and the Academy in the Nineteenth Century*, Manchester University Press: Manchester, 2000, pp. 102–16

3 *Panoramania!*, exhibition catalogue, London, Barbican, 1988–89; Altick, Richard, *The Shows of London*, Harvard University Press: Cambridge, Massachusetts., 1978; Meisel, Martin, *Realizations*, Princeton University Press: Princeton, N J, 1983

4 For further discussion of the correlation between eye and globe see Caroline Arscott, 'Representations of the Victorian City' in Daunton, M, Ed., *Cambridge Urban History of Britain: Volume Three (1840–1950)*, Cambridge University Press: Cambridge, 2000, pp. 811–32

5 Harley, J B, 'Maps, knowledge and power, in Cosgrove, D, and Daniels, S, *The Iconography of Landscape*, Cambridge University Press: Cambridge, 1988, pp. 277–312; Pollock, G, 'Vicarious excitements: *London: A Pilgrimage* by Gustave Doré and Blanchard Jerrold, 1872', *New Formations*, No. 4, Spring 1988; Pollock, G, 'Power and visibility in the city (review article), *Art History*, Vol. 11, No. 2, June 1988, pp. 275–83; Tagg, John, 'The discontinuous city', in Tagg, J, *Grounds of Dispute*, Macmillan: London, 1992

6 Buck-Morss, Susan, *The Dialectics of Seeing: Walter Benjamin and the Arcades Project*, MIT Press: Cambridge Massachusetts and London, 1989, pp.65–77 and 210–212

7 Key European figures are Jean-Baptiste Lamark (1744–1829), Lorenz Oken (1779–1851) and Etienne Geoffroy Saint-Hilaire (1772–1844). See Appel, Toby, *The Cuvier-Geoffroy debate: French biology in the decades before Darwin*, Oxford University Press: New York and Oxford, 1987; Desmond, Adrian, *Archetypes and Ancestors: Palaeontology in Victorian London, 1850–1875*, Blond and Briggs: University of London, 1982; Desmond, Adrian *The Politics of Evolution: Morphology, Medicine, and Reform in Radical London*, University of Chicago: Chicago and London 1989; Rudwick, Martin J S, *Georges Cuvier, fossil bones, and geological catastrophes: new translations & interpretations of the primary texts*, Chicago University Press: Chicago and London, 1997

8 Some of the scenes of railway construction produced by John C Bourne also include a vast number of labouring figures but their presentation is very different from that to be found in Scharf's work. Bourne, John C, *Drawings of the London and Birmingham Railway*, London, J C Bourne, Ackermann & Co., C Tilt, 1839

9 Yale Center for British Art, New Haven, Prints and Drawings Department, Paul Mellon Collection, B.1977.14.19090

10 Peter Jackson in his monograph of 1987 sees Scharf's paid scientific work as mere drudgery and his financially unsuccessful topographical work as his delight and hobby and focus of his artistic ambitions. Peter Jackson, *George Scharf's London: Sketches and Watercolours of a Changing City, 1820–50*, John Murray: London, 1987, pp. 6–7. The question of the aspirations and status and degrees of alienation involved in these different departments is an interesting one, but not my main concern here. It seems to me important to stress the proper pride he expressed *as an artist* in his dispute with Lonsdale, the Secretary of the Geological Society: 'I told him that consideration ought to be made that I might have been hindered, in fact that Artists ought not to be treated or spoken to like a common mechanic or servant, as he then did, and has done before, I did not like to be used in that way', Journal entry 7 Oct 1841

11 Charles Lyell (1797–1875), Charles Darwin (1809–1882), Gideon Mantell (1790–1852), Roderick Impey Murchison (1792–1871)

12 Thomas Webster (1773–1844) was trained as an architect, became curator, draughtsman and librarian at the Geological Society in London, 1812–26, and undertook editorial work on the *Transactions of the Geological Society* prior to his appointment at University College, London. Scharf recorded Webster's death with great sadness and was one of his only legatees. Journal entry 26 Dec 1844

13 William Buckland, *Geology and Mineralogy Considered with Reference to Natural Theology*, 2 vols William Pickering, London, 1836, (Sixth Bridgewater Treatise). Journal entry 15 Oct 1836

14 The mapping of the pre- and early Victorian London scientific community in terms of political positions has been vividly and effectively undertaken by Desmond. See Desmond, Adrian, 1982, op. cit. See also Rudwick, Martin J S, *The Great Devonian Controversy: The Shaping of Scientific Knowledge among Gentlemanly Specialists*, University of Chicago Press: Chicago and London, 1985

15 Sir John Frederick William Herschel (1792–1871), Louis Agassiz (1807–1873), Richard Owen (1804–1892). Scharf, journal entries, on Lyell 2 June 1844, on Herschel, 17 May 1837, on Bowerbank, 11 June 1840

16 Journal entries 20 Jan 1841 and 1 Dec 1841, 16 May 1838 and 4 May 1842

17 Journal entry 2 May 1837

18 Journal entry 26 May 1838

19 http://www.npg.org.uk Henry William Pickersgill, *Sir Richard Owen, c.* 1845, London, National Portrait Gallery, NPG 938

20 Owen, Richard, *Palaeontology*, Black: Edinburgh, 1860, p. 80

21 Ibid. p. 90

22 Owen was attacked by the Anglo-Catholics for his ideas which appeared to some to imply pantheism. He was equally attacked by those materialists and atheists/agnostics in the scientific community for his churchy idealist position

23 British Parliamentary Papers, *Second Report of the Commissioners on the State of Large Towns*, 1845, Part II, Appendix, 'Lancaster, Report on its Sanatory Condition by R.Owen, Esq.', p. 217, citing *An Historical and Descriptive Account of the Town of Lancaster*

24 Ibid., p. 226

25 Ibid., p. 230

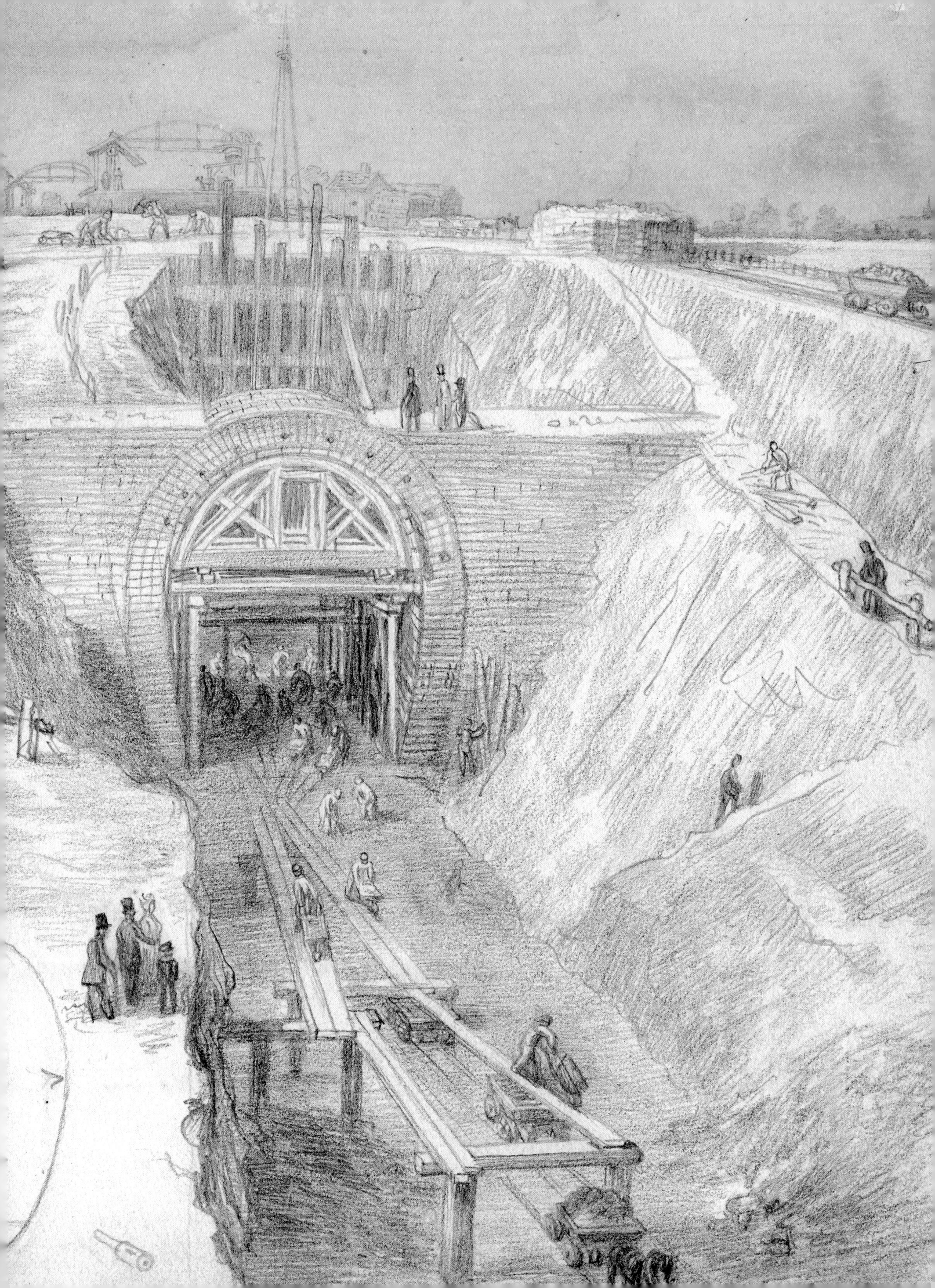

THE CHANGING FACE OF SCHARF'S LONDON (1816–1860)

Susan Palmer

The London of 11 November 1860, the day on which George Scharf died, was a very different city from the one that he first encountered as a young man of twenty-eight in January 1816. The intervening forty-four years had witnessed the inexorable growth both of the city and of its population. Many new public buildings had become familiar landmarks and services such as lighting and transport had undergone revolutionary changes. The aim of this short essay is to outline these changes and to set them in context against the background of Scharf's drawings and watercolours illustrated in this catalogue.[1]

The growth of London's population

The population of London in 1801 stood at just under a million (958,863). By 1821 it had reached almost one and half million (1,378,947) and by 1871 it had increased to over three and a quarter million (3,254,260). 1816, the year in which Scharf came to London, saw London's population swollen by soldiers and sailors discharged at the end of the Napoleonic Wars. In later years they were joined by migrants from elsewhere in the United Kingdom, drawn to the capital in the hope of finding work. Before 1841, the majority of migrants to London were from the south-east, but gradually the net widened.[2] Between 1841 and 1851 there were some 330,000 migrants to London (17% of the total population), 46,000 of whom were escaping famine in Ireland. They were joined in the 1850s by a further 286,000.[3]

The growth of London

The rapid growth of London in the years following the end of the Napoleonic Wars is graphically illustrated by a quotation from Richard Rush, American Minister in London from the end of 1817 to 1825, who later published an account of his time in England. In a preliminary 'Note to the Reader' he writes: '... I went to England again on a short visit in 1829. An interval of but four years had elapsed; yet I was amazed at the increase of London. The Regent's Park, which, when I first knew the west-end of town, disclosed nothing but lawns and fields, was now a city. You saw long rows of lofty buildings, in their outward aspect magnificent. On this whole space was set down a population of probably not less than fifty or sixty thousand souls. Another city, hardly smaller, seemed to have sprung up in the neighbourhood of St Pancras Church and the London University. Belgrave Square, in an opposite region, broke upon me with like surprise. The road from Westminster Bridge to Greenwich exhibited for several miles compact ranges of new houses. Finchley Common, desolate in 1819, was covered with neat cottages, and indeed villages. In whatever direction I went, indications were similar. I say nothing of Carlton Terrace, for Carlton House was gone, or of the street, of two miles, from that point to Park Crescent, surpassing any other in London, or any that I saw in Europe. To make room for this new and spacious street, old ones had been pulled down, of which no vestige remained. I could scarcely, but for the evidence of my senses, have believed it all ...'

In the same year the satirist George Cruikshank issued his famous etching – 'London Going out of Town – or – The March of Bricks & Mortar!' Aside from the satire, the etching gives a detailed picture of the brick-making and house-building processes: the clay is dug and bricks are made from the clay mixed with domestic ash and fired in kilns; the pits left behind are filled with domestic rubbish and shortly afterwards rows of houses are erected on top, supported on brick vaults, with streets between made up with more rubbish. This was a more or less continuous process, interrupted by periodic slumps. 1829 fell in one such period and Cruikshank depicted rows of unlet and collapsing houses.

Between 1840 and 1850 43,000 new houses were built and by 1851 over 66,500 people were engaged in building in London and it had become the capital's biggest industry.

A crucial part in this explosion of the building industry was played by London's canal network. Coastal shipping and a network of canals had long been important means of shipping goods and building materials around the country. In 1801 the Grand Junction Canal had been extended from Uxbridge to Paddington, providing a direct link between

London and the Midlands and bringing business to the terminus at Paddington Basin. In 1820 the new Regent's Canal, constructed from 1812, joined with the Grand Junction Canal at Paddington, going eastward from there via a series of tunnels to join the Thames at Limehouse, where another basin was constructed. Much used for the shipment of coal and timber, it linked all of north London to the national canal network and brought trade to Hackney, Hoxton, St Pancras and Camden. Cat. 43 shows a lime kiln on the Regent's Canal near Kingsland, ideally located to receive the limestone used to make mortar for bricklaying from quarries outside London and then to transport it to the various construction sites.

The Regent's Canal also stimulated smaller imitations, such as the Grosvenor Canal (1824–26) and the Kensington Canal (1824–28), sponsored by landowners seeking to open up their property for development.

The greatest schemes of metropolitan improvements in Regency London were designed by the architect John Nash. Prominent among these was Regent Street, a new and elegant thoroughfare designed to connect Carlton House, home of the Prince Regent, with Regent's Park. The Quadrant (seen in cat. 45) was a key part of Nash's scheme. Curving north from Piccadilly Circus it linked Lower Regent Street (as it then was) with the central part of the street with its shops with houses above. Completed by 1820, it soon became a fashionable shopping street.[4]

Regent's Park was planned as a suitable northern terminus for his new Regent Street, and also represented a chance to exploit the development potential of the old Marylebone Park. Between 1819 and 1823 the terraces on the east, south and west sides of the park were completed and a few private villas erected in the park itself. Regent's Park was completed by 1828, the same year that the Zoological Gardens, laid out by Decimus Burton, were opened. They became a fashionable place of resort and in 1835 Scharf published a series of six lithographs of the zoo which were for sale in the gardens (see also fig. 4). Another popular attraction was Decimus Burton's Colosseum, erected in the south-east corner of the park between 1824 and 1826. Modelled on the Pantheon in Rome, it housed a 360° panorama of London. It also boasted London's first passenger lift – the Ascending Room.

Nash was also employed to enlarge and remodel Buckingham House, where George III had lived since the 1760s. Finished in 1827, it was renamed Buckingham Palace.[5] In the same year Marble Arch, designed by Nash and based on the Arch of Constantine in Rome, was erected in front of Buckingham Palace.[6] Decimus Burton was also employed to enrich the setting of Buckingham Palace with suitable gateways and lodges for Hyde Park, and he drew up a scheme for Hyde Park Corner in 1825 which consisted of a long Ionic screen next to Apsley House with a central and subsidiary arches. On axis across the public road was a grand triumphal arch based on the Arch of Titus in Rome and leading to Green Park and Buckingham Palace.[7]

Having moved to the newly remodelled Buckingham Palace, George IV gave up Carlton House in Lower Regent Street. This facilitated another of Nash's schemes of

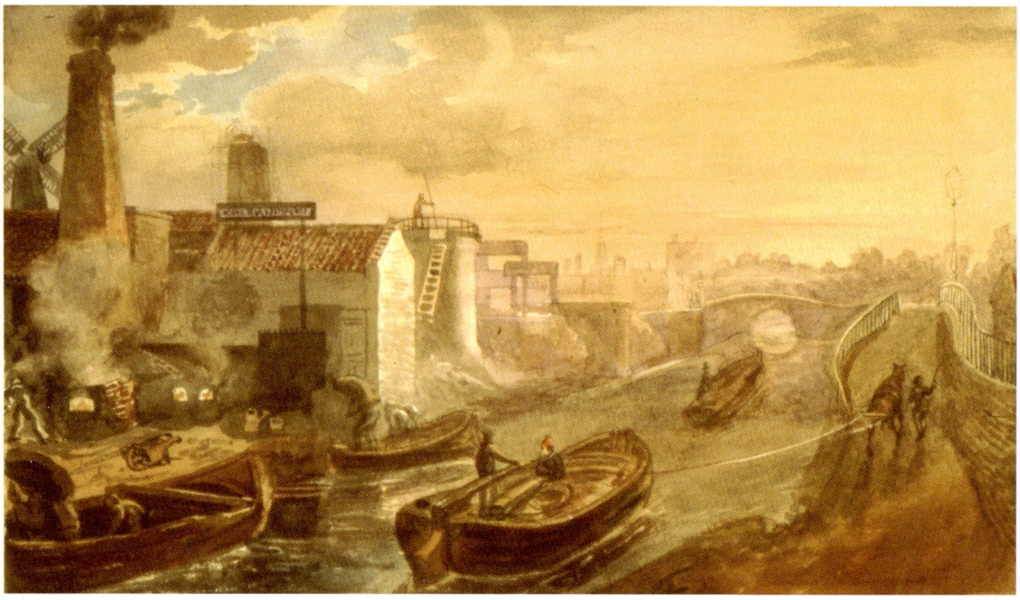

Cat. 43. Lime kiln on the canal near Kingsland, London

improvement. Carlton House was demolished and Nash designed three long terraces of houses for the north and south sides of St James's Park, flanking the vista from Buckingham Palace. In the event, only two of these terraces were built: Waterloo Place, on the site of Carlton House itself and Carlton House Terrace East and West. A proposed grand fountain between the two terraces did not materialise, but in 1834 the Duke of York's column by Benjamin Dean Wyatt was erected.

The last scheme of improvement in which Nash was involved (although he did not complete it, falling out of public favour after King George IV's death in 1830), was the West Strand (or Charing Cross) Improvements of 1830–32, a development to create a more convenient communication between the east and west ends of town, linking Lower Regent Street, Whitehall and the Strand and to include a new public square (to become Trafalgar Square). Cat.21 shows the Strand from the corner of Villiers Street a few years earlier in 1824. Church Lane (cat. 5), running between the Strand and Chandos Street, was demolished as part of the Strand Improvements, as was the south end of St Martin's Lane where Scharf was living up until 1830. As with Regent Street, the whole Strand frontage was treated as a single architectural entity.

The square (which became known as Trafalgar Square from about 1835) was laid out by Charles Barry, with the later, 1845, addition of two granite fountains and basins. The 145 ft Nelson Column was erected on the south side of the square in 1839–42, after a competition won by William Railton, the money having been raised by voluntary subscription by the Nelson Memorial Committee. The statue of Nelson by E H Baily was raised in 1843 and the bronze bas-reliefs at the base of the column added in 1849.[8]

A later improvement scheme which similarly cut through a notorious slum area (the St Giles Rookery) was the building of New Oxford Street in 1847. An extension of Oxford Street, it was designed to allow traffic to reach Holborn without passing through St Giles High Street. However, although it ameliorated the problem of traffic congestion it did little to deal with the problem of poor housing conditions. Some 5,000 people were displaced and the population of the surrounding streets increased by 76% (people being obliged to stay near their sources of casual employment).

Apart from these central improvement works, London was also expanding apace from the 1820s. Indeed, referring to the development of Marylebone, Leigh Hunt feelingly welcomed the creation of Regent's Park as 'it has checked in that quarter at least the monstrous brick cancer that was extending its arms in every direction and has prevented Harley and Wimpole Streets from going further [north]'. Regent's Park did indeed effectively block further northward building and Portland Place remained a relatively isolated backwater for the next half century.

From 1821 Thomas Cubitt completed the work begun by James Burton in Bloomsbury, completing Tavistock Square and building Endsleigh Street, Gordon Square, Woburn Place and Woburn Walk. To the west, the remodelling of Buckingham Palace stimulated development on the Grosvenor Estate in Knightsbridge from 1825 in what is now known as Belgravia. Thomas Cubitt's ten-acre Belgrave Square was the centrepiece of the development, which included Eaton Square and Eaton Place. North of Hyde Park, development spread beyond Marble Arch and Edgware Road into Tyburnia or Paddington. The cutting of the Grand Junction Canal in 1801, with its wharf just west of Edgware Road, provided the initial stimulus for the growth of this area; by the 1830s Sussex Gardens had been completed and by the 1840s Paddington became a fashionable residential colony. The development of Bayswater began in the 1840s, with villas lining Westbourne Park. In the 1850s larger town houses were built in Lancaster Gate by Kensington Gardens, and long terraces linking Westbourne Grove with the Bayswater Road.

To the south of Hyde Park, South Kensington, which had formerly been market gardens, developed, its elegant terraces and squares growing up around the museums which were built after 1856 on land purchased from the profits of the Great Exhibition staged in Hyde Park in 1851.[9] Three new roads were created: Queens Gate and Exhibition Road running south from Hyde Park and Cromwell Road running west.[10] Brompton, depicted by Scharf in 1822 (see cat. 54), changed a great deal during the period of Scharf's residence in London. It was described in 1862[11] as 'essentially a new suburb of the great metropolis . . . Michael's Place and Brompton Crescent were built upon Flounders Fields . . . Alexander Square was built between 1827 and 1831. On 6 June 1829 the Church of the Holy Trinity, near Brompton Square, was consecrated. The large cemetery between the Richmond and Fulham Roads was consecrated on 12 June 1840.[12] The celebrated Oratory . . . first established in King William Street, Strand . . . removed to Brompton on 22 March 1851 . . . The first stone of the Hospital for Consumption was laid on 11 July 1844 . . . and the Cancer Hospital opened in 1861.'

Further north, a number of semi-detached villas were

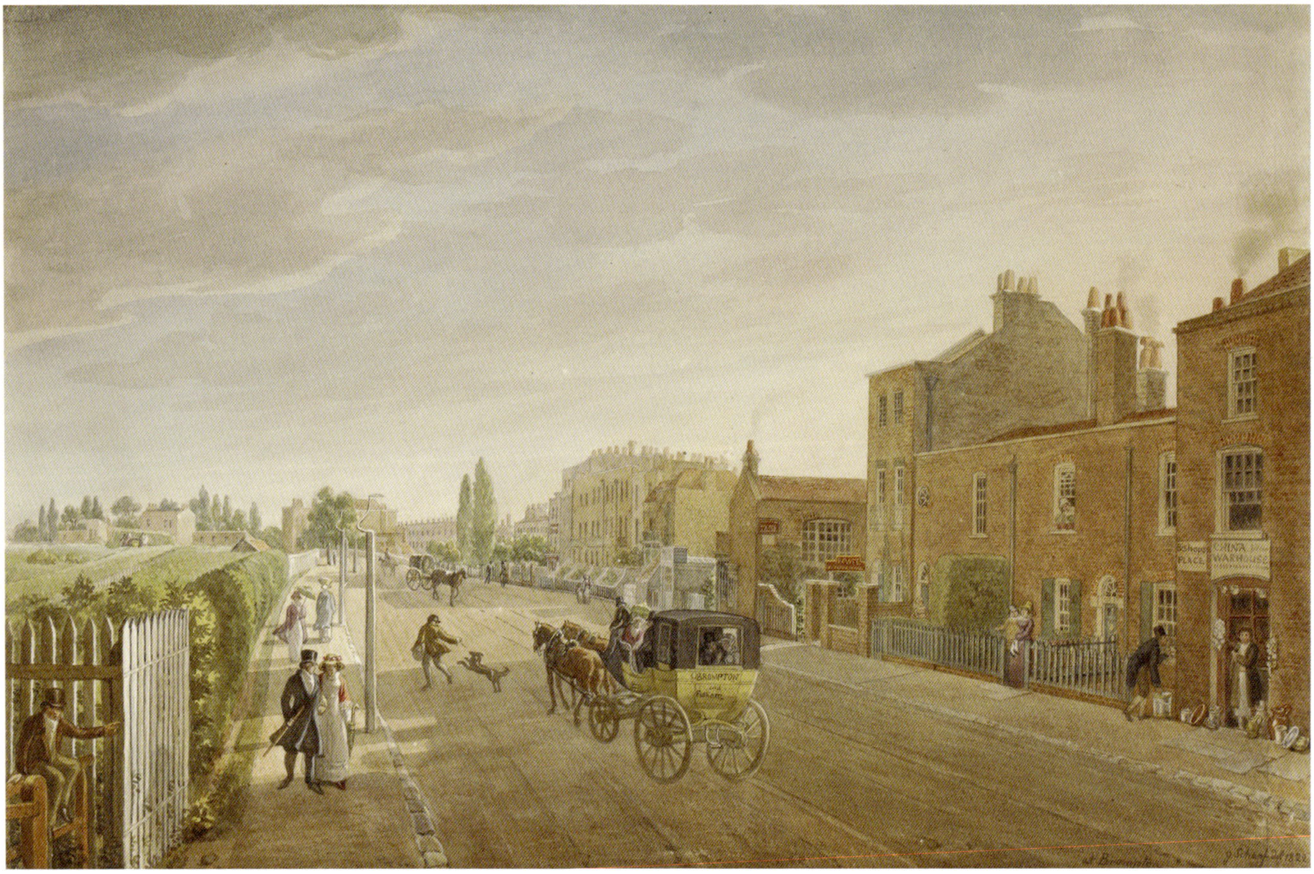

Cat.54. A view in Brompton

built in St John's Wood, with the development of the Eyre Estate between 1794 and 1830, marking the beginnings of middle-class outer suburbia beyond the Marylebone Road. Camden Town developed rapidly after the completion of the Regent's Canal in 1820. Coal wharves and builders' yards grew up and the area in general became an industrial and manufacturing suburb. By the time of Scharf's death Gospel Oak was becoming covered with terraces and crescents and Kentish Town was beginning to expand towards rural Hampstead Heath.

To the east, Hackney, largely rural at the beginning of the nineteenth century, had changed considerably, its population growing from 12,370 in 1801 to 22,494 in 1821 and 53,589 in 1851. Neighbouring Dalston and Clapton were expanding too.

South of the Thames, growth was stimulated by the erection of three new bridges at Vauxhall, Waterloo and Southwark between 1816 and 1819 (see below), and a network of turnpike roads leading out to Kennington, Newington Butts and Camberwell. In the 1820s the population of both Lambeth and Camberwell increased by over half, and new houses were built in Stockwell, Brixton and Peckham too. Further out, in Denmark Hill, Tulse Hill and Brixton Hill large detached villas set in spacious gardens were built.

Lighting

Arriving in London at the end of 1817, one of the first things on which Richard Rush, the American Minister in London, commented was the darkness: 'December 31 [1817] The fog was so thick that the shops in Bond Street had lights at noon. I could not see people in the street from my windows. I am tempted to ask, how the English became great with so little day-light? It seems not to come fully out until nine in the morning and immediately after four is gone . . .' Fog continued as the great winter scourge of London right up until the early 1960s,[13] exacerbated by the industrial growth of the Victorian era, but on a day-to-day basis the streets of the capital were rendered considerably brighter by improvements in street lighting. When Scharf first arrived in London, the streets were lit by oil lamps mounted on posts and railings. These were lit at dusk by lamplighters and left to burn through the night. But if the lamplighter failed to trim the wick properly or fill the reservoir full enough of oil, the light would fail before the end of the night. The Gas, Light and Coke Company was the first company chartered to light the City, Westminster and Southwark by gas in 1812 with rival companies soon following, and from that date the oil lamps were gradually replaced by gas lanterns as the necessary network of gas mains was laid. To take Lincoln's Inn Fields as a fairly typical area in central London: in 1819 four large gas lamps were erected on the north and south sides of the square and twenty oil lamps were discontinued; repaving in 1824 gave the opportunity to lay gas mains on the east and west sides of the square and 20 more gas lamps were erected around the square, together with one over each gate on the north and south sides of the garden and the old stone obelisks to which the oil lamps had been fixed were removed (see cat. 62). In cat. 54, a watercolour of Brompton of 1822, the semi-rural area is still lit by oil lamps. Gas light was considerably brighter than that provided by oil lamps and it became the more so as various improvements in the design of the burner were made over the years. As early as January 1827 Prince Pückler Muskau, a German visitor to London, prefaces one of his letters with the comment: 'By bright gas-light, which is always like a festal illumination here, we drove into town . . .'.

Cats 28 and 60 illustrate well the great disruption caused by the installation and need for periodic repair of the necessary miles of gas pipes under London's streets during the first quarter of the nineteenth century.

Sewers and water supply

Considerable disruption was also caused to London's streets by the frequent need to dig them up to repair the antiquated and inadequate sewers. Sir Joseph Balzalgette's great interceptory sewage system (still largely in use today) was not completed until 1875. Some new sewers were, however, laid as part of metropolitan improvement work, for instance below Nash's Regent Street. Fig. 10 depicts the construction of the new Fleet Sewer in 1825 and fig. 7 shows sewers being laid at the corner of Drury Lane in 1845. In the main, however, London's system of drains and sewers was vastly inadequate, with many houses reliant on cesspits. When the use of cesspits was banned by the Metropolitan Commission of Sewers, formed in 1847, all the main sewers and underground streams began to discharge their new contents into the Thames and the river became a huge open sewer in which no fish could survive. The climax was reached in the hot dry summer of 1858 in what came to be called 'The Great Stink' when the windows of the Houses of Parliament had to be draped with curtains soaked in chloride of lime to mitigate the disgusting smell.

Various rival water companies supplied London with water from the seventeenth century. One of these was the New River Company which brought water to London from the River Lee in Hertfordshire, via an artificial river 'the New River' cut in 1613. In cat. 53 Scharf depicts the river near its terminus at New River Head, Clerkenwell, in a charmingly rural scene of 1816. From here the water was supplied to London by large elm pipes, seen in fig. 17, drawn two years earlier, in 1814, as an illustration to one of Sir John Soane's lectures as Professor of Architecture at the Royal Academy. From these wooden pipes the water was fed into such houses as were equipped, and paid a water rate to the company, through an iron pipe. Because the wooden pipes leaked and could not withstand high pressure the Metropolitan Paving Act of 1817 laid down that all new water pipes be of iron.

However, as late as 1850 there were 80,000 houses in London, inhabited by 640,000 people, without a piped water supply. Charles Kingsley wrote in 1849: 'I was yesterday . . . over the cholera districts of Bermondsey, and oh God! What I saw! People having no water to drink – hundreds of them – but the water of the common sewer . . .

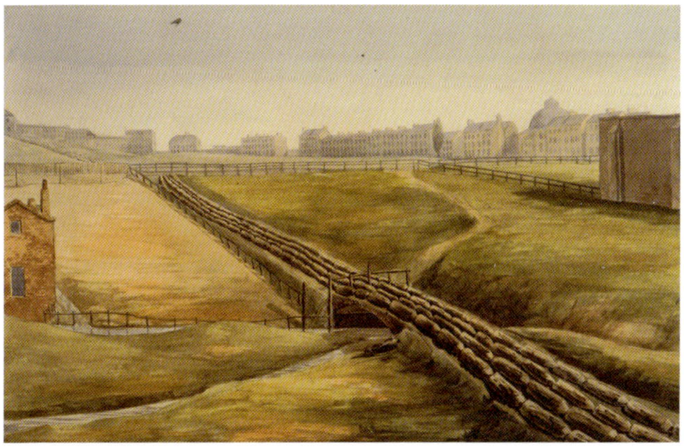

Fig. 17. Wooden pipes of the New River Water Company at Spa Fields, 1814. Illustration prepared for one of Sir John Soane's lectures as Professor of Architecture at the Royal Academy. The Trustees of Sir John Soane's Museum, SM 76/9/8. Cf. cat. 53, p. 14

full of . . . dead fish, cats and dogs.' And a report published in the following year showed that the companies supplying water derived from the Thames were supplying very impure water. The Metropolitan Water Act of 1852 tackled some of the worst abuses of the water companies and forced those supplying Thames water to move their intakes above Teddington Lock into the non-tidal river, but the supply remained uncertain and cholera remained rife. The completion of the Bazalgette sewage scheme removed a major danger of pollution to the water supplies, and the last major epidemic of cholera was in 1868, but a Metropolitan Water Board was not founded until 1902.

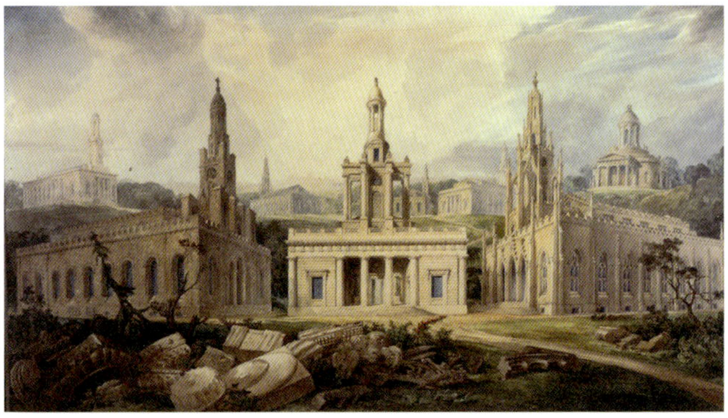

Fig. 18. Composite view of Sir John Soane's designs for three London churches: Holy Trinity Marylebone, St John Bethnal Green and St Peter Walworth, Joseph Michael Gandy, 1825. The Trustees of Sir John Soane's Museum, SM P259

New Public Buildings

A number of new public buildings also changed the face of London during Scharf's years in the city. To describe just a few will give a flavour of the change. Between 1818 and 1856 the Church Building Commission were responsible for erecting a number of new churches to accommodate London's swelling population and in particular to provide free church accommodation for the poor. A number of London's ancient parishes were subdivided and given new churches. Between 1822 and 1826 no less than 17 were opened and by 1837 the number had grown to 53. Sir John Soane himself was responsible for the design of three of them: Holy Trinity Marylebone, St John Bethnal Green and St Peter Walworth (see fig. 18).

These new 'Commissioners' Churches' were, in the main, built without burial grounds. Just as the number of churches were, after the Napoleonic wars, inadequate for London's growing population, so their ancient burial grounds became full to overflowing, and a potential source of disease. In response to this, cemeteries were established by joint stock companies outside the built-up areas. These had landscaped grounds with cemetery chapels and a proper system of management. The first of these to open, at Kensal Green, was consecrated in 1833. It was followed by the South Metropolitan Cemetery at Norwood in 1837, Highgate Cemetery in 1839 and Nunhead and Abney Park, Stoke Newington in 1840.

The British Museum in Bloomsbury, a building which featured in many of Scharf's sketches and drawings (see cats 29–32, 34 and 59) was considerably enlarged between 1823 and 1857 to the designs of Robert, and later Sydney, Smirke. The King's Library was built between 1823 and 1826, followed by a west wing in 1831–34 and a north wing in 1833–38. Work began on a new front in 1842 and the new Central Hall was opened in April 1847. In 1852–57 the courtyard was converted into the Reading Room, with its magnificent copper dome.

In 1828 the University of London building (later University College) was opened in Malet Street, with its imposing classical façade designed by William Wilkins. From 1830 it included a school – University College School – where Scharf enrolled his two sons (see cat. 6) as pupils. In 1833 he produced a lithograph of the school playground with the college in the background. King's College followed University College in 1829–31 on a site next to Somerset House on the Strand, to designs by Robert Smirke.

Gentlemen's Clubs became a prominent part of the London social scene from the 1820s, and a number of grand buildings sprang up to house them. The first, the United Services Club, was built to the designs of John Nash in 1827 on the corner of Waterloo Place and Pall Mall East. The Travellers Club, in the Italian Renaissance style by Charles Barry, was built at 106 Pall Mall between 1829 and 1832, and next door at 107 Pall Mall, Decimus Burton's building for the Athenaeum was opened in 1830. Charles Barry's Reform Club building completed the triumvirate at 104–105 Pall Mall in 1837–41, while further down the street at No. 71, Sir Robert Smirke's Oxford and Cambridge University Club had opened in 1836.

Another prominent London landmark which engaged Scharf's attention more than once (see cats 50–52) was the Bank of England. Standing on a large irregularly-shaped site bounded by Threadneedle Street, Princes Street. Lothbury and Bartholomew Lane, it was bounded by high stone windowless walls surmounted by a castellated skyline of Greco-Roman acroteria and attics. Sir John Soane, who was Architect to the Bank from 1788–1833, greatly enlarged the existing building by Sir Robert Taylor and designed the imposing curtain walls. Most of his major building campaigns were over before Scharf arrived in London, but the years 1824–27 saw the rebuilding of the Threadneedle Street façade, recasing the crumbling entrance block of the first Bank building of 1734 by George Sampson. Cat. 52 records the early work of Charles Robert Cockerell, who succeeded Soane as Architect to the Bank in 1833.

The years 1832–38 witnessed the erection of William Wilkins's new building for the National Gallery on the north side of the new Trafalgar Square and on the site of the Old King's Mews, demolished in 1830 (see cat. 20). The Royal Academy of Arts also moved to the new building from Somerset House, moving to its current home in Burlington House in 1868.

A major change to London's skyline was wrought in October 1834 by the fire which gutted the Palace of Westminster, a scene graphically captured by Scharf (see cat. 56). The building by Charles Barry, with decoration by Augustus Pugin, which is now such an iconic London landmark, was the result of a competition to design new, purpose-built Houses of Parliament 'in the Gothic or Elizabethan style'. Scharf monitored the progress of the demolition and reconstruction (see cats 57–58), which began in 1837. The House of Lords opened in 1847 and the House of Commons in 1851. The Clock Tower was finished in 1858 and the new Palace of Westminster was finally completed in 1860 when the roof was put on the Victoria Tower.

Another public building recorded by Scharf was Charles Barry's new building for the Royal College of Surgeons on the south side of Lincoln's Inn Fields, opposite the house and museum of Sir John Soane, built between 1834–38 to replace George Dance the Younger's building of 1813 (see cats 61 and 62).

Transport

In 1816, transport through the streets of London was exclusively horse-drawn, from the various delivery vehicles of the tradesmen to the variety of open and closed carriages owned or hired by its wealthier citizens. A network of public stage-coaches, operating from the many coaching inns which had grown up at various strategic places in London connected the capital with the rest of the country and plied a busy trade both in passengers and in the

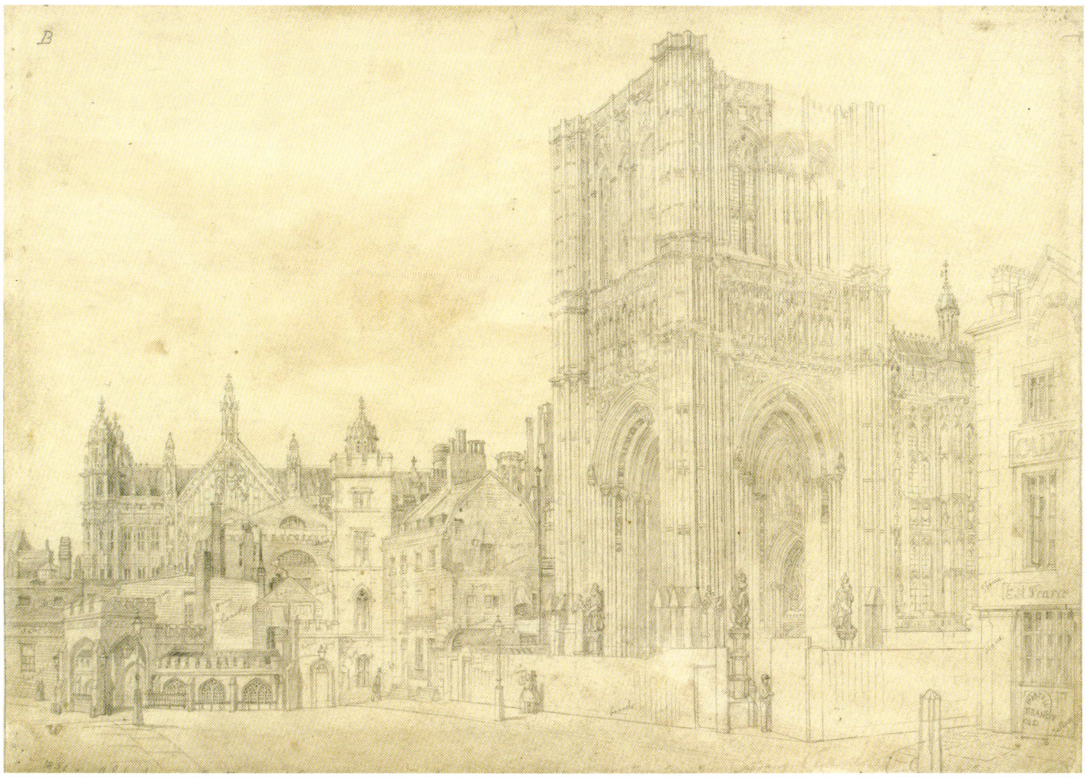

Cat. 58. Part of the Old Houses of Parliament and the New in progress, including the Victoria Tower

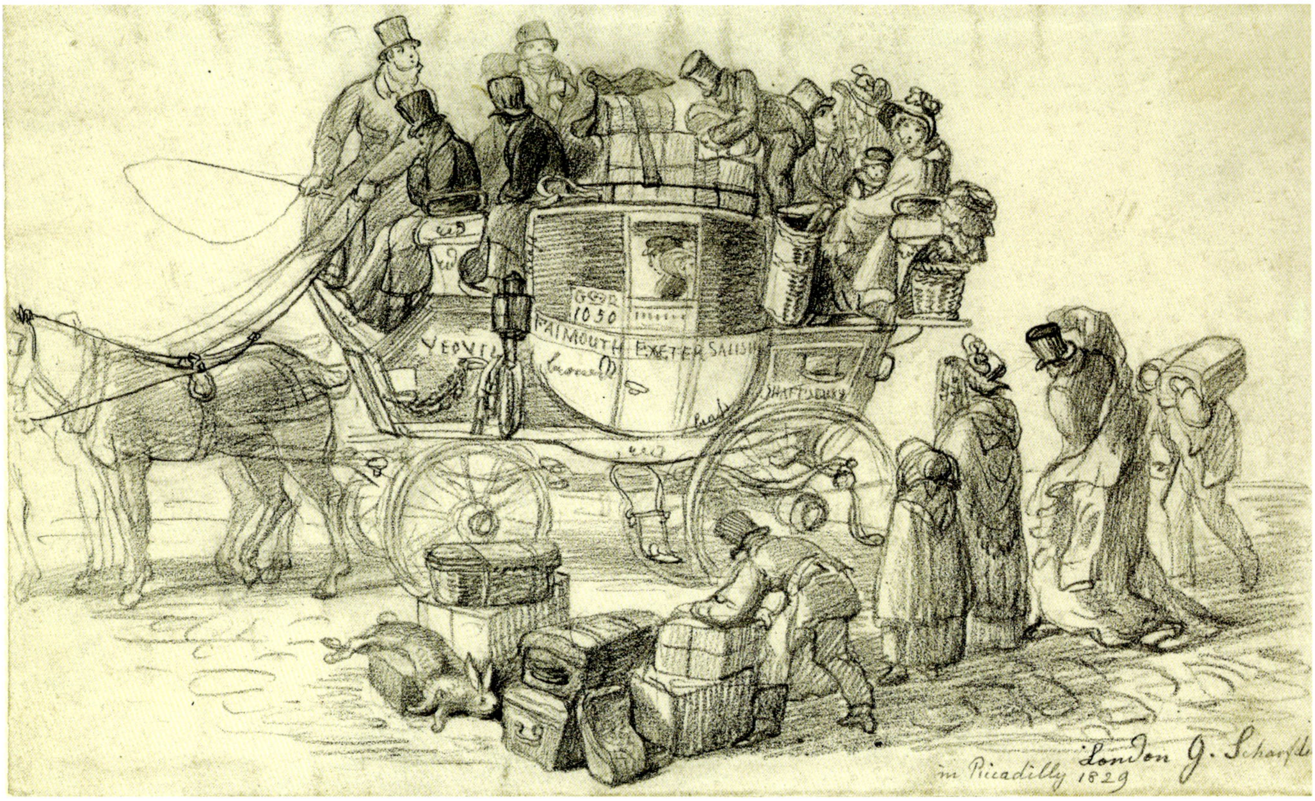

Cat. 39. Coach in Piccadilly

carriage of goods. Cat. 39 depicts the London to Plymouth stage-coach preparing to depart from Piccadilly in 1829.

The first omnibus service was begun in July 1829 by George Shillibeer, who ran long, three-horse vehicles with benches for 20 passengers (more than the capacity of a short-stage coach) on a route from the Stingo public house in Paddington to the Bank along the New Road (today's Marylebone, Euston and Pentonville Roads) (one can be seen at the extreme right of cat. 50, p. 87). His operation was short-lived, and went bankrupt in 1831. But the Stage Carriages Act of 1832, which abolished the monopoly of the hackney carriages and allowed omnibuses into the central area meant that a number of omnibus companies grew up, in particular the London General Omnibus Company, which in the 1850s started to buy up the other companies.

However, the 1820s also saw the development of other forms of experimental locomotion. One of these was the steam carriage, invented by Sir Goldsworthy Gurney, which is described in more detail in cat. 40, and which first appeared on the London streets in 1827. Even though Londoners had been familiar with steam from the second decade of the century through the paddle-driven steamboats that plied the Thames between London and Gravesend, these new steam carriages must have proved quite a sensation at the time. They were, however, a short-lived phenomenon, superseded by the opening of the first railways in the 1830s.

The streets in the central area were very busy and terrible traffic jams were not uncommon, with no modern aids such as traffic lights or one-way systems to alleviate them. Apart from all the horses and carriages and tradesmen's barrows, cattle were still being driven through the streets to Smithfield market until 1855[14] when the live cattle market was moved to Islington and the Central Meat Market built at Smithfield.

By the 1830s the constant roar of the ever-growing London traffic, caused not only by the clatter of horses' hooves but also by the rumble of iron-shod wheels on uneven paving, was a cause of considerable concern. Experiments were carried out to determine the ideal paving material. In 1839 a stretch of just under 150 yards of Oxford Street between Tottenham Court Road and Charles Street was laid with twelve specimens of pavement consisting of combinations of bitumen, stone, asphalt,

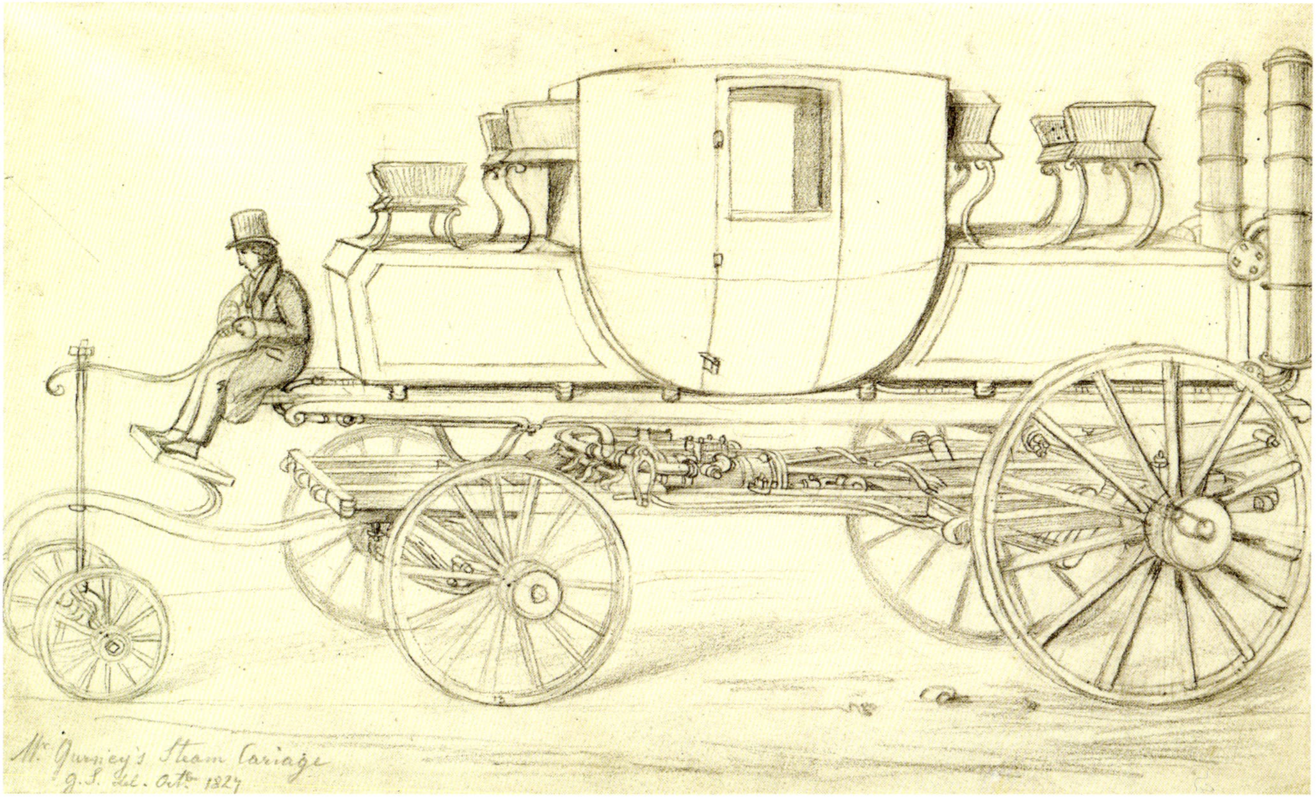

Cat. 40. Mr Gurney's steam carriage

granite and wood. Wood was found to be much the best material and the whole of Oxford Street was subsequently paved in this way. Following the success of this experiment, wood paving was used all over London. Fig. 12 shows patent wooden blocks being laid in the Strand in May 1840.

Arguably the revolution that most changed the face of London at this period was the coming of the railway. London's first railway, from Bricklayer's Arms, Southwark to Deptford, began operating in December 1836 and was soon extended to London Bridge and Greenwich. The next year saw the opening of the London and Birmingham Railway at Euston Station (see cat. 42), to be followed in 1838 by Paddington Station (terminus of the Great Western railway), Fenchurch Street Station (the first City terminus) in 1841, King's Cross Station (terminus of the Great Northern railway) in 1852 and Victoria Station in 1860.

The huge disruption occasioned by the building of these railway lines is graphically illustrated in cat. 41 – *Constructing the Birmingham Railroad, near Chalk Farm, London* – and in the description from Dickens's *Dombey and Son* cited in the catalogue entry.

From the 1840s a number of stations were built a few miles from the centre, in places such as Battersea,

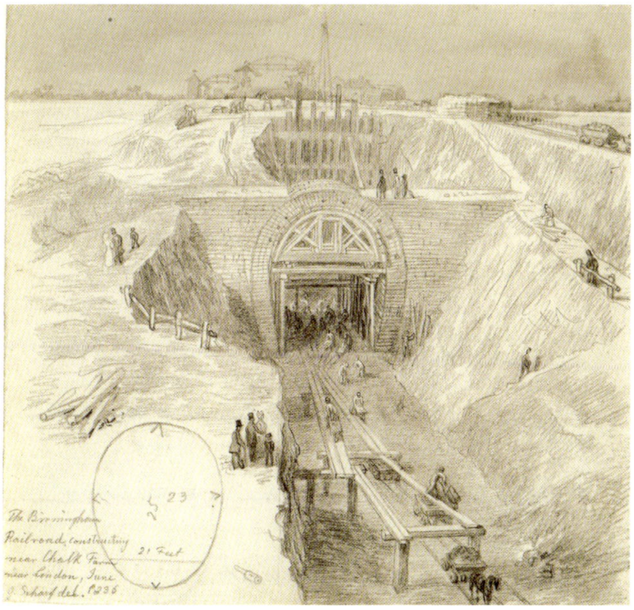

Cat. 41. Constructing the Birmingham Railroad, near Chalk Farm, London

Lewisham, Kilburn and Crouch End and this encouraged the move of the middle classes out to these areas and the growth of suburban London.

The Docks and the River

When Scharf first came to London the first enclosed wet docks with warehouses, cut off from the tides in the Thames by locks to allow ships to lie safely at the quays, were well established: the West India Docks, opened in 1802; and the London Docks and East India Docks, both opened in 1805. The 21-year monopoly on trade in various goods held by these three companies meant that no further docks were constructed for some years. On 25 October 1828 St Katherine's Dock was opened, constructed on a site close to the City between the Tower and the London Docks to designs by Thomas Telford and Philip Hardwicke. Some 1,250 houses and tenements were pulled down to make way for it, as was the Royal Hospital and Collegiate Church of St-Katharine-by-the-Tower, and over 11,000 inhabitants were displaced.

Twenty-seven years later in 1855, the St Katherine's Dock Company opened the Royal Victoria Dock on the Plaistow Marshes. The soil from the excavations was used to consolidate the marshy land of Battersea Park, opened in 1859 (see below). The Victoria Dock was the first to use the new railways to the full, and this compensated for its distance of four miles from the City. It was also the first to be built for the new iron steamships which were gradually replacing sailing ships, and the first to use hydraulic cranes and lifts for raising ships in a pontoon dock.

With his interest in construction, Scharf no doubt watched with fascination the building of the Thames Tunnel between Rotherhithe and Wapping, the first underwater tunnel in the world. Marc Brunel's plan was authorised by Parliament in 1823, but the 1,200 foot long, brick-lined tunnel, a huge and pioneering engineering feat for the period, was not completed until 1843. It had been intended for vehicular traffic, but for financial reasons remained a foot tunnel until the 1860s when it was converted into a railway tunnel for the East London Railway.

New Bridges over the Thames

In Scharf's first couple of years in London two new bridges were completed. The first, Vauxhall Bridge[15] was opened in 1816 to the designs of James Walker and was the first iron bridge over the Thames in London. Vauxhall Bridge Road was constructed at the same time, as an approach to the new bridge.

18 June 1817, the second anniversary of the Battle of Waterloo, saw the opening by the Prince Regent of Waterloo Bridge,[16] a nine-arched granite structure designed by John Rennie, which had been under construction since 1811.

Two years later in 1819, Southwark Bridge, also by John Rennie, and under construction since 1814, was completed. This three-arch bridge had a central span of 240 feet – the largest ever constructed in cast-iron at that date.[17]

The new Vauxhall, Waterloo and Southwark bridges opened up south London to more than ribbon development and a network of factories transformed the south bank into the industrial powerhouse of post-Napoleonic London.

The years 1824 to 1831 saw the construction of a new London Bridge of five arches upstream of the old one (which was subsequently demolished). Designed by John Rennie, it was opened by William IV on 1 August 1831. Sir John Soane was among those present at the opening ceremony, and he subsequently commissioned a painting to commemorate the event from the artist George Jones, which can be seen on the staircase at 13 Lincoln's Inn Fields, just above the first-floor landing. Scharf recorded the massive disruption caused by the construction of the northern and southern approaches to the bridge in two vivid and detailed watercolours subsequently made into lithographs. The lithograph illustrated in fig. 8 shows the view looking northwards from the middle of the bridge's approach as it cuts into the heart of the City to continue as far as the Bank of England and become King William Street. It demolished 318 houses and carved through nine ancient thoroughfares. In the centre is the church of St Michael, Crooked Lane, demolished soon after Scharf recorded this view.[18]

Hungerford Suspension Bridge, designed by Brunel, was built between 1841 and 1845 to serve Hungerford Market. It was replaced in 1864 by the current wrought-iron nine-span girder bridge designed by Sir John Hawkshaw to carry the South-East Railway over the river to its new terminus at Charing Cross.

The last new bridge to be built in the period under

discussion was Westminster Bridge. The present cast-iron bridge of seven arches by Thomas Page was constructed between 1854 and 1862, replacing the mid-eighteenth century stone bridge, the foundations of which were showing signs of structural weakness.

Changes in shopping habits

Scharf, who frequently included shop-fronts in his streetscapes, himself pointed up the beginnings of a change in shopping habits in two contrasting views of shops made in 1825 – *A Cowkeeper's shop in Golden Lane* (cat. 44) and *The Westminster Dairy in the Quadrant, Regent Street* (cat. 45). The cowkeeper's shop, with its old-fashioned plaster sign and the cows in their stalls at the back, is a relic of a London ringed by market gardens, nurseries and dairy farms, when the only means of transporting perishable foodstuffs was by horse and cart. The Westminster Dairy is part of the fashionable new Regent Street, laid out by John Nash and completed in 1820. The move of fashionable shops, particularly drapers, away from the City and Fleet Street to the West End and particularly Oxford Street, and later Regent Street, had begun in the late eighteenth century. In 1790 Dickins and Smith moved to 54 Oxford Street and thence in 1835 to Regent Street (where they were known as Dickins and Jones from the 1890s). In 1833 Peter Robinson opened at 103 Oxford Street and included a separate dressmaking department. The era of the department store, however, began just after Scharf's death with William Whiteley whose empire was founded in 1863.

The development of plate glass and interior gas-lighting in the late 1820s revolutionised shop-window display. Charles Dickens in *Sketches by Boz* (1834) records the phenomenon: 'Six or eight years ago the epidemic began to display itself among the linen drapers and haberdashers. The primary symptoms were an inordinate love of plate-glass, and a passion for gas-lights and gilding. The disease gradually progressed, and at last attained a fearful height. Quiet, dusty old shops in different parts of town were pulled down; spacious premises with stuccoed fronts and gold letters were erected instead.'

London's meat and produce markets continued to thrive during the period in question, Covent Garden (depicted in a vibrant watercolour by Scharf in 1825 – cat. 46) so much so that new market buildings were built to replace the old stalls between 1828 and 1831. Besides Covent Garden the principal fruit and vegetable markets remained Borough

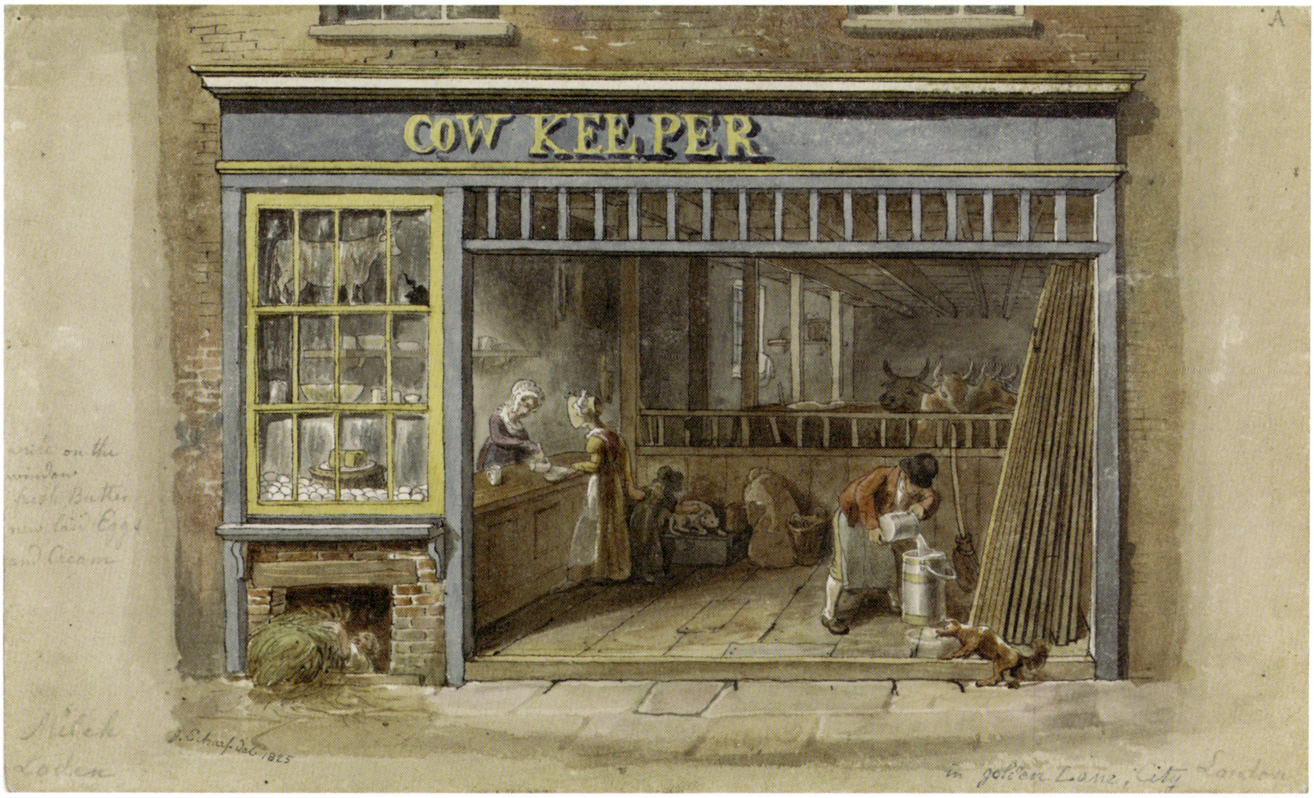

Cat. 44. *A Cowkeeper's shop in Golden Lane*

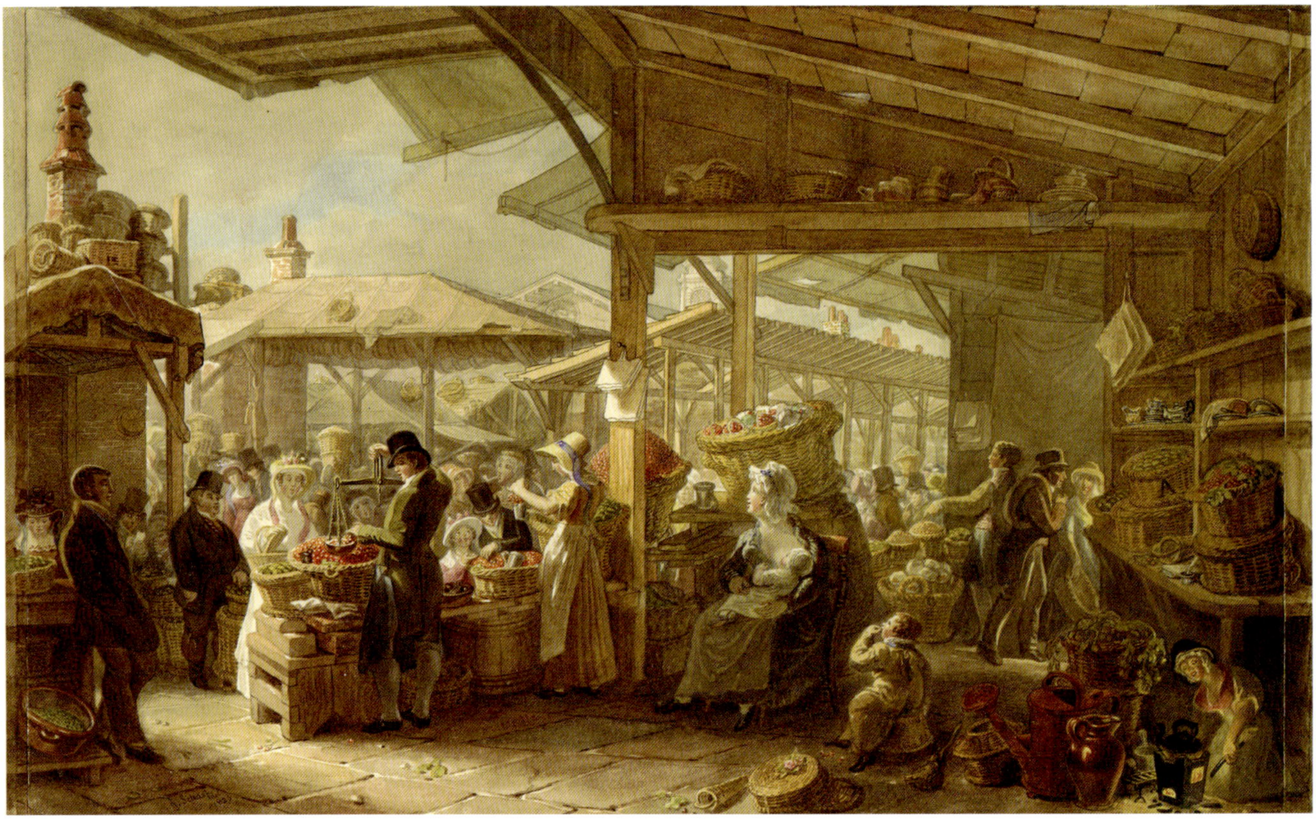

Cat. 46. Old Covent Garden Market

Market in Southwark and Spitalfields. Fleet Market between Holborn Bridge and Fleet Street was demolished in 1826–30 prior to the construction of Farringdon Street. By the end of the period under discussion others were in decline, and Hungerford Market closed in 1862 to make way for Charing Cross Station.

In 1855, as we have seen, Smithfield ceased to be a live cattle market when new slaughterhouses were built in Islington and the Central Meat Market erected in their stead. Billingsgate fish market in Lower Thames Street was rebuilt in the 1850s, and Leadenhall Market in Gracechurch Street continued to thrive, specialising in meat, hides and poultry.

Pleasure Gardens to Parks

The second quarter of the nineteenth century saw the gradual demise of London's Pleasure Gardens. The Rotunda at Ranelagh, the grounds of which are now part of the gardens of Chelsea Hospital, was demolished in 1805. The gardens at New Tunbridge Wells, opposite Sadlers Wells, were built over in 1840, as were Vauxhall Gardens, closed in the 1840s, in 1858. The last survivor was Cremorne Gardens in Chelsea (the site of which is now mostly covered by the Lots Road Power Station), which hung on until 1877.

As the pleasure gardens declined they were superseded by a new style of public park. The first of these was Victoria Park in Hackney. Laid out by James Pennethorne and covering some 290 acres, it was opened to the public in 1845. Shortly afterwards the 198-acre Battersea Park was laid out in Battersea Fields, again to the designs of James Pennethorne, and opened in 1859.

Epilogue

It is perhaps fitting to end with a view from the top of Primrose Hill taken in the early 1860s, just after Scharf's death, by the journalist George Rose Emerson.[19] Commenting on the suburban progress spread out before him he writes: 'Sixty years ago even the hill was as secluded and rural, as completely removed from the hum and bustle of a great city, as any Sussex or Devonshire hillock. Now, as we look Londonwards, we find that the metropolis has thrown out its arms and embraced us, not yet with a stifling clutch, but with ominous closeness. We do not look, as our grandfathers did, on waste uncultivated fields, where the hare and the rabbit still couched and burrowed in silent safety . . . A trim park, with green sward and shell-paths, flower patches and gymnasium, is immediately at our feet; then the narrow stream of the Regent's Canal, designed by Nash, but now in imminent danger of being converted into a railway; and beyond spread, like a variegated carpet, the Regent's Park, with its broad walks, lakes, villas and the gardens of the Zoological Society, the slender spires of St Katherine's Church and the massive domes of the Colosseum breaking the lines of the stately terraces marking the outline of the park. In the background lies the Great City, with its thousand spires and tall chimneys piercing to the cloud which overhangs the mighty mass. St John's Wood, spruce and trim, invades us on the right, and on the opposite side are huge railway stations, circular engine factories, house upon house, and street upon street. We turn away from London, only to find that bricks and mortar are fast invading the pleasant Hampstead fields dear to our boyhood for the buttercups and hedgerows, the myriads of wonderfully-coloured moths, and the lark singing far up in the blue expanse. A huge cutting [the Euston railway] traverses the valley at our feet, and pierces the bowels of the green hill, and the snorting and panting of mighty engines have long since scared away the lark and the goldfinch, the throstle and the thrush, for whom the cunning bird-catcher used to set his snares on this very spot . . . But the tall trees crowning the ridge of Hampstead Hill are yet untouched; there, too, is the spire of the church, still, as of old, a landmark; and away to our right, beyond the groves of Caen Wood, the white church of Highgate, gracefully conspicuous, overtops the sombre cedars of the cemetery; and we willingly forget, that farther eastward, the once green slopes of Holloway are crowded with houses, and that castellated prisons rear their dismal and defiant towers . . .'.

1 The subject is a vast and complex one, and to treat it in a detailed or analytical way far beyond the scope of this essay. I have therefore confined myself to broad themes and illustrative examples. Much has been written on the subject, but three books (all of which have their own bibliographies) make a good starting point: Francis Sheppard *London 1808–1870: The Infernal Wen*, Secker and Warburg: London 1971; Celina Fox Ed. *London – World City 1800–1840*, Yale University Press: New Haven and London, 1992 and Roy Porter *London A Social History*, Hamish Hamilton: London, 1994.

The diaries of Richard Rush and Prince Pückler-Muskau, quoted from in this essay, are both available in modern editions: Richard Rush *A Residence at the Court of London*, Century Hutchison Ltd: London, 1987; E M Butler Ed. *A RegencyVisitor: The English Tour of Prince Pückler-Muskau Described in his Letters 1826–1828*, Collins: London, 1957.

Strictly speaking, 'London' did not exist as an entity at this period. There were the Cities of London and Westminster and the Borough of Southwark and the surrounding Counties of Middlesex, Essex, Surrey and Kent. Until the formation of the London County Council in 1888 there was no County of London and no overall governing authority. Instead London was governed by a network of jurisdictions – parish vestries, justices of the peace, turnpike trusts, commissions of sewers, guardians of the poor, the Metropolitan Police (from 1829) and the forerunner of the LCC, the Metropolitan Board of Works (from 1855). However, for clarity this essay refers to 'London' throughout

2 This was particularly true after the agricultural crisis of the 1860s

3 A further 331,000 migrants came to London in the 1860s

4 As part of this scheme Sir John Soane designed a terrace of shops, Nos 156–170 Regent Street, for John Robins, furniture maker and auctioneer

5 Further remodelling work was done by Edward Blore between 1832 and 1837

6 It was moved to its current site at the north-east corner of Hyde Park in 1851

7 The arch was later moved to the top of Constitution Hill

8 The four bronze lions designed by Landseer, though part of the original scheme, were not placed into position until 1867

9 The first of these was the South Kensington Museum, the forerunner of the V&A, opened on 24 June 1857

10 In the decades after 1850, Kensington grew steadily south and west towards Fulham, still a market-gardening village until the 1870s, and Hammersmith

11 George Rose Emerson *London: How the Great City Grew*, Routledge, Warne & Routledge: London, 1862, p.239

12 Scharf is buried in the Brompton Cemetery

13 The first Clean Air Act was passed in 1956

14 The survivial of the name 'Cowcross Street' is a reminder of this practice

15 It was replaced by the current bridge in 1895–1906

16 It was replaced by the current bridge in 1937–42

17 It was replaced by the current steel structure in 1912–21

18 Rennie's London Bridge was replaced in 1967–72 and famously dismantled and sold to the USA

19 George Rose Emerson (*c.*1825–1885). George Rose Emerson op. cit., p.253 ff.

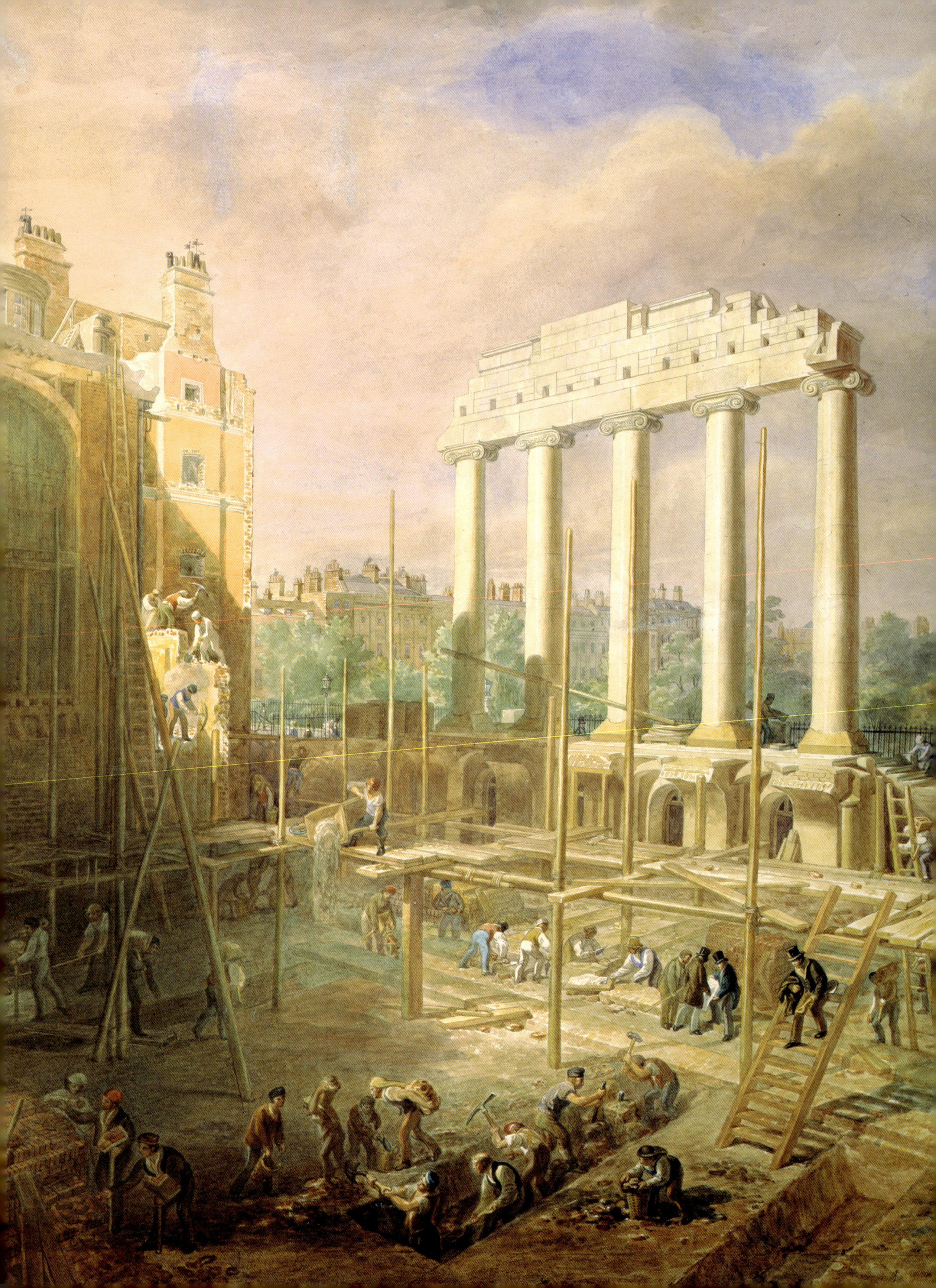

THE CATALOGUE

Jerzy J Kierkuć-Bieliński

All works are borrowed from the British Museum (BM) unless otherwise stated.
All measurements are given in millimetres, height before width.

The Journey to London

1. *Albrecht Dürer's house, Nuremberg*

1845
Pencil, heightened with white, on buff paper, (322 x 243)
1868,0822.7605

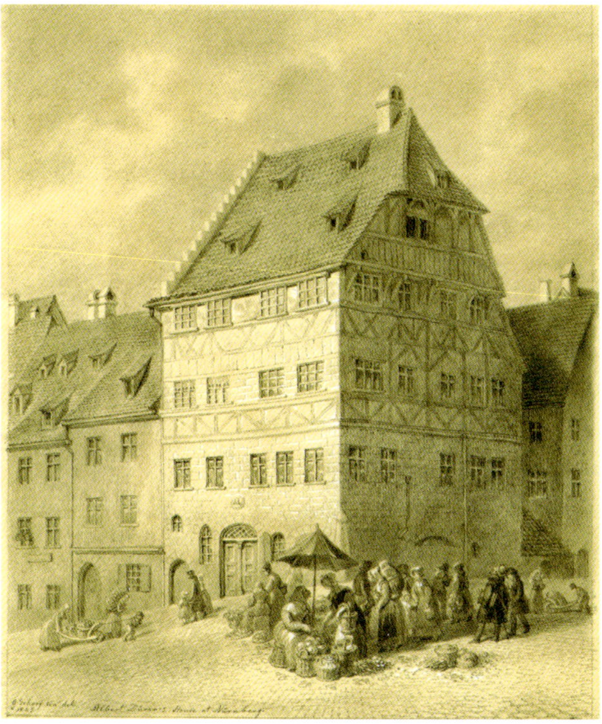

There are now few works by Scharf that can be attributed to his early years in Bavaria, before he came to England. However, throughout his life his ties to Bavaria remained strong. In 1845, due to his brother's terminal illness, he returned to his native country. This highly finished drawing dates from this trip. The cult of Albrecht Dürer (1471–1528), particularly in Germany where he was seen as the equal of the great artists of the Italian Renaissance, received renewed impetus in the 1840s, when Scharf was visiting. This was especially the case of Dürer's home town of Nuremberg, where his house, the subject of this drawing was located.[1] Scharf, by making reference to his far greater predecessor in drawing his house, not only provides an interesting topographical detail of the historical city of Nuremberg but also places his own work within the context of the *longue durée* of German art. Like the great Dürer, Scharf was a topographical artist and printmaker.

2. *Military costumes*

1828 and 1831
Watercolour, (222 x 131)
1900,0725.95

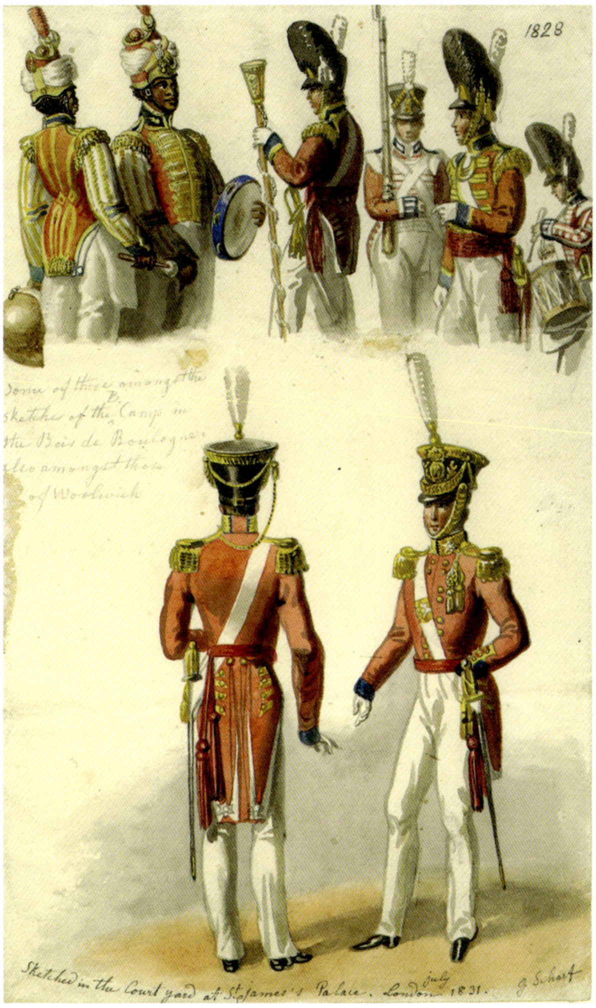

Of the miniatures and drawings that Scharf produced during the period of the Napoleonic Wars, little if anything can be securely attributed. In his journal, he records that several drawings of military subjects were confiscated at the Customs House, when he arrived in England.[2] This drawing is perhaps related to a sketch Scharf mentions in his journal. On 11 June 1840 he records that: 'I retouched my old drawings of the British troops encamped in the Bois de Boulogne near Paris in 1815 particularly the lead pencil outlines, which had almost been rubbed out.' The annotation mentions the British Camp in the Bois de Boulogne but the style of the soldiers' uniforms accords with the dates Scharf has noted. However, the

Cat. 62. View of the Royal College of Surgeons from the south-east

identity of the regiments depicted is unclear. The upper register shows what appear to be fusiliers alongside two 'oriental' bandsmen who were often used in Regency-period military bands. The lower register possibly shows front and back views of a Coldstream Guard's uniform, although the tall cylindrical hat or *shako* does not appear to be regulation.[3]

3. *Royal Horse Artillery, Woolwich*

1825
Watercolour, (149 x 139)
1900,0725.96

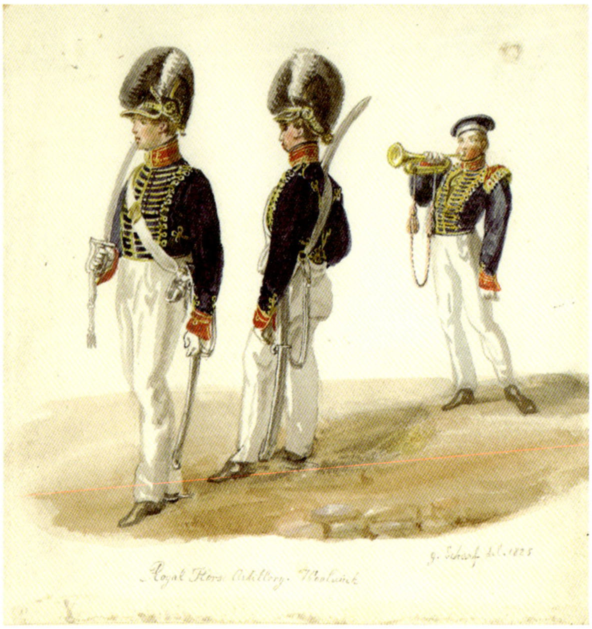

Scharf's interest in uniforms, first developed whilst painting portraits of officers during the Napoleonic Wars and furthered when he enlisted with the British Army as a lieutenant of baggage in the Engineers, continued throughout his career, as evidenced in this drawing which shows soldiers in the Royal Horse Artillery (see also cat. 20).[4] Scharf has accurately shown the distinctive gold braiding of the Horse Gunners' uniform. The Royal Horse Artillery played a decisive role in the victories over Napoleon. Even the French General Foy, who witnessed their effectiveness at the Battle of Waterloo, 1815, expressed his admiration for them: 'In battle they [British gunners] display judicious activity, a perfect *coup d'oeil*, and stoical bravery'.

4. *Dover Castle* (*see p.12*)

1816
Watercolour over pencil, (187 x 385)
1862,0614.540

This sketch is of particular poignancy as it is the first drawing Scharf produced on English soil. It shows the approach to Dover Castle, situated above the prominent white cliffs, clearly showing Henry II's (1133–1189) inner and outer baileys dominated by the great keep in the centre. Scharf has commemorated this important moment in his life – his arrival in England – in the inscription, which reads: 'Dover Cliffs painted on the spot on my arrival in England 5 of January 1816.' This drawing is eloquent testimony of Scharf's passion for sketching. As soon as he sets foot on English soil he begins to sketch what would become his adopted country. Throughout his life he would record the anniversary of his arrival in this country in his journal entries.

Scharf's London

5. *View looking west along Church Lane*

1828
Watercolour over pencil, on grey paper, (256 x 173)
1862,0614.107

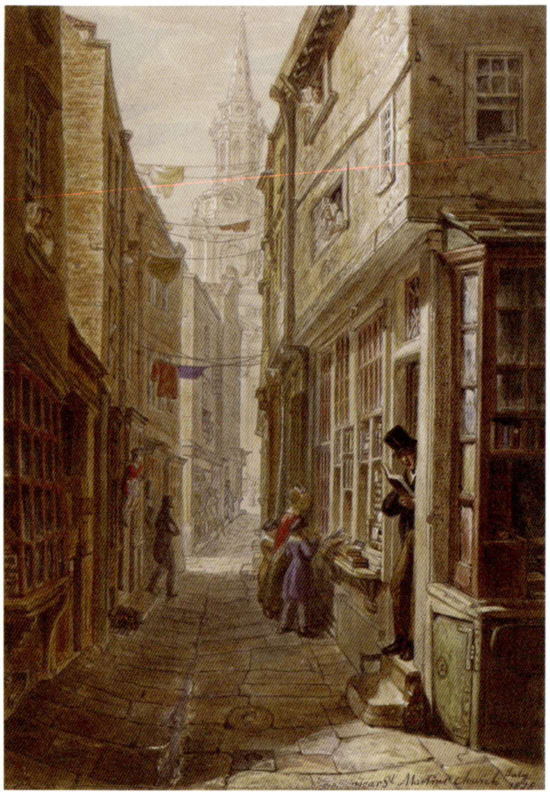

Scharf's first home in London was at No. 3 St Martin's Lane above a grocer's shop owned by a Mary Hicks. This area of London had long been associated with artists and artisans. It was also a part of the West End that was characterised by its tangle of narrow alleyways and passages, such as Church Lane, shown here. These were so notorious, with slum tenements isolated by the winding lanes, that in the late sixteenth century they were called colloquially 'The Bermudas'.[5] Scharf has shown the narrowness of the lane, with a central gutter running along its length and washing lines stretching between the upper storeys of the tenements. Just discernible and to the left, opposite the book shop, Scharf has shown a wig shop, an advert for hair in the shop window. In the distance rises the spire of St Martin's-in-the-Fields. This distinctive London landmark was built by James Gibbs (1682–1754) and was consecrated in 1726. Scharf would marry Elizabeth Hicks, the sister of Mary, there on 20 August 1820. Church Lane, which ran from the Strand to Chandos Street, with a branch leading to Church Yard (shown here) was demolished as part of John Nash's (1752–1835), improvements to the Strand (see cat. 21). The southern end of St Martin's Lane, where Scharf and his family lived, would also disappear when, in 1830, work was begun on creating Trafalgar Square. As a consequence the Scharfs moved to 14 Francis Street off Tottenham Court Road.

6. *Portrait of the artist's family*

1830
Watercolour, (261 x 196)
1900,0725.5

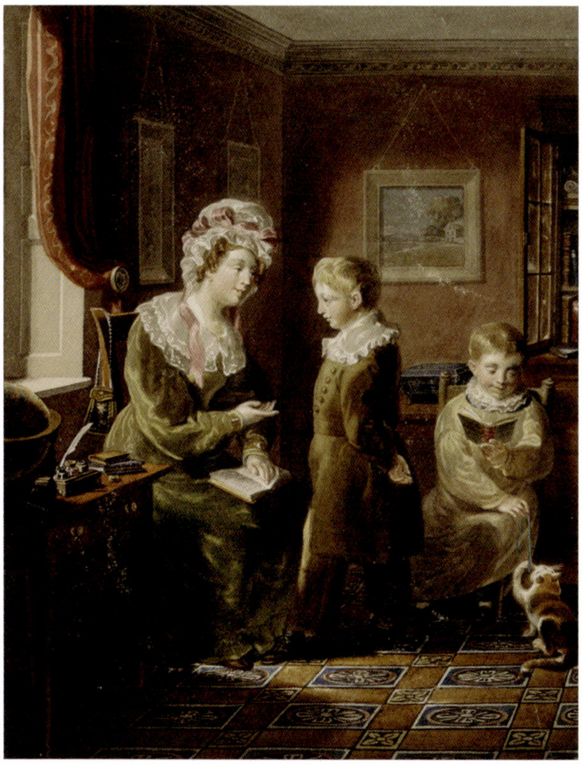

George Scharf and Elizabeth *née* Hicks had two children. George Scharf the Younger who was born on 16 December 1820, four months after his parents married, and Henry born on 8 December 1822. This sketch, made in 1830, shows George at the age of twelve and Henry at ten years old. It is plausible that George can be identified with the figure of the boy standing in front of Elizabeth, whilst Henry sits reading towards the right. It is not clear whether the interior shown is that of the Scharfs' first house at No. 3 St Martin's Lane, shortly before it was demolished, or whether it is a room in their new house in Francis Street. Scharf has shown his family in an idealised, 'sentimental' scene echoing the conventional composition of a 'conversation piece'. The furnishing of the room is simple but elegant, reflecting middle-class taste. The decorated floor covering is probably a painted and sealed floor cloth rather than a wall-to-wall carpet as this would have been an expensive item in the 1820s.

George Scharf the Younger would become an important figure for nineteenth-century museology (see cat. 8), and showed his father's flair for drawing. George was his father's favoured child. His younger brother was less artistically inclined. Together they were educated at the University College School, where they were amongst the first pupils. Although Scharf also taught Henry how to draw, he failed as an artist. Instead, he had always shown a talent for amateur dramatics. Having worked for a period from 1841 as Articulator and General Assistant to the Museum of the Royal College of Surgeons (see cats 61 and 62), he entered the theatre. In 1842 he started work at the Newcastle Theatre. This was followed by appearances at Sadler's Wells back in London. It is only when he began to develop a moderately successful career in this profession, from the 1840s onwards, that Scharf begins to speak of *both* his sons' careers with some pride, as he wrote in his journal whilst in Germany in 1847: 'I am the more delighted with all this good news of my dear sons . . .'.[6] Henry continued his theatrical career in America, to a certain level of acclaim dying there in 1887.[7] Scharf has inscribed this drawing 'The artist's family' in German.

7. *Portrait of Elizabeth Fry*

1819
Pencil, (98 x 124)
1900,0725.22

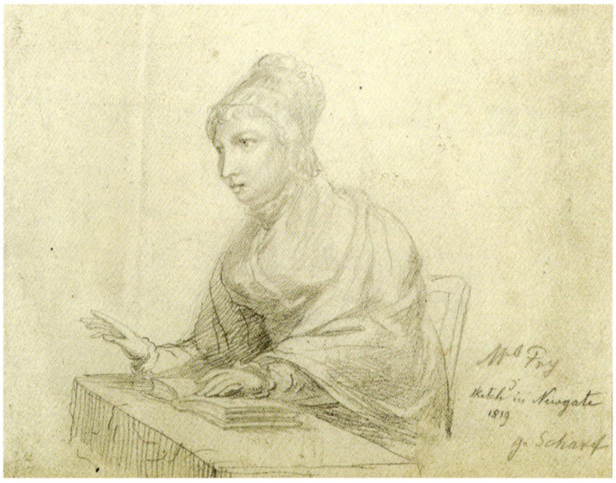

When he moved to London, initially Scharf hoped to continue his work as a painter of portrait miniatures. However, he met with no success and was forced to deploy his knowledge of printmaking instead. This small pencil sketch is representative of this earlier, unsuccessful phase of his career in London. The sitter is the philanthropist and penal reformer Elizabeth Fry (1780–1845). Following a religious conversion in 1798, she started her philanthropic work, which, in 1813 led her to visit the female section of Newgate Gaol. Horrified by the crowded conditions that the female prisoners (and their children) had to endure, she became a pioneer in penal (particularly female) reform.[8] In this sketch, Scharf has shown Fry in Newgate gaol, perhaps expounding upon her reformist theories that called for prisoners to be treated with kindness and humanity so, as she put it, to '. . . change the character and change the heart . . .'.[9] As a trained minituarist Scharf has captured her likeness well; she is shown wearing her distinctive 'Quaker bonnet', which can be seen in later representations of her such as George Richmond's 1844 watercolour (private collection), and uses delicate, short strokes of the pencil to describe the contour and shading of Fry's face. It is clear, though, that Scharf is less able to integrate the sitter's face and head with the rest of her anatomy as required by a three-quarter-length portrait. Scharf has shown her with disproportionately small hands and short arms. His line is less assured when describing her torso. These shortcomings in his technique may explain why he had no success in London as a portraitist. Although there is no evidence to suggest it, this sketch may have been produced with a print in mind. The three-quarter-length format is similar to that used in the four sketches of the Spa Fields Rioters (see fig. 2).

8. *Portrait of Sir George Scharf the younger in court dress*

Brush drawing in grey wash with watercolour, (266 x 172)
1900,0725.21

It is clear from reading Scharf's journal that his eldest son, George Scharf the Younger (1820–1895), was his favourite. He is mentioned often in the journals, far more so than his brother Henry. George Scharf the Elder notes his 19th birthday in an entry for 1838. He also records his eldest son's success at school, something he does not do in relation to Henry, and later makes a note of the day that George the Younger is admitted to the Royal Academy to study.[10] Indeed, George the Younger's progress as an artist is often recorded in the journals. Scharf makes notes when he and George sketch together (see cat. 41). He teaches both sons to etch, but it is George the Younger's immediate mastery of this difficult technique that his father records.[11] With equal pride he also recorded George's first attempt at drawing a portrait.[12] However, this close relationship between father and son would deteriorate in later years.[13] Scharf drew his eldest son's portrait on at least three occasions (see cat. 34).[14] Here, Scharf the Younger is shown wearing the black mourning court dress (indicated by the unusual black waistcoat) that was reserved for a courtier of unspecific rank. The lace ruffles on George the Younger's cuffs and on his *jabot* indicate that this drawing was made sometime either in the 1840s or 1850s.[15] Scharf the Younger's career developed rapidly through his ability as a draughtsman and his interest in art. At the age of fifteen he was awarded a silver plate by the Royal Society of Arts for his work which was followed, in 1836, by a silver medal for a drawing. In 1838 he enrolled at the Royal Academy Schools and Scharf the Elder noted the occasion in his journal.[16] Whilst at the Academy, he published his first portfolio of prints: a series of etchings entitled *Recollections of Scenic Effects*, which illustrated productions by contemporary playwrights and scenes from Shakespeare. Having drawn as a boy in the British Museum (see cat. 34), he was also interested in antiquity and in 1840 and again in 1843 he was called upon to accompany Sir Charles Fellows on two archaeological expeditions to ancient Lycia in modern Turkey. The result of these expeditions was the excavation and acquisition by the British Museum of several important antiquities, including most notably the Nereid Monument. Scharf the Younger published a series of prints based on the drawings he made on his trips to Turkey in 1847 and would also provide illustrations to other archaeological texts, including Layard's publications on Nineveh.[17] Amongst his other undertakings during this period was a cartoon showing King Caractacus that he submitted to the competition held at Westminster Hall for frescoes to decorate the new Palace of Westminster. However, Scharf the Younger was also making a name for himself as a scholar in his own right. In 1850 he identified a hitherto unrecognised fragment of the Parthenon Frieze in a country-house collection which led to his being elected a fellow of the Society of Antiquaires in 1852. He taught at Queen's College, London and lectured at the Society, contributing seventeen papers to the Society's periodical *Archaeologia*. However, the most important aspect of his work was the central role he played in the newly founded National Portrait Gallery. In 1857 he was appointed the National Portrait Gallery's first Secretary – a post he would hold for some forty years. Scharf the Younger became the pre-eminent authority on historical portraiture in Britain and over his lengthy period at the Gallery he identified countless sitters and made numerous attributions. In 1882 he was made Director and in recognition of his achievements he was made a Companion of the Order of the Bath in 1885. Scharf the Younger's final achievement was to implement the relocation of the National Portrait Gallery to its present site behind the National Gallery. Although, he was by then in his seventies and well past the compulsory retirement age he was allowed to supervise the complex task of transferring the Gallery's collections from their temporary home at the Bethnal Green Museum. Work on the new building started in 1890 but Scharf the Younger would not live to see it completed. He died on 19 April 1895, having been made a Knight Commander of the Order of the Bath a few months before.[18]

8

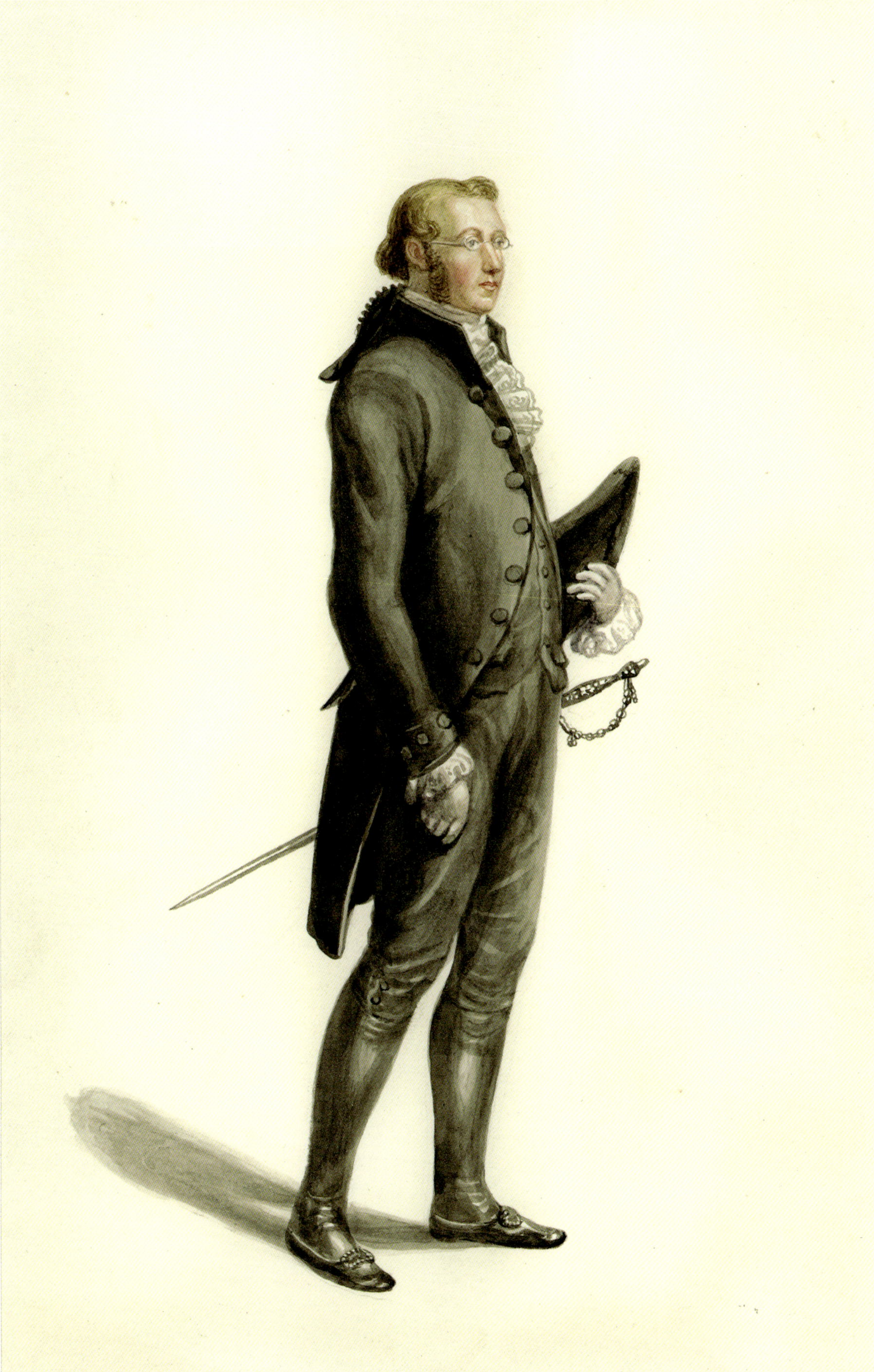

Drawing techniques

9. *Shops in Bishopsgate Street*

Watercolour over pencil, (180 x 254)
1862,0614.457

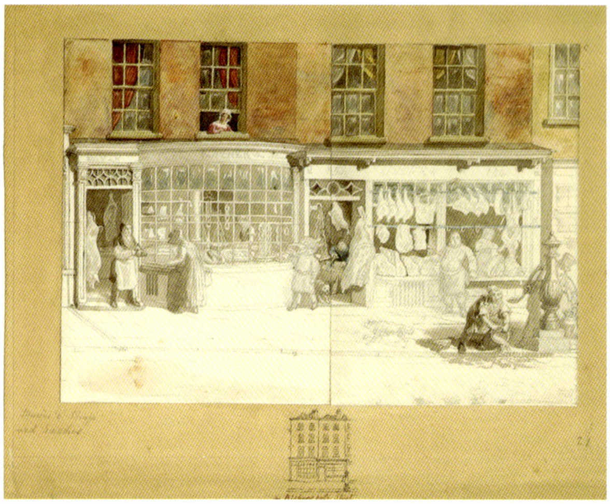

It is clear from Scharf's journals that his commissioned lithographs of fossils and medical specimens preoccupied him greatly and his journals accord them greater prominence than his other artistic subjects, although we do know that he produced finished paintings of London's monuments for sale and for exhibition as well as lithographs of these subjects (see cats 30, 51 and 55). His drawings, both topographical and the studies of London's inhabitants, served specific functions in relation to these, later, printmaking and painting projects. In the case of this drawing and cats 10 and 20, below, we can see that they were produced as records of a London that was fast disappearing. These drawings could then be used as studies for the later, more developed compositions. This drawing of Bishopsgate Street can possibly be related to a journal entry, dated 6 September 1841, in which Scharf described making several sketches of houses in Bishopsgate Street that were about to be demolished.[19] We can clearly see in this unfinished drawing how Scharf has drawn the composition in pencil, over which he then describes the shading of the architecture using a grey wash applied with a brush. The whiteness of the paper support is left untouched to describe the highlights of the composition. Finally, working from the top of the composition downwards, watercolour is used. This would indicate that this study was intended as a preliminary stage in a more fully developed painting of the same subject and perhaps was never intended to be fully coloured. Inscriptions on the mount of the sheet, noting that the sashes of Davis's Butchers should be coloured red, and a small pen and ink sketch, that roughly outlines the composition would help Scharf use the drawing for the final, fully resolved painting. Bishopsgate Street was redeveloped in the later nineteenth century, when the Georgian houses we see in Scharf's view were demolished.

10. *Mr Mcnab's house and chemist's shop in St Martin's Lane*

1827
Watercolour and pencil, (227 x 134)
1862,0614.121

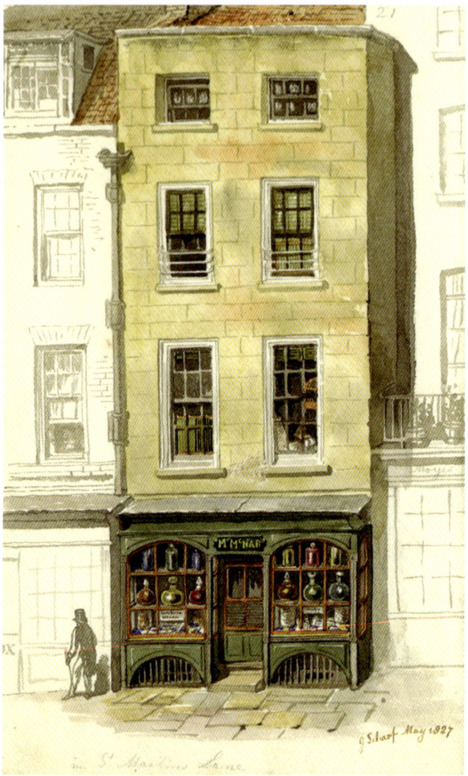

Watercolour was considered a less important medium than oil paint in the nineteenth century. For this reason the New Watercolour Society was founded to promote the technique. Although Scharf did experiment with oil paint on at least one occasion (see cat. 56), his preferred medium was watercolour. This was also the medium that most readily lent itself to the painting of miniatures and in the case of Scharf's streetscapes it allowed him to create highly detailed images. In this sketch he has carefully described the bottles and packages on display in the shop's window. Scharf has focused on one specific house in the street, finishing this part of the composition to a high degree whilst leaving the buildings on both sides as sketches in grey wash. This type of close focusing on one element of a street can often be found in Scharf's working sketches and contrasts with his resolved views of London's streets such as cat. 21, showing the Strand. Instead of delineating the composition in pencil, here Scharf outlines the drawing solely using grey wash over which he then applies colour. This would have allowed him to explore the tonal aspects of the composition in a more painterly manner and contrasts with his pencil studies of architectural subjects such as cat. 12, below, where he focuses upon the structure of the composition.

11. *Dinner Time, Sunday, One O'Clock* (*see also p. 8*)

1841
Pencil, (223 x 137)
1862,0614.339

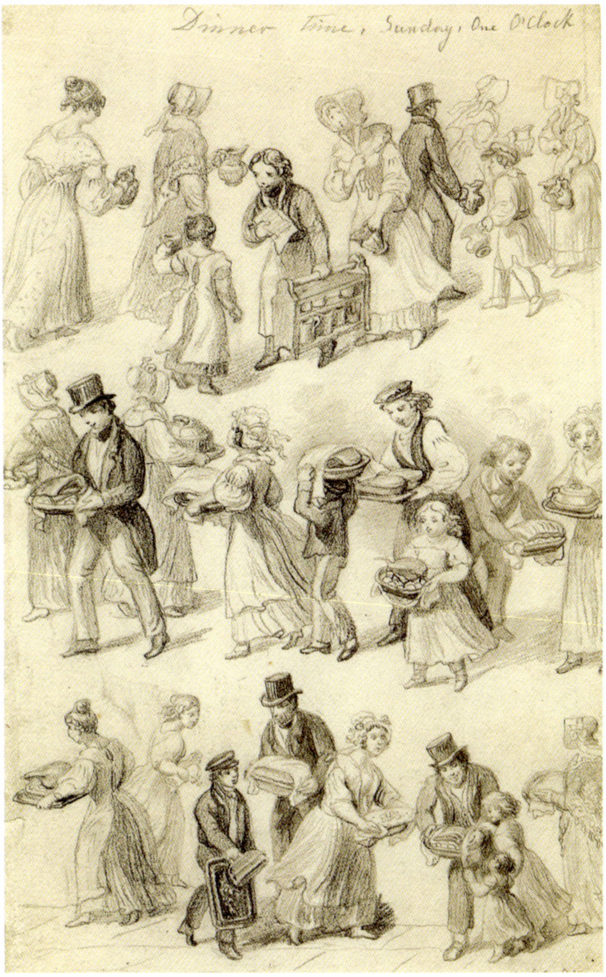

In the first half of the nineteenth century it was common for working-class London households not to have kitchens. The baked or roasted food for Sunday dinner, and the ale to wash it down, would have to be bought at a cookshop and inn. The indication of the time 1 o'clock is significant. The middle and upper classes would have eaten dinner much later in the evening. Only servants and working men had their main meal at around midday. This drawing does not represent a single scene but rather is an amalgamation of individual *vignettes* sketched on one sheet. The features of the figures are largely conventionalised; Scharf has not really attempted to show individual facial types. Instead he wanted to convey the bustle of the figures rushing home with their food before it got cold and he does this through the swishing of skirts and the fluttering of ribbons on the women's bonnets described using rapid strokes of the pencil. He has also conveyed the wide-eyed anticipation on the faces of several of the children particularly the boy carrying a pie in the mid-right of the drawing. Scharf used these figure studies as a type of 'stock' of images that could be referred to for later compositions.[20] He notes in his journal that he would return to these earlier drawings and 'outline' them again, as he put it.[21] Presumably, the need to go over the pencil sketches once more to reassert the contours of the figures arose from the fact that these were working drawings (see also cat. 2), and would become indistinct through constant handling.

12. *The back of Scharf's house in Francis Street* (*see p. 31*)

1844
Pencil on buff paper, (286 x 204)
1862,0614.71

The Scharfs moved into this house on Francis Street, off Tottenham Court Road, in 1830 as their former house on St Martin's Lane was due to be demolished (see cat. 5). Scharf, in this sketch, has shown the narrow, flagged back yard, with an outdoor privy in the corner and a water butt towards the right that collected rain water from the house's guttering. In the background a group of builders are working on scaffolding in the neighbouring house. As well as a record of the Scharf's second London home, this drawing acts as a good indicator of how Scharf composed his sketches. The narrowness of the yard is described through the quite acutely foreshortened ranges of houses to the left and right. The sketch is quite detailed. Scharf has shown the heart-shaped aperture in the half-open privy door, the tap at the bottom of the water butt and even the cracks in the flagstones of the yard. However, we can also see how he has structured the composition through the clearly delineated perspectival lines that converge upon a vanishing point, indicated by a mark just under the roof line of the privy, towards the top centre of the wall. These are particularly evident on the right-hand side of the sketch. Once the structure of the architectural elements was resolved, Scharf then integrated the *staffage* into the composition – in this case the workmen on the scaffolding. Individual and group figure studies, such as those in cat. 11 would be used for this. Scharf also very often carefully annotated his sketches with notes recording the colour, texture or other details of certain elements of the scene. In this case he has made colour notes as well as making other observations such as '. . . 10 bricks . . . this ledge projects 8 inches . . . this window higher'. Along with the pictorial record of the scene formed by the sketch, these notes would have provided additional information when using the drawing as the basis of either a finished painting or for a lithograph. Scharf often returned to earlier drawings and, on the basis of such annotated instructions, would redraw certain parts or even add colour (see cat. 2). The Scharfs lived on Francis Street until 1848 when they moved to Torrington Square.

13. *Sketchbook by George Scharf*

1820–30
Watercolour over pencil, (175 x 260)
1900,0725.120.1

Most of Scharf's drawings are no longer arranged in his original sketchbooks. When Elizabeth Scharf sold many of her husband's drawings to the British Museum they were unbound and mounted in new albums. In spite of having been rebound, this sketchbook, bequeathed by Sir George Scharf the Younger, is a rare survival. It shows the small scale of the sketchbooks Scharf would have carried around the streets of London, allowing him quickly to capture his impressions of the city on the spot. The book also indicates how Scharf used his sketches. Scharf made notes as to where he used the figures from the sketchbook in his finished compositions. A note on the verso of the flyleaf of the book states: 'This x mark signifies that the figures have been introduced into my arranged quarto sketches.' The book also contains two indexes, which refer to the subject matter and dates of the drawings, allowing Scharf readily to locate a stock figure type that could be then incorporated into a composition.

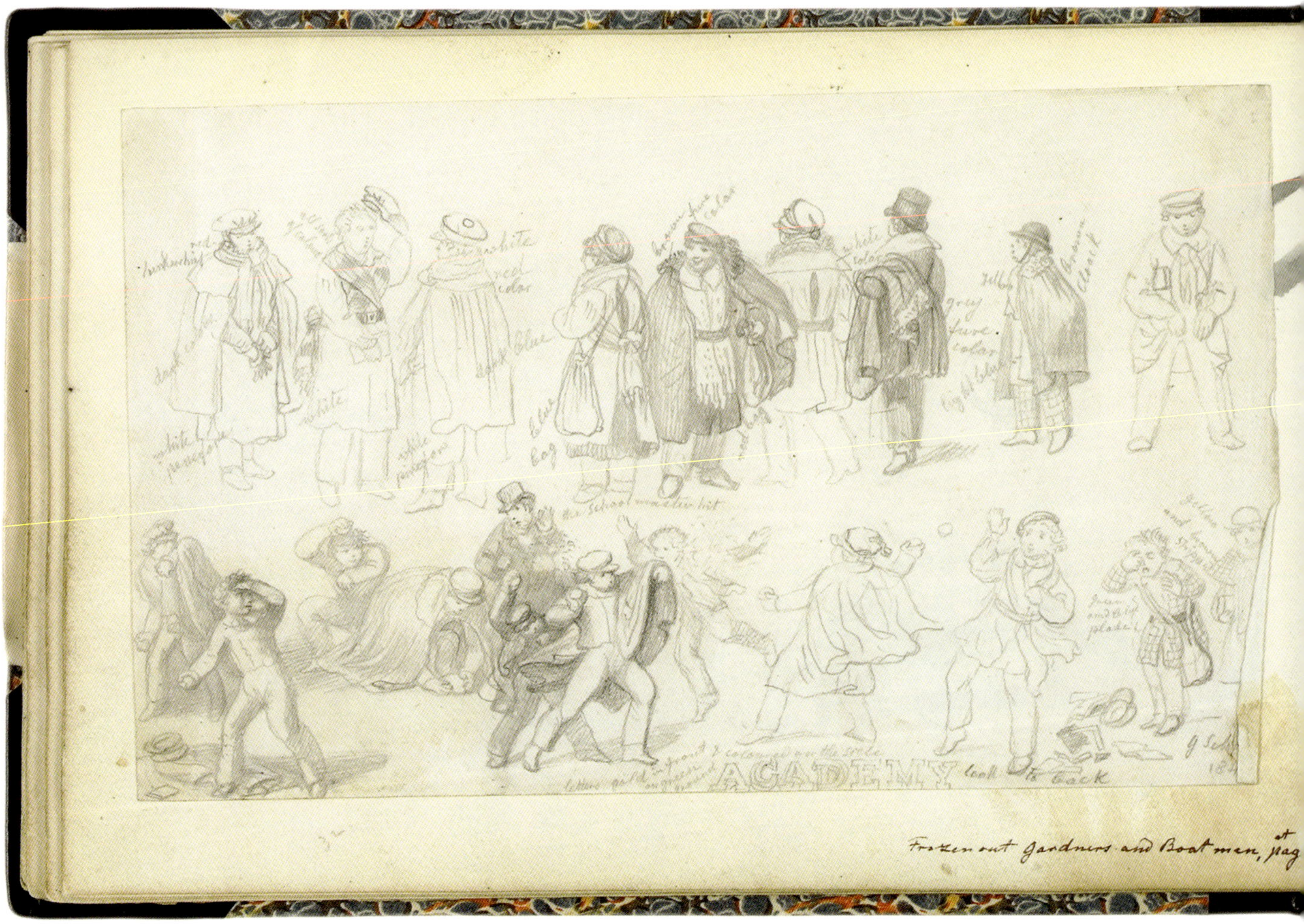

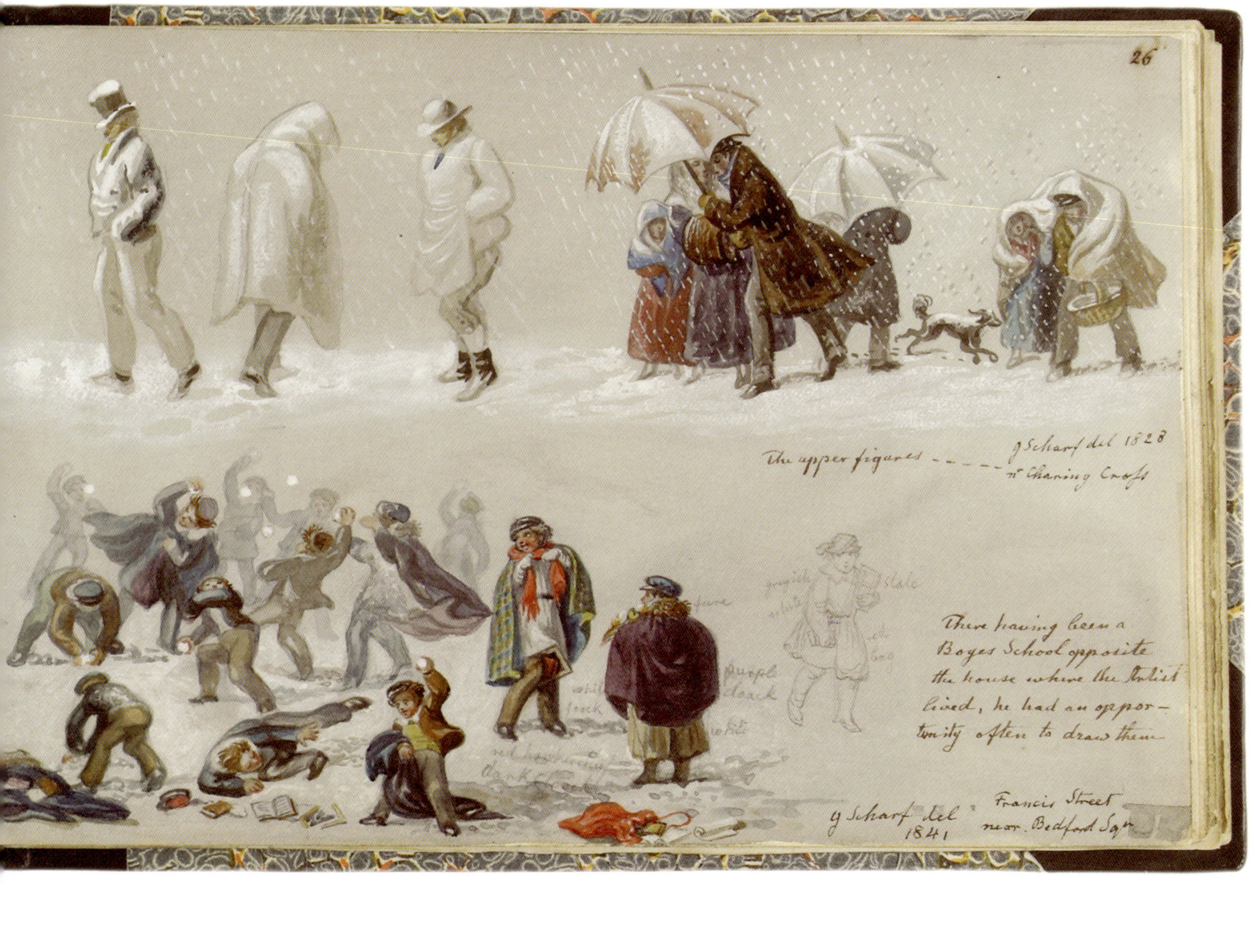
26
The upper figures
G Scharf del 1828
nr Charing Cross
There having been a
Boyes School opposite
the house where the Artist
lived, he had an oppor-
tunity often to draw them
G Scharf del
1841
Francis Street
near Bedford Sqr

Public London

14. *Representation of the election of Members of Parliament for Westminster*

1818
Hand-coloured aquatint and etching, (382 x 491)
1880,1113.3088

This aquatint is one of Scharf's earliest print commissions undertaken on his arrival in London. It shows the scene on polling day for the election of the two Members of Parliament for Westminster which had the largest electorate of any borough before the Reform Act of 1832. Before 1872, voting, which was restricted to male constituents who owned property worth a certain amount, was done in public and from the early eighteenth century, in the Westminster constituency, this took place in front of Inigo Jones' church of St Paul, Covent Garden. Scharf shows the large milling crowd and includes many anecdotal details in the foreground, such as the small fallen boy whose hat has been knocked off in the excitement. He also has shown the temporary wooden shed or hustings from which the prospective candidates made their speeches; a grandstand has been erected to the right of this with people also precariously sitting on the lead roof of one of the timber stalls that were used by the marketers (see also cat. 46). The names of the candidates are clearly visible on the flyposters attached to the hustings. Supporters in the crowd carry banners with political slogans: 'Maxwell to the last . . . Magna Charta [sic]'. In the foreground, towards the right, a figure can be seen holding a placard giving the results of the last day's poll which has the candidates Sir Samuel Romilly (1757–1818) and Sir Francis Burdett (1770–1844) in the lead and who would eventually be elected the Members for Westminster.[22] Both were reformist politicians. Romilly wished to reform criminal laws, having published *Thoughts on Executive Justice* in 1786. Burdett supported Roman Catholic emancipation and universal (male) suffrage (see Scharf and Politics pp. 13–16). This aquatint was based on a highly detailed preparatory drawing. Two related sketches show Burdett making an address in Palace Yard, Westminster, and Burdett's supporters celebrating in the Strand (BM 1862,0614.666 and 1900,0725.16). Alongside the print, Scharf included a key, identifying costume types of the figures in the crowd scene. The print was engraved by Robert Havell and Sons, of 3 Chapel Street, Tottenham Court Road and was published by Scharf at No. 3 St Martin's Lane and by Colnaghi and Co. Printsellers of Cockspur Street. Scharf reissued this print, with minor adjustments to dates and names when, following the death of George III in January 1820, Parliament was dissolved and new elections were held.

15. *The coronation procession of His Majesty King George the Fourth*

1821
Lithograph, (338 x 452)
1862,1108.556

The Coronation of George the Fourth was one of the most spectacular ceremonies that Westminster Abbey had witnessed.[23] George, who had acted as Prince Regent from 1811 to 1820 during his father George III's long illness, was aware of the precedent set by Napoleon's Imperial Coronation in Paris in 1804 for splendour. The British Coronation should outdo the Napoleonic one, as was befitting the status of the sovereign whose armies had defeated the French, and to this end Parliament voted £243,000 towards the costs of the lavish ceremony. George was dressed in a costume that re-worked seventeenth-century English ceremonial robes.[24] Some £2,0044 was paid to William Webb the robemaker for the various ceremonial mantles that were worn by the various dignitaries at the coronation. However, the King's vision was somewhat short of the reality of the ceremony in certain aspects. As one German observer noted of the spectacle:

> It excited in me a strong feeling of the comic, to see how the most powerful monarch of the earth was obliged to present himself, as chief actor in a pantomime, before an audience he deems so infinitely beneath him. In fact, the whole pageant, including the King's costume, reminded me strikingly of one of those historical plays which are here got up so well; nothing was wanting but the 'flourish of trumpets' which accompanies the entrance and exit of one of Shakespeare's Kings, to make the illusion complete.[25]

The mantle of the King's robes was so massive that eight, rather than the normal six, pages had to hold it and the King nearly fainted in the Abbey due to the heat and weight of the crimson velvet and because his vanity had forced him to corset tightly his corpulent frame.[26] His estranged wife, Queen Caroline, who had not been invited to participate in the ceremony, tried to force her way into the Abbey through the barred doors. In spite of this, the coronation of King George the Fourth was considered '. . . the most splendid ever celebrated in England'.[27] Following the Coronation ceremony, the newly crowned George the Fourth processed to Westminster Hall for the banquet that was traditionally held there afterwards. This is the part of the ceremony that Scharf has depicted in his lithograph. The King is shown, wearing the crown and carrying the orb and sceptre, beneath a canopy of cloth of gold held up by the sixteen Barons of the Cinque Ports.[28] In front of the King process Peers of the Realm and other dignitaries that took part in the coronation with guards lining the route. Scharf has removed the blue canopy that ran the length of the processional route and which protected the King and other participants from the elements, for clarity. As

14

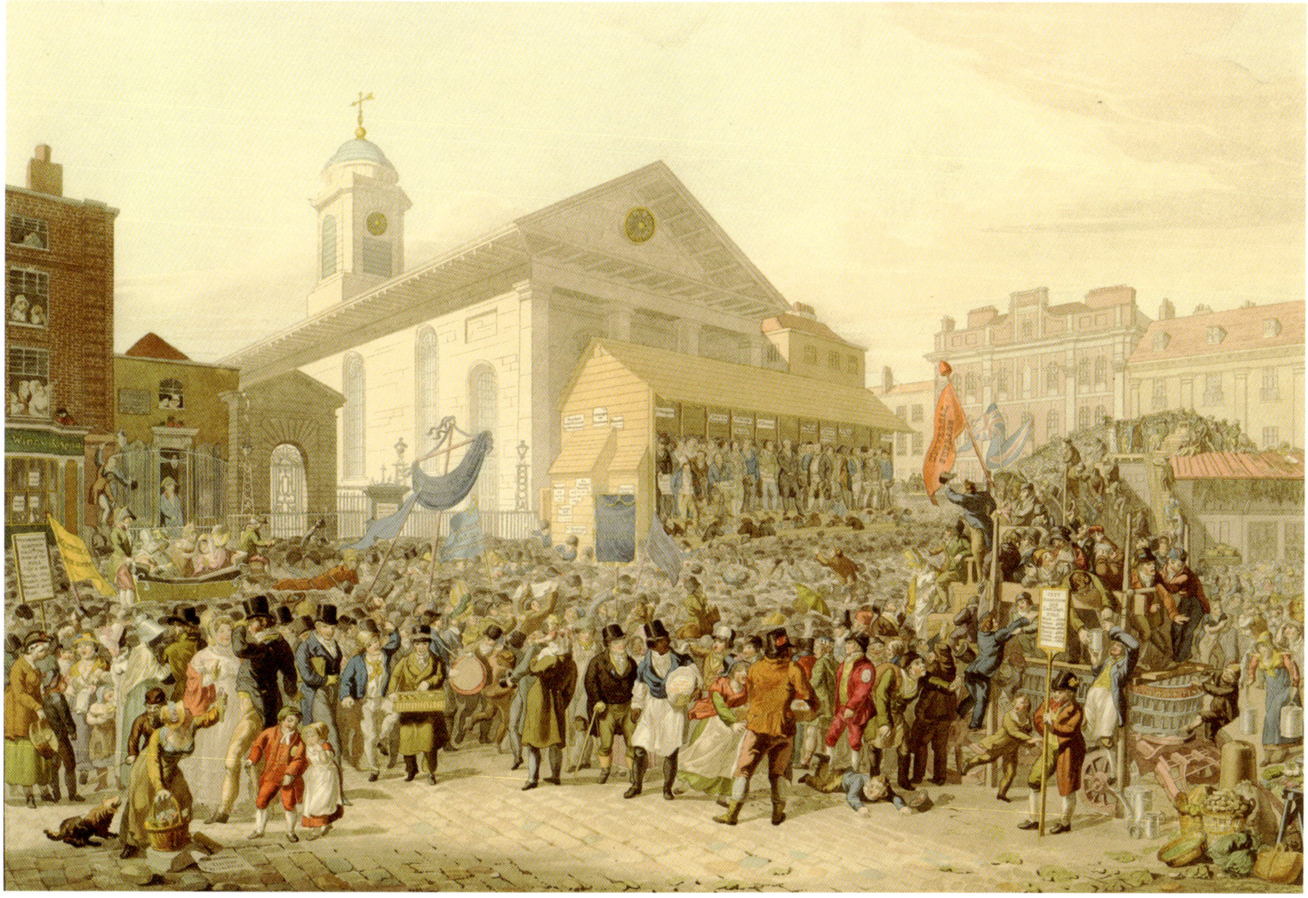

15

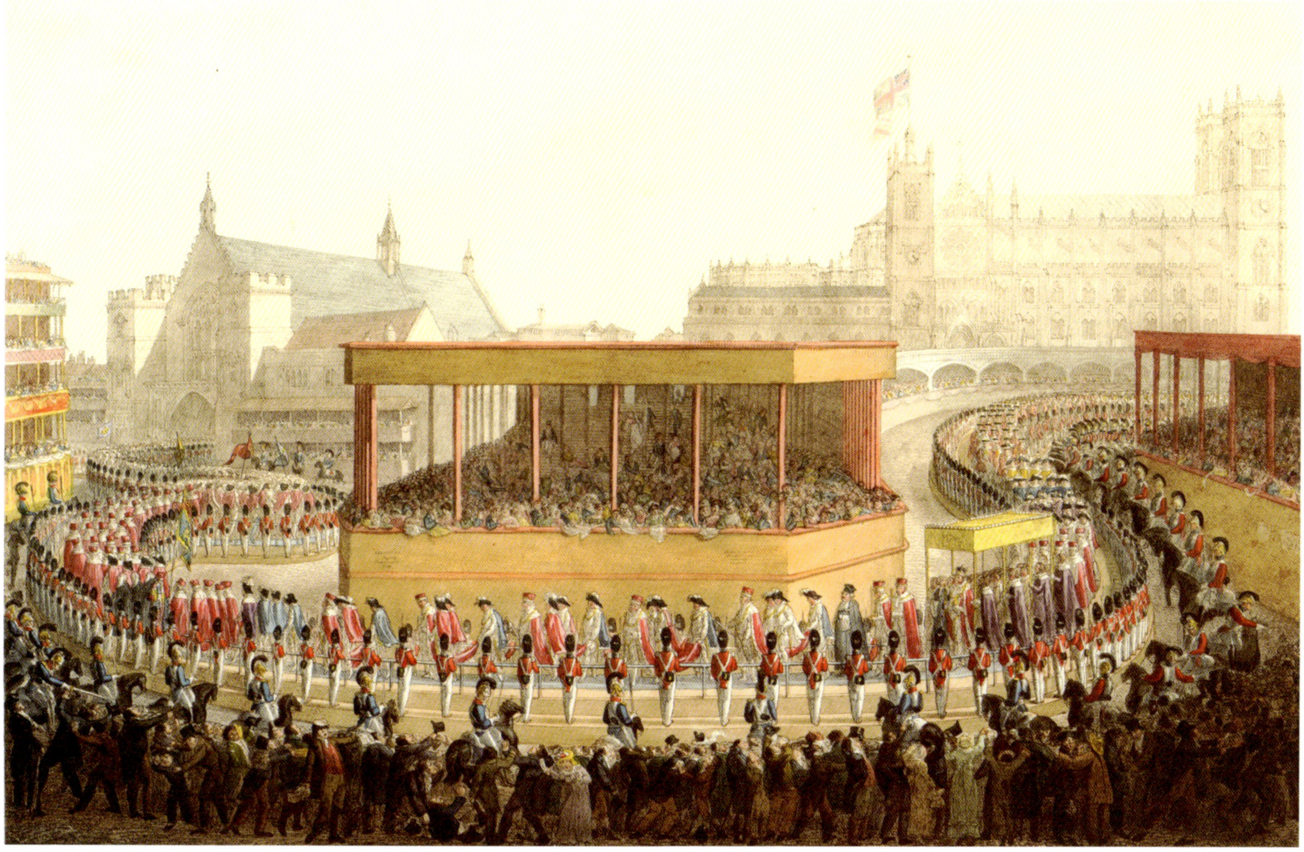

with the previous work (cat. 14), this was one of Scharf's earliest print commissions in London and one of his most successful ones.[29] The lithograph was pulled from the stone by Hullmandel and published by Thomas Clay (*fl.* 1811–22) of Clay and Scriven, 18 Ludgate Hill.

16. *Lord Mayor's state coach*

1827
Watercolour, (142 x 227)
1862,0614.864.2

17. *Lord Mayor's state coach; view of front half*

1827
Watercolour, (141 x 125)
1862,0614.864.1

One of the more splendid and popular events in London's public calendar was (and still is) the Lord Mayor's Procession, which has been taking place in some form since 1215 when King John granted the citizens of the City of London a charter allowing them freely to elect their Lord Mayor (from 1752, this was always held on 9 November and nowadays on the second Saturday of November). The Lord Mayor Elect was required to process from the City to Westminster in order to swear fealty to the Crown. By the eighteenth century this had developed into the present pageant. Initially, up until 1711, the Lord Mayor was required to make the journey on horseback. However, following an accident to one of the Lord Mayors Elect, where a drunken flower girl knocked him off his horse and he fell, breaking his leg, coaches were hired out for the procession.[30] In 1757, the new Lord Mayor Elect, Sir Charles Asgillit (1713–88) decided to commission a new Lord Mayor's Coach from Joseph Berry of Holborn to the designs of Robert Taylor at a cost of £1,065.[31] Scharf erroneously states in a note inscribed on the recto of the smaller study of the coachman's seat and foot rest that it had been purchased from the King. Scharf records seeing the Lord Mayor's Procession on a number of occasions, although it could interfere with his work, as he stated in his journal: 'Went into the city to draw, but was prevented on account of there being a great crowd, but I stayed to see the Lord Mayor's procession.'[32] When he sketched these two studies of the coach, in 1827, the Lord Mayor of the City of London was Matthias Prime Lucas (1761–1848). His procession was considered to be one of the most lavish, although the banquet that followed was marred when a lamp fell on his head. Lucas and other guests near him were injured, including the Duke of Clarence, the future King William IV. The highly ornate and gilded woodwork of the coach frames a series of allegorical *panneaux* by the Italian painter Giovanni Battista Cipriani (1727–85), who also decorated the slightly later Golden State Coach, used at British coronations. Scharf has shown the side with an allegory representing the Genius of the City of London with Mars, the patron god of the City. The figure of the City's Genius points to the figure of Truth who holds a scroll (just discernable) upon which is inscribed the name of the first Lord Mayor of London – Henri Fitz Alwin – who held the post from 1189 to 1211. Less clearly shown is the back panel of

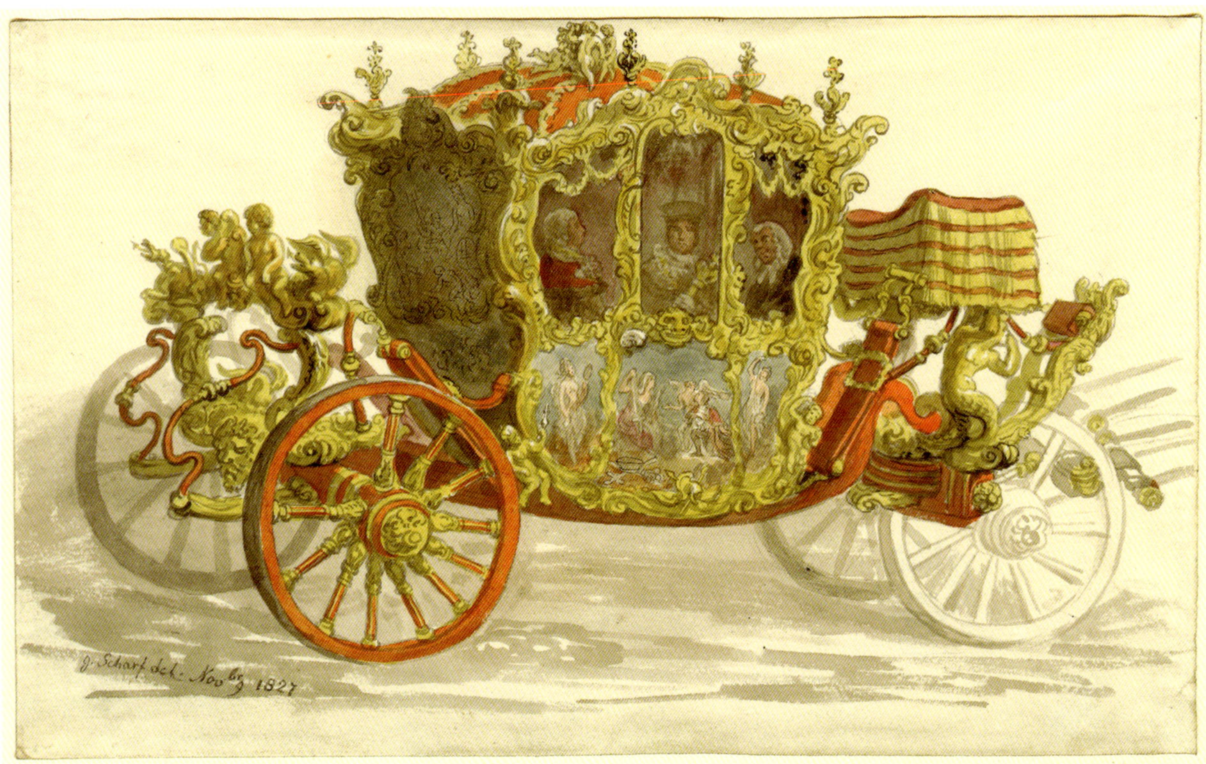

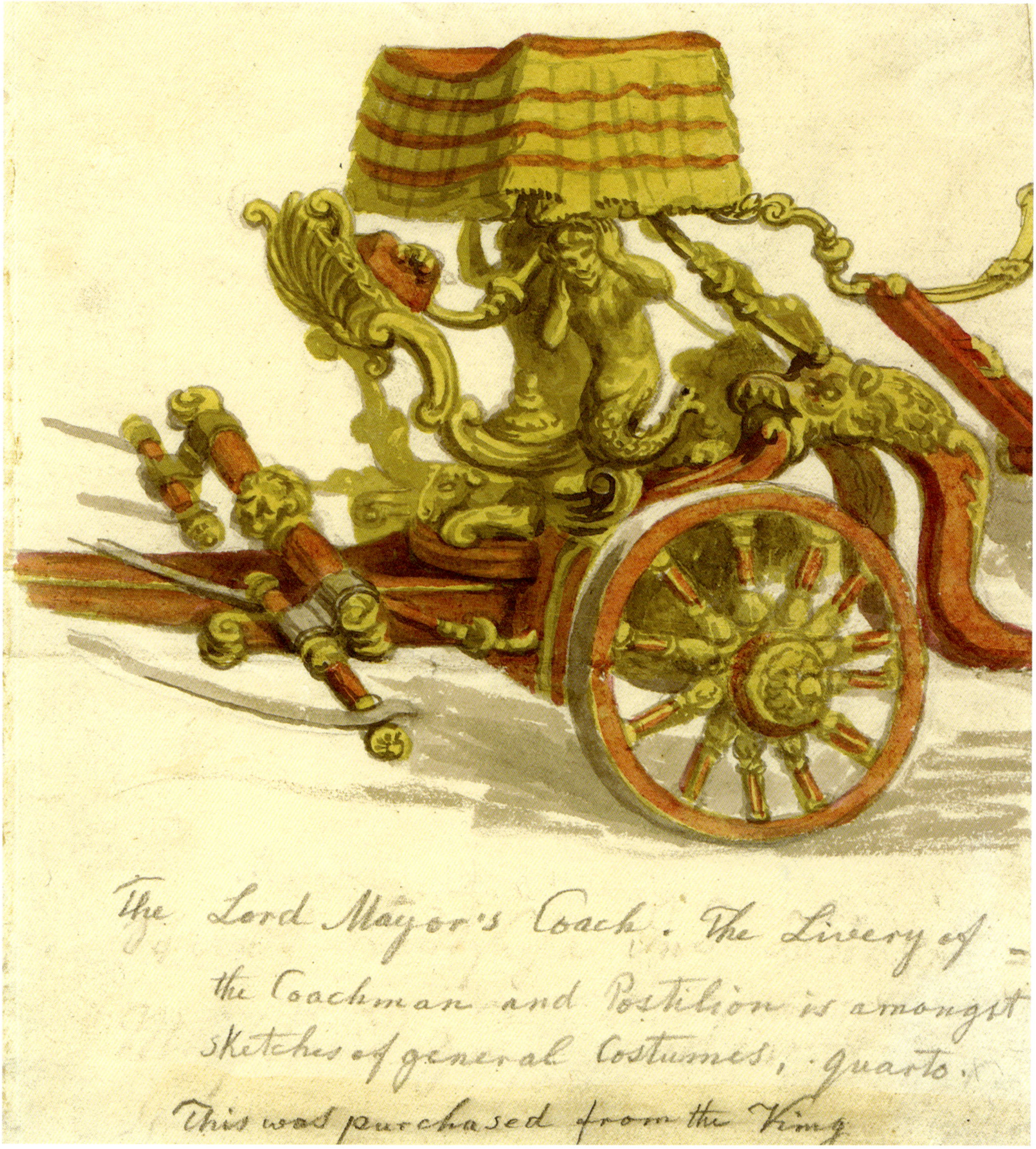

the Coach with an allegory of the Genius of London greeting Riches and Plenty in the upper register. In the lower register she is shown receiving Trade and Commerce, alongside Neptune.[33] Scharf has also shown the construction of the coach, paying particular attention to the red leather braces on which the box is sprung. Also visible, towards the right of the drawing, is the coachman's seat, supported by carved *Tritons*, representing London's maritime trade and a foot rest carved in the form of a large scallop shell (see detail cat. 17). Within the coach can be seen three figures, including Lucas, shown in profile seated in the rear of the coach, and in his crimson robes of office. Seated before him are the two Sheriffs of London, one of whom holds the Lord Mayor's crowned mace of office or 'Sceptre' as it is more properly referred to.[34]

18. *The Lord Mayor's Dinner*

1829
Hand-coloured lithograph, (514 x 340)
1978,U.1979

On the Monday following the Lord Mayor's procession, it was customary for the new Lord Mayor to hold a banquet in the Guildhall in honour of 'the late Lord Mayor' as the outgoing incumbent is styled.[35] In this lithograph Scharf has shown the dinner held by William Thompson (1793–1854) who was Lord Mayor from 1828 to 1829 in honour of his predecessor Matthias Prime Lucas (see cat. 16). Among those guests invited it was customary to include representatives of the Church, the armed forces, commerce and the government; the Prime Minister would give a speech.[36] The location for the banquet was the Guildhall, building work on which began in 1411 and lasted until 1501.[37] The main part of the structure – the Hall itself – was some 152 ft by 40ft in size. Completed in 1439, it was one of the largest secular Gothic structures in Britain.[38] The Hall was severely damaged in 1666 during the Great Fire of London and was subsequently rebuilt with a new flat roof replacing the old hammer-beam wooden one.[39] Scharf shows the interior of the Guildhall as it appeared following this rebuilding and a further remodelling by George Dance the Younger in 1789. The hall is decorated with the banners bearing the arms of Livery Companies, the walls hung with crimson, festooned lights down the length of the hall with a large star of the Order of the Garter at the far end, below which can just be discerned the figure of Thompson, wearing his ceremonial chain of office. Scharf has also shown several statues to national heroes that had been erected in the hall, including one to Admiral Lord Horatio Nelson (1758–1805), by James Smith, which can been seen to the left. In the foreground liveried butlers can be seen serving various dishes to the guests, the arrival of the most distinguished of whom would be announced by the two trumpeters. This print was published by Engelmann, Graf, Coindet and Co. of Newman Square, Soho and is dedicated to the Lord Mayor, the Sheriff and the Common Council of the City of London '. . . by their most obedient servant G. Scharf'. This print was exhibited at the National Gallery of Practical Science, Adelaide Street.[40] The subject of the lithograph has also been given by Scharf in German and French, possibly with an eye to a European market as well as a British one.[41] We know that he consigned a number of this lithograph on commission to a dealer in St Petersburg.[42] The lithographs did not make it to Russia – they were lost in a shipwreck.

Street Life

19. *Men with billboards*

c.1818–25
Watercolour, (139 x 229)
1862,0614.1192

Scharf was an avid consumer of the various entertainments that Regency and early Victorian London had to offer, such as the many exhibitions and zoological collections advertised by the figures in these drawings and seen in cat. 22 below. In his journal entry for 15 April 1840 he notes that he saw a number of shows in the space of a single day.[43] Of particular importance is the placard advertising the exhibition of Belzoni's Egyptian Tomb. This referred to a reconstruction of the wall paintings and bas reliefs found in the tomb of the Nineteenth-Dynasty Egyptian King Seti I (reigned 1291–1278 BC), discovered in 1817 by the pioneer Egyptologist, Giovanni

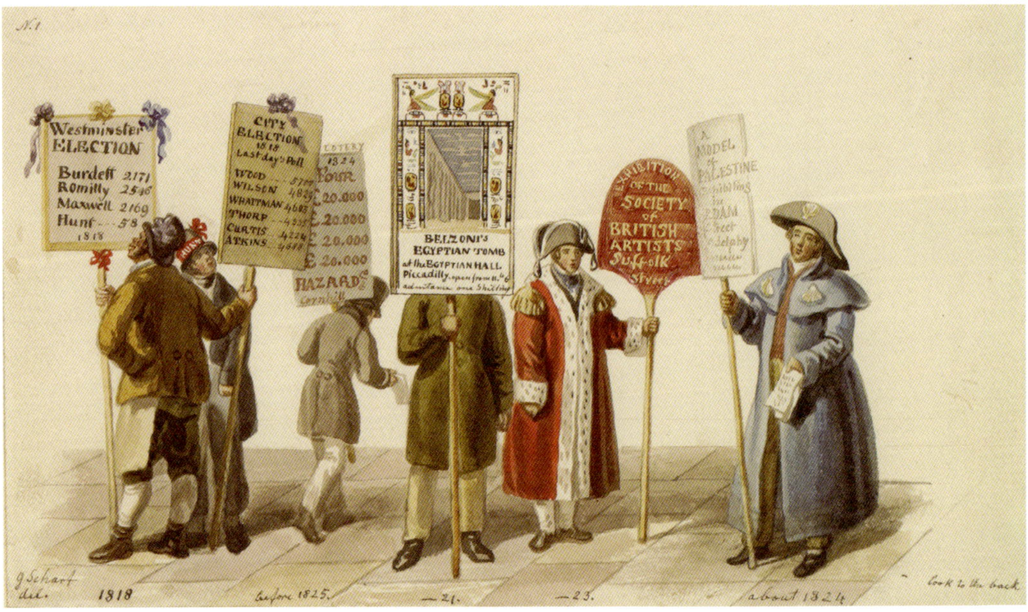

18

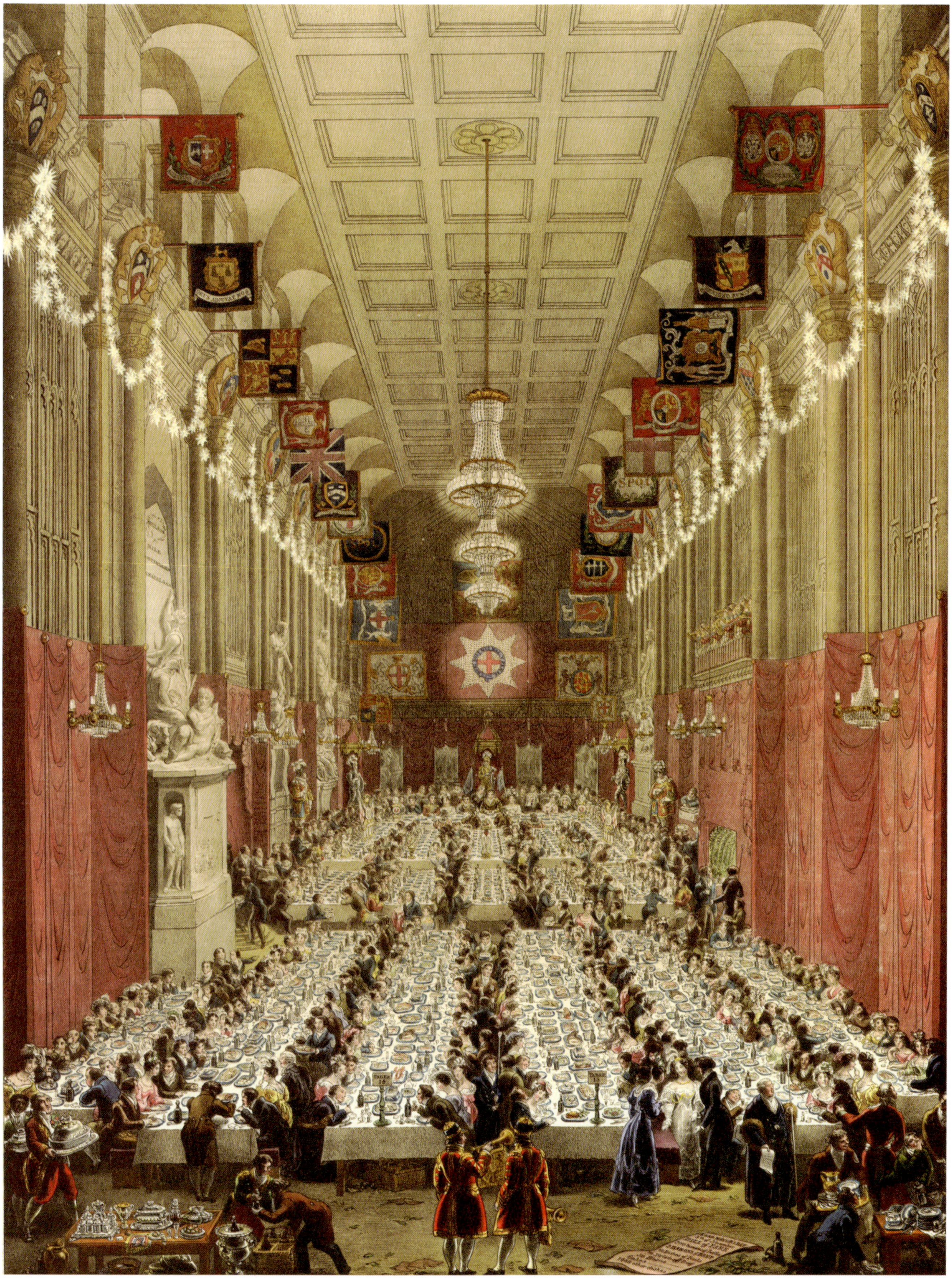

Battista Belzoni (1778–1823). The tomb, located in the Valley of the Kings, is the largest tomb in the Valley at over 100 metres deep and 100 metres long. The extent and quality of the wall paintings and reliefs marked out the tomb as the most significant Egyptological discovery of the nineteenth century. Although the tomb had been plundered in antiquity and the body of the King removed to another tomb for safety, Belzoni did find his original alabaster sarcophagus, which can now be seen in the Sepulchral Chamber in the basement of Sir John Soane's Museum, and on the foot of which Belzoni inscribed his name. In addition, Belzoni took casts of the reliefs of the tomb and detailed, coloured studies of the wall paintings. These served as the basis of a reconstruction of the interior of the tomb, which opened in the Egyptian Hall in Piccadilly in 1821.[44] Scharf includes a view of one of the tomb's painted corridors, surrounded by hieroglyphs, at the top of the placard. The Egyptian Hall was also used for the display of other exhibitions such as the Indian Exhibition being advertised by the figure to the far right in cat. 23, below. Along the bottom of the sketch, Scharf has noted the years in which he drew the figures and includes placard holders announcing the results of the 1818 Westminster election which was won by Sir Francis Burdett and Sir Samuel Romilly (see also cat. 14).

20. *Yeomen of the Guard at King's Mews, Charing Cross*

1830
Watercolour, (226 x 138)
1900,0725.20

In 1826, Scharf was asked by the Bavarian Ambassador to provide detailed drawings of the Horse Guards' uniforms. These sketches were to be sent to Bavaria as King Ludwig I wanted to style the uniforms of his own palace guard in Munich after those of the British regiment.[45] Although this sketch is not related to the earlier commission, we can nevertheless see Scharf's careful attention to the details of the uniform of the Yeomen of the Guard, who acted as bodyguards to the sovereign. He has accurately depicted the red tunics, trimmed with gold lace and their distinctive ruffs and hats, all based on sixteenth-century historical costume.[46] To the left Scharf has made a separate study of the front of one of the Guard's tunics, showing the Scottish thistle, Irish shamrock and English rose surmounted by a royal crown. He has annotated the sketch with explanatory texts in English and German. Below he has shown a study of the livery worn by coachmen of the postal service, which operated out of Golden Cross Coach-Yard located just off St Martin's Lane and Charing Cross, near Scharf's first house in London. The coach-yard was demolished when Trafalgar Square was laid out in the 1830s.[47]

21. *The Strand from the corner of Villiers Street*

1824
Watercolour, with pen and black ink; on two conjoined sheets, (218 x 371)
1862,0614.19

This is one of several sketches Scharf produced of the Strand. This important street had a long history, having developed from a simple track (or strand) running parallel to the Thames during the Anglo-Saxon period. By the 1100s several important residences were located along the Strand, the most prominent being the Savoy Palace. By the sixteenth century the number of mansions increased to include amongst others such notable residences as Northumberland House and Somerset House. When Scharf drew this sketch in 1824, only these two mansions still stood and of these Somerset House had been totally remodelled by William Chambers to act as the seat of the Royal Academy, the Society of Antiquaries and the Admiralty. The Strand was now dominated by the smaller town houses, shops and coffee houses as shown in this view of its north side. Scharf has depicted a dramatic moment:

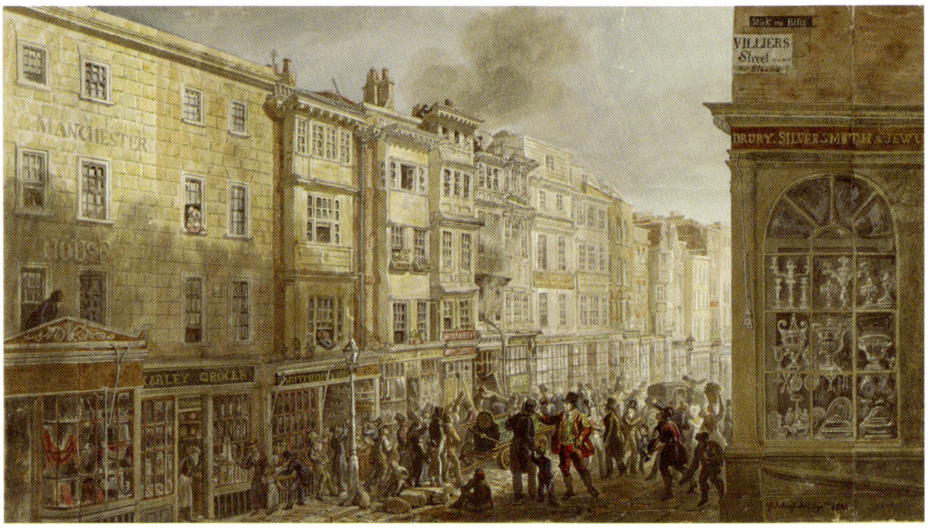

21

20

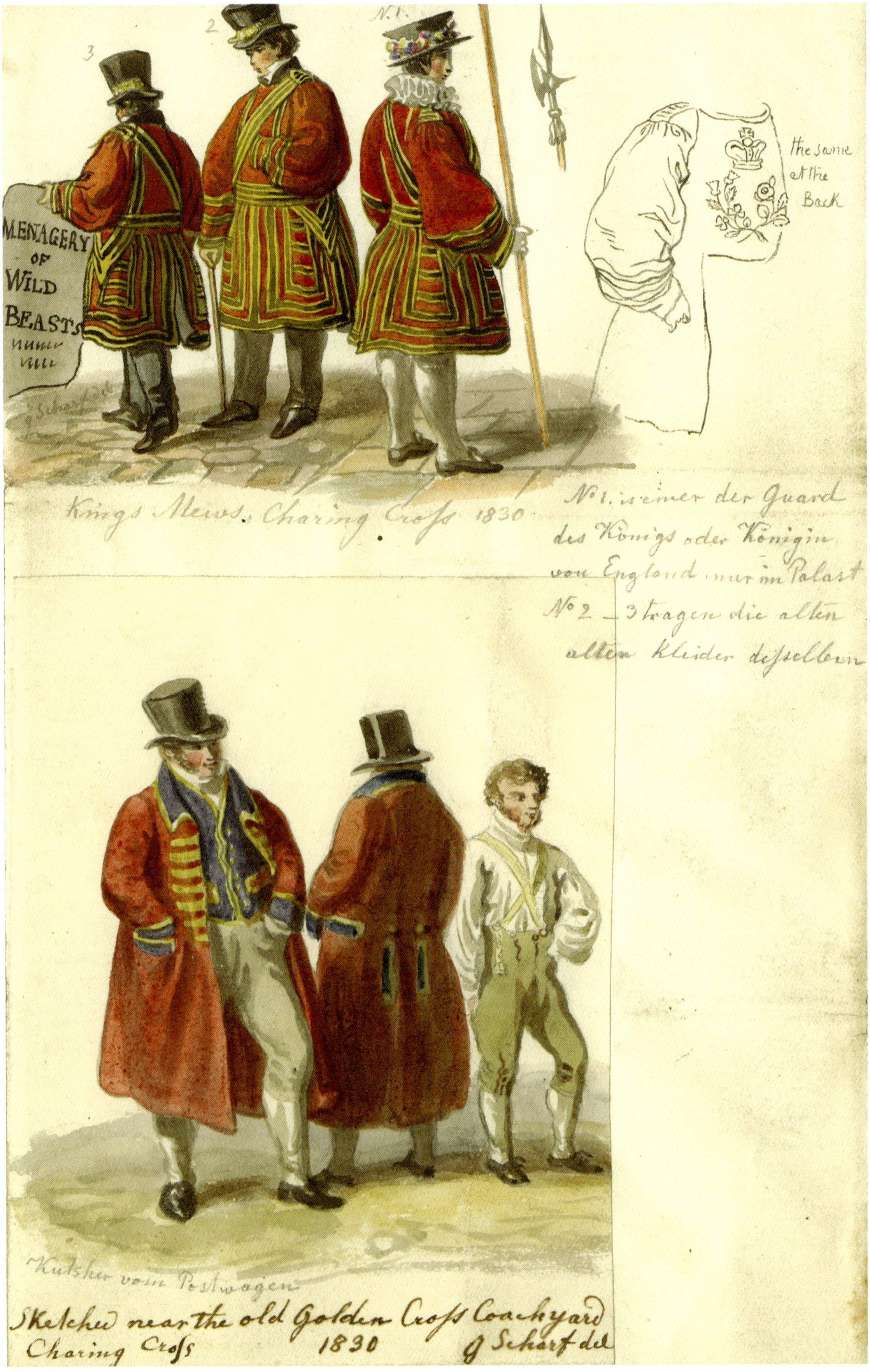
3
2
N.1
MENAGERY
OF
WILD
BEASTS
the same
at the
Back
G Scharf del
Kings Mews, Charing Cross 1830
No 1. is einer der Guard
des Königs oder Königin
von England nur im Palast
No 2 _ 3 tragen die alten
alten kleider dieselben
Kutsher vom Postwagen
Sketched near the old Golden Cross Coachyard
Charing Cross
1830
G Scharf del

Mr Martin the sausage maker's shop caught fire on 5 September 1824 and the firemen of the Sun Fire Office are attempting to extinguish the blaze. In the foreground, and in front of the crowd gathered to watch the conflagration, one of the men from the Office is shown in his distinctive red and gold uniform. The early 'fire-engine' used to pump water through the hose to the first floor is clearly shown. Scharf has heightened the effects of the flames and smoke by scratching into the surface of the paper to describe the flying sparks. The view of this section of Strand documents how it appeared before a series of major improvements undertaken in the 1830s by Nash (see also cat. 44), swept away the seventeenth- and eighteenth-century buildings seen here. This sketch was one of a series Scharf produced of different parts of the old Strand and another sketch of this scene in the British Museum (BM 1862,0614.20) shows the same view just after the fire. The crowds have dispersed and a lone fireman is rolling up the hose used to extinguish the blaze. Scharf notes in his journal that, in 1835, he returned once more to these earlier sketches of the old Strand, including this one, and touched them up in the hope of publishing a print through Ackermann's based on the compositions.[48] As he had no luck in creating interest in a print, the next day he tried to sell the drawings themselves, returning to Ackermann's and then going to a number of other dealers including Colnhaghi's, 'Mr. Marten's at Messrs Boyes and Graves' and Evans of Great Queen Street. He sadly records '. . . neither of whom bought any, saying they did not want to buy but sell drawings, or else that the subjects did not suit them; I felt of course much disappointed as I was much in want of money'.[49]

22. *Men and boys with advertising boards* (*see p. 40*)

c.1825
Watercolour, with pen and black ink, (137 x 221)
1862,0614.1187

23. *Men and boys with advertising boards* (*see p. 40*)

1834–40
Watercolour, with pen and black ink, (135 x 219)
1862,0614.1188

The outlandish costumes worn by the figures in these two sketches were another way through which people's attention was caught by advertisers. In particular the black male figure (cat. 22), wearing a striking yellow coat trimmed with what appears to be red-dyed fur, stands out from his group as does the man wearing a strange green bonnet, advertising an anatomical model in cat. 23. As in cat. 19, the figures in these two sketches hold placards advertising various attractions, such as a masquerade at the Argyll Rooms, the display of giraffes at the Surrey Zoological Gardens or the various dioramas that were popular during the period. These 'peripatetic placards', as this type of advertising was called, was compared to the Roman army's use of standard bearers in antiquity.[50] However, the days of the 'peripatetic placard' were numbered. A new mode of advertising would soon take its place in the London street – the sandwich man. Dickens described these figures as '. . . a piece of human flesh between two slices of pasteboard . . .'.[51] Scharf has included two such figures in these two sketches, the man advertising an exhibition at the Egyptian Hall in Piccadilly showing the 'Battles of the French Army' and, more unusually, a small boy wearing the carapace of a large turtle, painted with an advertisement for port. The Argyll Rooms, on Little Argyll Street, were a very popular venue for social gatherings with balls and gambling being held there. Set up by Henry Francis Greville, who was a cousin of the 1st Earl of Warwick, visitors included the Prince Regent and Beau Brummel. It was at the Argyll Rooms that, following the Prince Regent's refusal to speak to his former friend, Brummel was heard to utter: 'Alvanley, who is your fat friend?' The real target, to whom this barbed comment was addressed, was of course the Prince.

24. *Foreign street musicians*

1838–42
Pencil and watercolour, (139 x 235)
1862,0614.940

25. *Sketches of four street hawkers*

1820–1844
Watercolour, (179 x 139)
1862,0614.1154

Apart from using his figures as *staffage* in his more fully developed paintings and prints (see cat. 14), Scharf also saw the potential of these types of studies for the markets outside London and Britain. Whilst visiting Munich, he was advised by a printseller and picture dealer that prints and watercolours showing 'British costume and manners' would be very popular in Germany.[52] These two sheets of sketches show just such studies of ordinary Londoners, their 'costume' and their 'manners'. However, they also reflect earlier graphic traditions and in particular the popularity of prints of the 'Cries of London'.[53] In cat. 25, Scharf has even noted: 'They call, "Ornaments for your fire stoves"'. The more *picaresque* images of entertainers and vagabonds, in cat. 24, can be seen in relation to other graphic works nearer in date. Thomas Barker of Bath had produced a portfolio of lithographs depicting 'rustic' types. Scharf's sketches can, on one level, be understood to be urban analogues of this type of 'picturesque' depiction of individuals. Unlike the more generic images of Barker's 'rustics', Scharf's images illustrating 'British costume and manners' are often located explicitly in London, either through the inclusion of attributes that reference the wider city or through Scharf's annotations that cite the location where the sketch was taken, such as Charing Cross in the case of cat. 25 (see also cats 20 and 23). Scharf's interest in anatomy and medical science appears in the case of

24

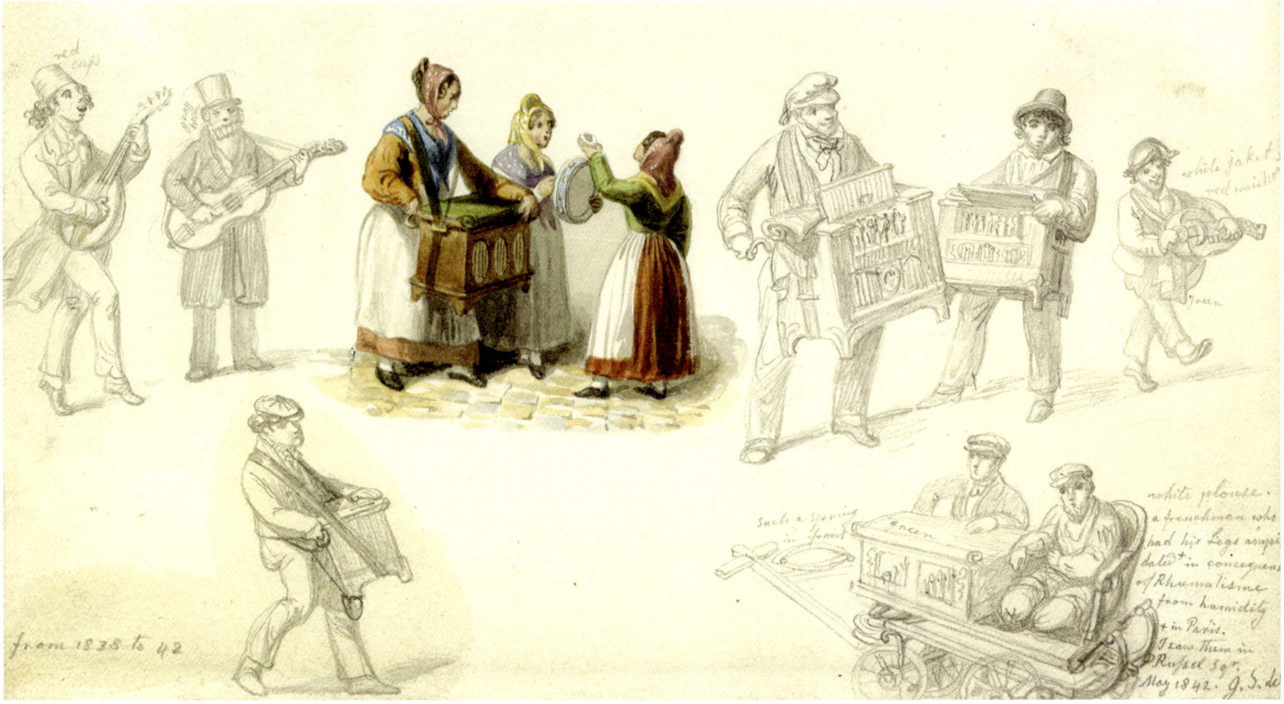
red cap
white jaket
green
Such a spring in front
green
white blouse.
a frenchman who had his Legs ampu-dated in consequen of Rhumatisme from humidity in Paris.
I saw them in Russel Sq. May 1842. J.S. del
from 1838 to 42

25

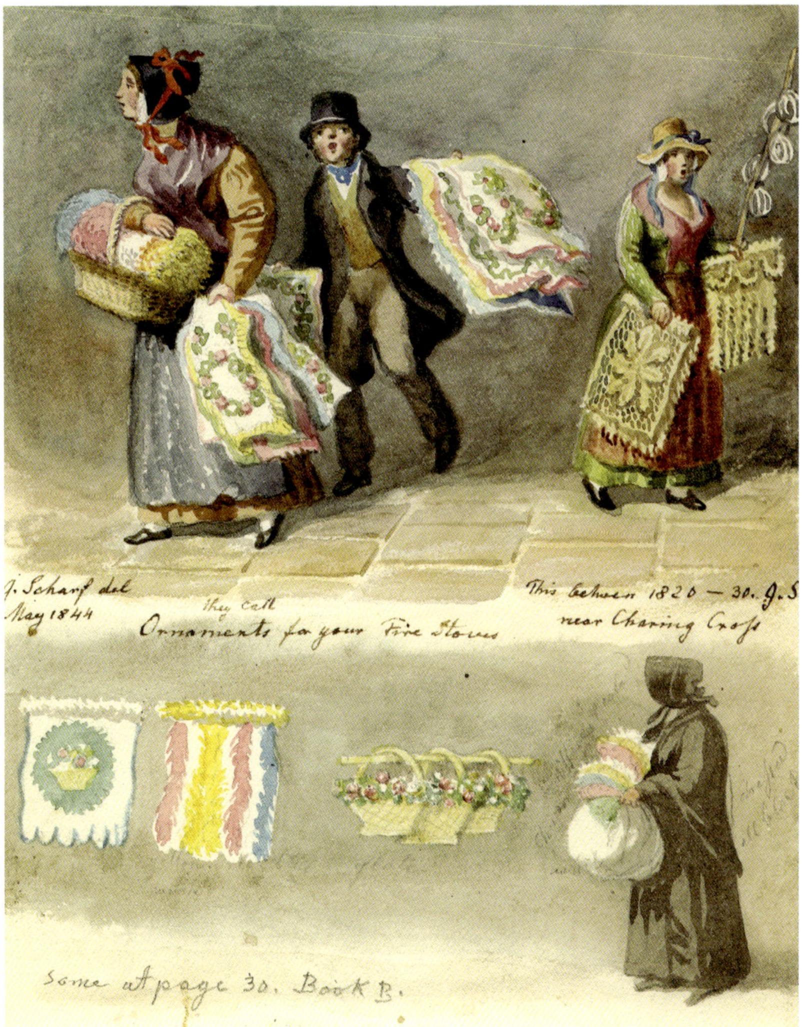
J. Scharf del May 1844
they call
Ornaments for your Fire Stoves
This between 1820 – 30. J.S
near Charing Cross
Some at page 30. Book B.

the study of the French soldier at the bottom right of the sheet in cat. 24. Shown in a type of musical organ-cum-wheelchair, Scharf's notes explain that the soldier has had both legs amputated just below the knee because of extreme rheumatism and 'humidity'. However, this sheet in particular also shows the underside of the industrialisation of London and its burgeoning consumer economy: the continued presence of an urban underclass, whose position had worsened due to the economic down turn in London during the period 1816 to 1825. The multiple dates for the sheet of sketches (1820–30 and 1844), in Scharf's hand in cat. 25 are explained by his habit of returning to earlier sketches, often after the lapse of a considerable length of time (see also cat. 2).

London at Work

26. *Figures on their way to the 'employment' of a summer's morning between 5 and 6 o'clock*

1840
Watercolour, (141 x 234)
1862,0614.1193

27. *Men going to work between 6 and 7 of a summer's morning*

c.1840
Watercolour, on a number of conjoined sheets, (166 x 296)
1862,0614.1194

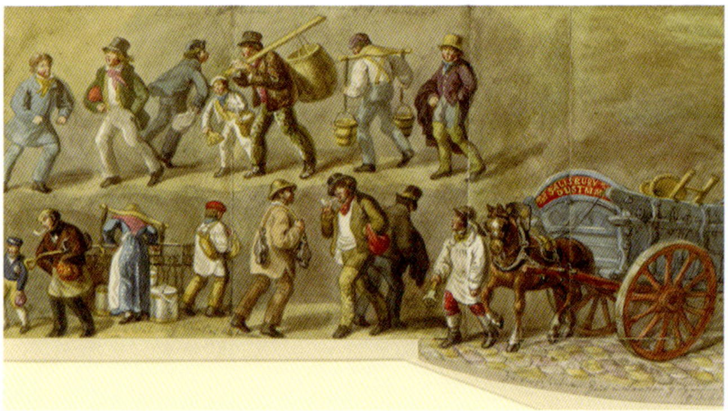

The first half of the nineteenth century saw dramatic changes in London's workforce as Britain's economy shifted from a largely rural to an industrial one. At the same time, the way in which the work force was seen by society also altered,[54] and this extended to how work, and those engaged in it, were represented in art. The link between the visual arts and labour was justified by John Ruskin: 'Life without industry is sin, and industry without art is brutality.'[55] Scharf, in his images of London's working masses, can be seen to be engaging in this new mode of representation. Amongst the distinctive figures are those of the milkmaid (left), and dustman (right), in cat. 27. Scharf has shown the milkmaid as she lowers a full tin pail over the railings at the front of a house down to the kitchens in the basement. The milkmaids' distinctive cry of 'milk below!', often shortened to 'Mi-o', referred to this. Scharf also shows a number of figures wearing traditional rustic smocks as in cat. 26, upper and lower right. Many cities such as London attracted itinerant rural workers in search of

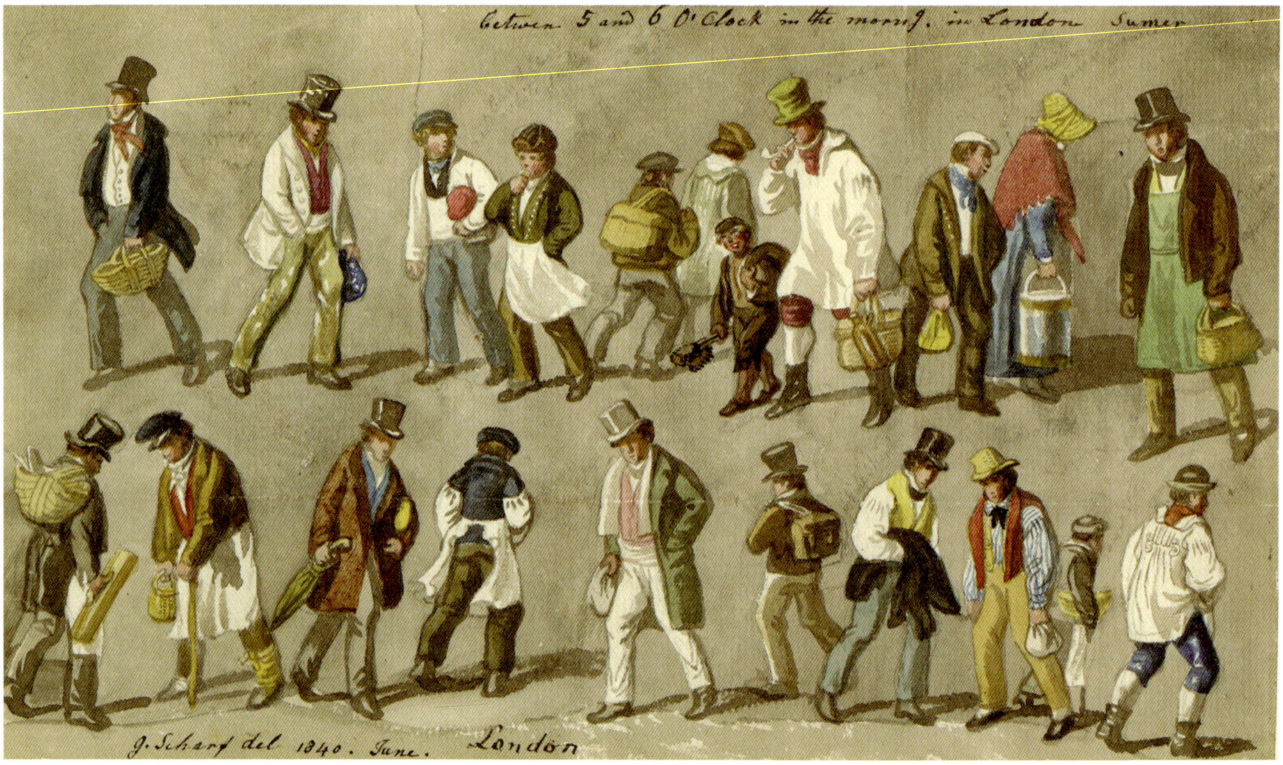

26

employment having been displaced by the industrial revolution. These sketches also document a period when the question of workers' rights and their exploitation at the hands of unscrupulous employers, was being debated.[56] In particular, two areas of working conditions are touched upon in these two drawings. Firstly Scharf has shown a number of children amongst the adults setting off to work, including a small chimney sweep holding his brushes (cat. 26, upper middle). Children as young as five were engaged in factory work. Secondly, in the case of both drawings, Scharf has noted the time 'between five and six o'clock in the morning' when workers set off to their employment. From 1831 a popular mass movement – the so-called 'short time' committees – began to lobby for the regulation of working hours and conditions in the workplace as, until 1833, factory owners were allowed to set the length of the working day as it suited them. Following the publication of the Sadler Report in 1832, which shocked the public with its descriptions of the conditions faced by the mass of employees in their workplaces, Parliament began the slow process of reform. In 1833 the Factory Act was passed, setting the working day from 5.30am to 8.30pm and restricting the use of child labour.[57] In 1840 the Children's Employment Commission further advocated children's rights. The contentious issue of child labour was highlighted by Dickens, notably in *Oliver Twist* and *Great Expectations.*

28. *Men repairing the gas pipes in Tottenham Court Road (see p. 38)*

1834
Watercolour, (250 x 442)
1862,0614.227

In this highly finished drawing, Scharf contrasts the vigour of the working men with the curious onlookers who have gathered to observe their toil. The figure bent over the cauldron of molten lead, whose rolled-up shirt sleeves reveal his muscled forearms, is juxtaposed alongside the school boys and woman, with a small child hiding from the heat of the fire. The workers are shown without protective clothing performing a hazardous job. The fumes from the molten lead would have been highly noxious. In the background a gentleman in a stove-pipe hat together with a boy, leans nonchalantly on an umbrella surveying the work. As observers, rather than participants in the scene, they are depicted in an almost passive manner, unlike the vigorous way in which Scharf has depicted the workers. Their removal from the central scene of action is compositionally enhanced by their position on the pavement, away from the workmen. Scharf has effectively depicted the clouds of black and toxic smoke that rise above the workers and the sparks of the fire that heats the lead, scratching into the white support in places.

29. *Stonemasons at work on the columns in the British Museum (see also p. 26)*

1844
Pencil, (226 x 138)
1862,0614.634

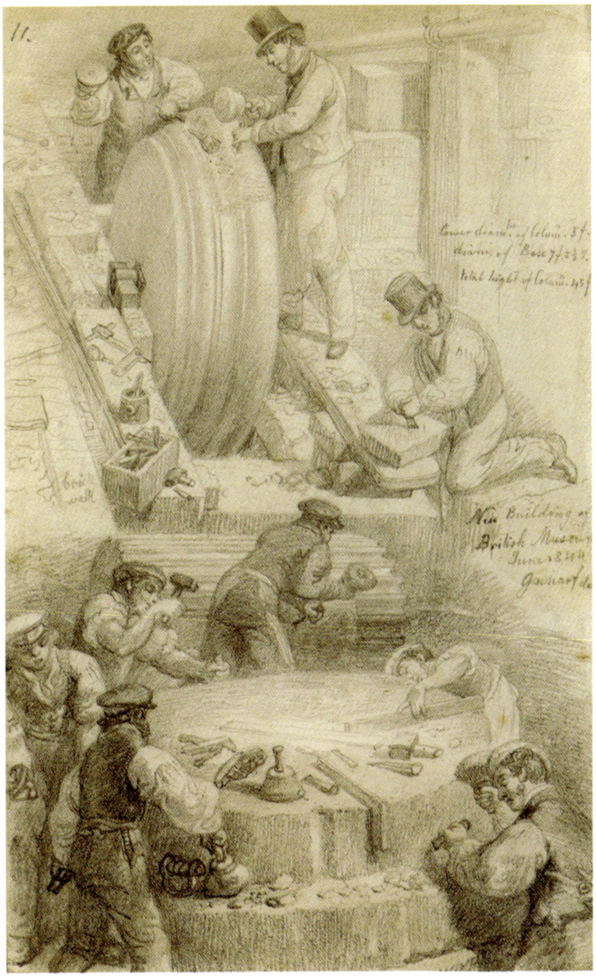

In this drawing, Scharf has shown the skilled stonemasons who cut and dressed the stonework of the columns of the front façade of the British Museum. Scharf has conflated several individual figure studies in this one composition in order to show how the columns were prepared. In the foreground, stonemasons are roughing out the basic form of the column bases, whilst behind them others are carving the fluting of the column shafts. In the background two men are smoothing the surface of a nearly complete column base that has been upended on its side like a wheel for ease of handling. Scharf has differentiated the types of chisel used for the work: the kneeling figure to the right is using a claw chisel and the striations that this makes are visible on the piece of stone he is working. Scharf has also noted the size of the columns on the right (see also cat. 59).

30. *Tarring the iron hooping used for binding the brickwork at the New Building of the British Museum (see p. 39)*

1844
Pencil, (140 x 227)
1862,0614.635

Scharf was also interested in the more prosaic aspects of construction and in this sketch he has shown workmen preparing the iron bands that would help strengthen the brickwork of the massive walls that were used in the construction of the British Museum. The iron bands would be passed through a container full of molten tar, heated over the furnace seen in the centre left of the drawing, to coat them. As one workman threads the tar through with his bare hands another pulls the now heated metal with a pair of pliers at the other end. Sand is then sprinkled through a sieve over the still sticky tar, seen to the right. This would give the metal bands a waterproof and resilient coating so that the iron would not rust and expand, causing the brickwork to blow out once in place. Scharf has noted the barrel of tar in the foreground as well as a barrel of beech wood chippings which fed the furnace. Beech was used as it burns with a high temperature. Scharf also notes that the distinctive cowl, decorated with a dragon, on top of the furnace's chimney, was reused from the Pantheon on Oxford Street. This public assembly room, built 1770–72 by James Wyatt (1746–1813) was converted into the 'Pantheon Bazaar' by Sidney Smirke in 1833–34 (see cat. 59) before being finally demolished in 1937.

31. *Accident of a rope breaking while hoisting a girder at the building of the Lycian Room of the British Museum*

1844
Pencil, (230 x 181)
1900,0725.30

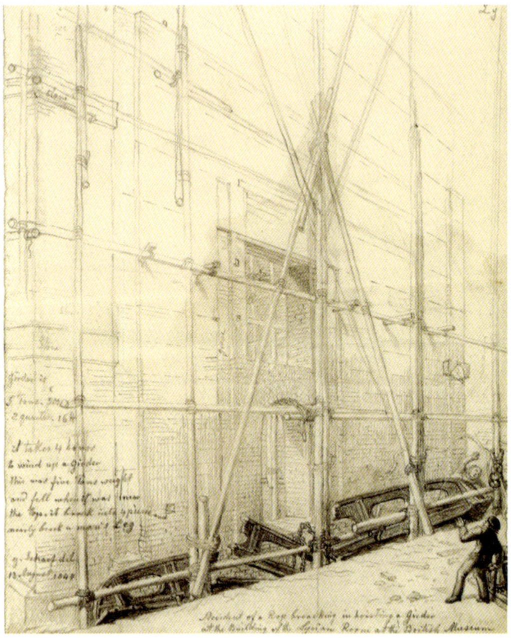

Large architectural projects, such as the rebuilding of the British Museum, involved the use of dangerous equipment and often extremely heavy building materials. In his designs for the British Musuem, Smirke envisioned several large open galleries, such as the King's Library and the Lycian Room, that required the use of substantial iron girders to span the width of these spaces. The use of these girders was innovative and required considerable power and skill in order to hoist them into position. As Scharf notes, the girders for the Lycian Room each weighed some five tons. It took four hours to winch each into position. In this sketch Scharf has shown just how dangerous these types of engineering procedures could be in the 1840s. The drawing records an accident that took place on 13 August 1848 when a rope broke whilst a girder was being hoisted on to the roof of the Lycian Room sending the iron beam crashing to the ground and in the process nearly breaking a workman's leg. His alarmed figure can be seen at the right. Although in this instance, apart from the girder which broke in four, no one was killed or seriously injured, accidents were prevalent before adequate safety regulations were implemented in the workplace.

32. *Traveller used in erecting the New Building at the British Museum 1844*

Pencil, on three conjoined sheets, (116 x 269)
1862,0614.639

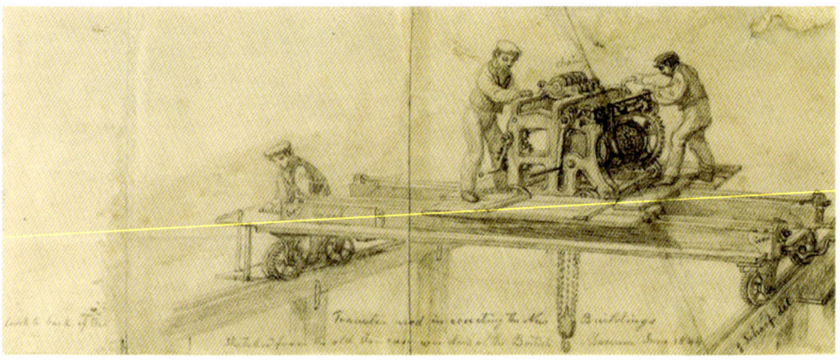

A 'hand traveller' was an early type of mechanical crane which was used in stonemasons' yards to carefully lift and precisely position heavy blocks of stonework. The 'traveller' consisted of the central piece of machinery or 'crab' which winched the block of stone into position. This 'crab' was then fixed on to a movable carriage that ran on rails that had been built up to the maximum height of the Museum's walls. The 'traveller' was hand-powered and Scharf has shown two workmen using cranks to turn the cogs that either propelled the machine along its tracks or raised and lowered the chain-block hoist (clearly shown in its raised position).[58] Scharf notes that this sketch was drawn on the site of the old British Museum's staircase (see cat. 34).

33. *Interior of the Royal Military Repository, the Rotunda, Woolwich*

1828
Watercolour, (274 x 446)
1862,0614.202

The Rotunda at Woolwich was originally a tent-like structure, designed by Nash, and erected in the grounds of Carlton House as part of the celebrations held to mark the abdication of the Emperor Napoleon in 1814. Although the peace proved short-lived, Tsar Alexander I of Russia and Frederick William II, King of Prussia visited London and were splendidly entertained by the Prince Regent.[59] Following the end of the festivities, the tent was taken to Woolwich, to house the collection of military models and exhibits of the Royal Artillery Institution Museum. Nash converted the temporary tent into a permanent structure in 1822 by replacing the original fabric covering of the Rotunda with sheet lead and adding the central supporting pillar. Scharf has carefully shown the exhibited models of strategic ports and other locations, models of guns and their emplacements as well as actual examples of artillery and firearms. The Rotunda stands to this day, although the historical collections are no longer displayed there. A later note in Scharf's journal, dated 28 July 1834, indicates that he intended to exhibit his drawing of the Rotunda in Liverpool.

34. *Staircase of the old British Museum in Montagu House* (*see p. 38*)

1845
Watercolour, (242 x 288)
1862,0614.629

Although founded in 1753 as the world's first public museum, the British Museum for a long time resisted allowing the general public in to view its collections of antiquities, books and also, at that time, *naturalia*.[60] This policy changed when the liberal and reformist Whig party came into power in 1832. Under the influence of such lobby groups as the Useful Knowledge Society museum going in the nineteenth century became a popular pastime as collections became accessible to the middle-class, and even working-class, public – if they were correctly attired![61] By the 1840s people flocked to see the British Museum's collections, so much so that on one occasion Scharf was forced to complain in his journal: '35,000 persons are said to have visited the British Museum this Whit Monday. I felt very much annoyed by the noise of so many people going continually in and out, talking etc. whilst I drew there.'[62] This drawing, one of Scharf's more well-known works, forms part of a series he undertook in the 1840s (see also cat. 59) recording the exterior and interiors of Old Montagu House which housed the collections of the British Museum and which stood on the site of the present Museum. It had been built in the seventeenth century for Robert Hooke, First Duke of Montagu, and the Ambassador of Charles II to France. As a result, the interiors showed a marked French taste and much of this earlier, beautiful

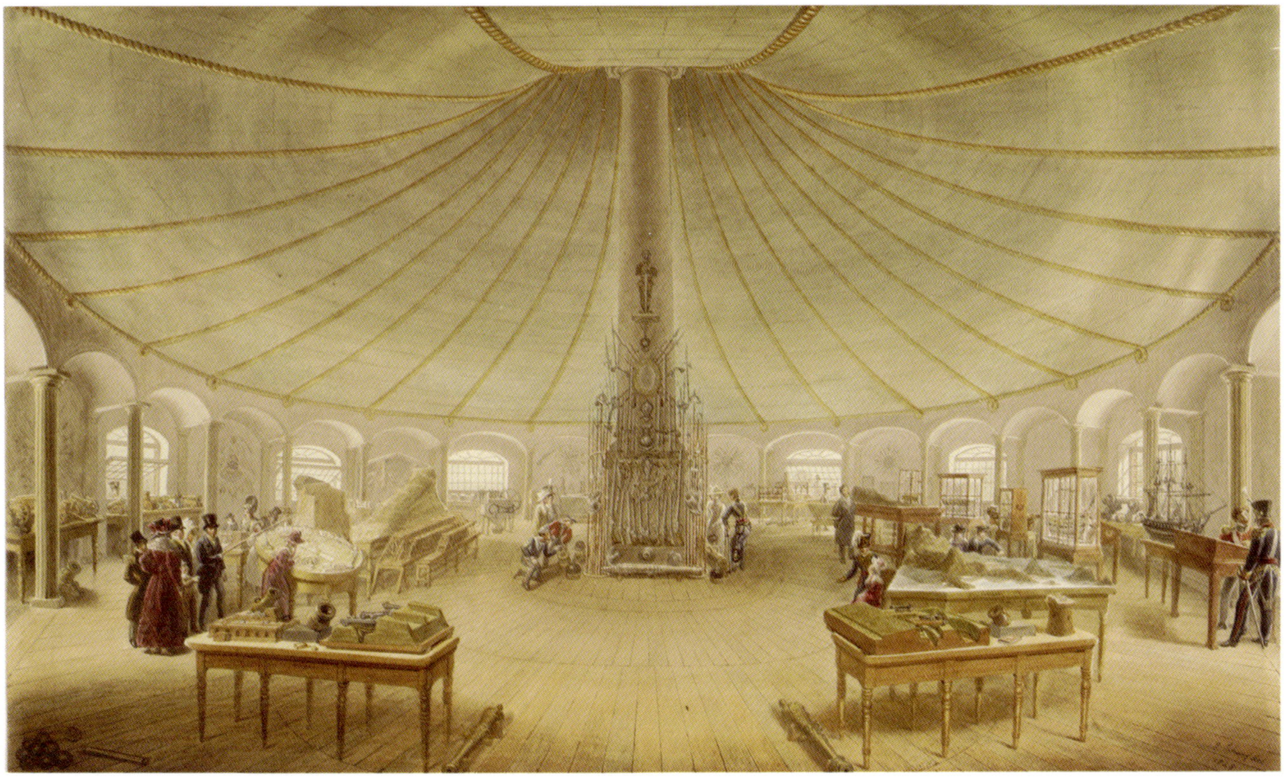

decoration survived in the rooms that were adapted to house the collections of the British Museum, such as the main staircase, which Scharf has shown here.[63] The stuffed giraffes are shown beneath a painted ceiling; the illusionistic balustrade with *putti* is clearly visible. Further *putti* adorn the pediments above the doorways leading off the landing. The German Prince Pückler-Muskau compared the two animals to 'stuffed guards' and declared them to be '. . . emblems of English taste . . .'.[64] Scharf chose to document old Montagu House as it was being pulled down in order for the present edifice by Sir Robert Smirke (1780–1867) to replace it. He records finishing this drawing on 14 August 1845. He also records that he took a number of fragments from the staircase as it was being demolished later in the year.[65] Scharf had several links with the British Museum. He was employed by them to draw and colour casts of fossils in their collection.[66] He also visited the Department of Prints and Drawings whilst his son, George, was put to sketching the collections of antiquities. Scharf the Younger would himself work for the British Museum. He travelled to the near east on an archaeological expedition which resulted in the transportation to the British Museum of many ancient artefacts and even monuments such as the so-called Lycian 'Tomb of the Harpies'.[67]

35. *A fountain of rock arches and live animals, exhibited at Joshua Brookes' Museum, Blenheim Street (now Ramillies Street)* (*see also p. 5*)

1830
Brush drawing in grey wash, (238 x 298)
1862,0614.691

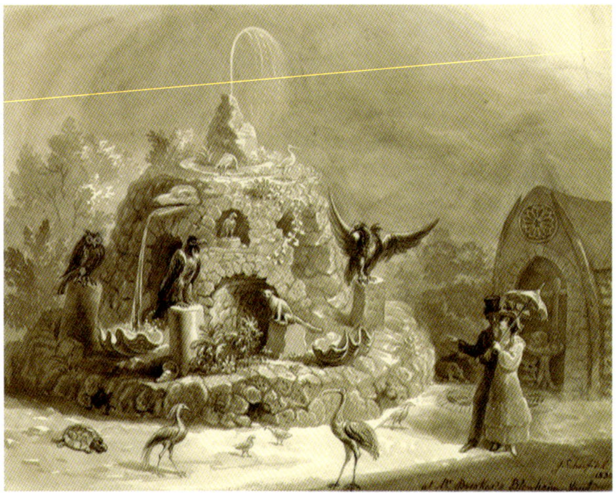

The Brookesian Museum of Comparative Anatomy was founded by the anatomist and naturalist Joshua Brookes (1761–1833), a member of both the Royal Society and the Linnean Society (for whom Scharf had possibly produced lithographs and drawings) and discoverer of the *genus* of the cheetah. The Museum, open to the public by appointment only, housed Brookes' collection of some 3,000 anatomical specimens, three mummies (two of which were Egyptian) and the numerous mammalian and bird specimens that formed the Museum's Comparative Department.[68] This view shows the *viviarium* of the Museum, where live specimens were kept chained to a rockery made from samples taken from the Rock of Gibraltar. The *vivarium*, located just off Oxford Street, was visible to passers by through its iron gate. It is possible that the rockwork, with its fountains and animals, were intended to act as an 'advertisement' for the Brookesian Museum.[69] Brookes also used the animals as ready subjects for his anatomical dissections.[70] Amongst the animals we can clearly see a tortoise and a vulture, as well as a lemur. A chain, tethering the vulture on the right by its foot, can also be discerned. Towards the right a 'Pilgrims Cell', lit with stained glass windows, has been constructed to display a skull, the arched frontage formed from the jaw bones of a whale.[71] Collections of crania and other skeletal specimens formed a large part of the Comparative Museum's collections. Public interest, in London, in the natural world was fuelled by the opening of the Zoological Society, Regent's Park, in 1826 and also by other collections of *naturalia* such as the Brookesian Museum. This drawing is a highly resolved preparatory study for Scharf's 1830 lithograph, published by Joshua Brookes, entitled 'A view of the Vivarium constructed principally with large masses of the Rock of Gibraltar in the Garden of Joshua Brookes Esq', a copy of which was in the possession of Sir John Soane (see cat. 36 below). The collections of the Museum were dispersed in 1828 and 1830 by public sale.

36. *A View of the Vivarium . . . in the Garden of Joshua Brookes Esq. 1830*

Lithograph on chine collé, (293 x 355)
Sir John Soane's Museum, 57/11/10

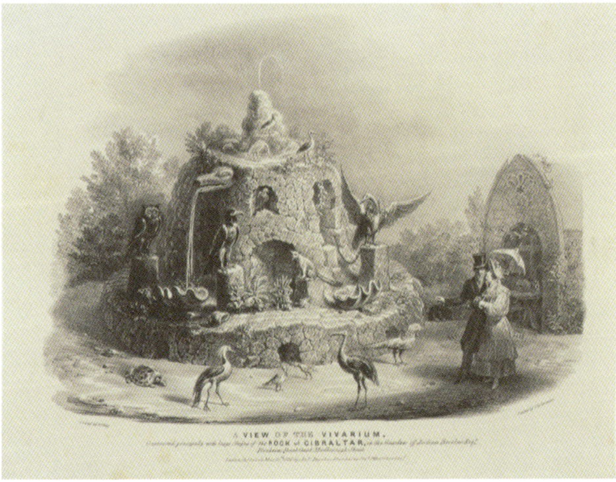

Scharf's lithograph of the *vivarium* at Sir Joshua Brookes' Museum very closely replicates his preparatory drawing (see cat. 35 above). There are a few minor differences such as his inclusion of a puffin at the apex of the fountain, the large Golden Pheasant (*Chrysolophus pictus*), before the admiring couple to the right, which replaces a smaller bird and the repositioning of the conch shell next to the Giant Clam (*Tridacna Gigas*), that acts as a basin for the jet of water emanating from '... an antique head of a large animal nearly resembling that of an ichthyosaurus'.[72] The lithograph was published by Brookes and was pulled from the stone by Hullmandel. Brookes wrote to Soane in 1830 offering to sell him both the rockwork of the *vivarium* and the 'Pilgrims Cell' explaining that they would make '... a noble rural ornament ...' Along with the letter, which carefully detailed both 'follies', Brookes included a copy of the lithograph.[73]

37. *The Garden at Jack Straw's Castle, Hampstead*

1830
Brush drawing in grey wash, (127 x 221)
1862,0614.693

Scharf was not a frequent visitor to the countless inns and taverns that were so much a part of the London streetscape. He occasionally records having made visits to such establishments in his journals. However, here he shows one of the more recognisable landmarks of Hampstead – the tea garden at the back of the renowned coaching inn. It was a favourite haunt of many well-known London figures including the writers Wilkie Collins, William Makepeace Thackeray and Charles Dickens. The latter frequented the inn whilst writing *Pickwick Papers*.[74] In the foreground a man appears to be lighting a pipe from a gas pipe, although how it would function fixed to a tree is unclear. On the left, patrons of the inn are seated dinning under a pergola. Their food is being brought by staff from a buffet with a hot water boiler in the background. Scharf has annotated the drawing with descriptions of the colour of the inn's chimney and that of the weather boarding, possibly intended as instructions for a more developed painting of the same subject. The unusual name of the inn refers to the name of one of the leaders of the Peasants' Revolt in 1381 who, having set fire to the Priory of the Knights of St John in Clerkenwell, is thought to have hidden in the vicinity from the troops of King Richard II. The present 'Jack Straw's Castle', now no longer an inn, was rebuilt in 1961 following severe war-time damage.[75]

38. *Interior of the National Gallery of Practical Science, Adelaide Street* (*see p. 18*)

1832
Watercolour, (329 x 226)
1862,0614.689

The National Gallery of Practical Science was housed on the north side of the Lowther Arcade, a shopping passage that formed part of the neo-classical triangular block, with its distinctive 'pepper-pot' corner towers, that had been built by Nash on the north side of the western end of the Strand in 1831. Popularly known as the Adelaide Gallery, it was opened in 1832, the year that Scharf drew this view of its long main hall. It is likely, given the relatively sparse number of exhibits that are yet displayed, that this view was made shortly after the opening. The main hall was used for the display of various scientific and mechanical models. The centre of the hall is dominated by the long water tank (100 ft), with two circular reservoirs at each end. This was used to display model, clockwork paddle boats that would sail up and

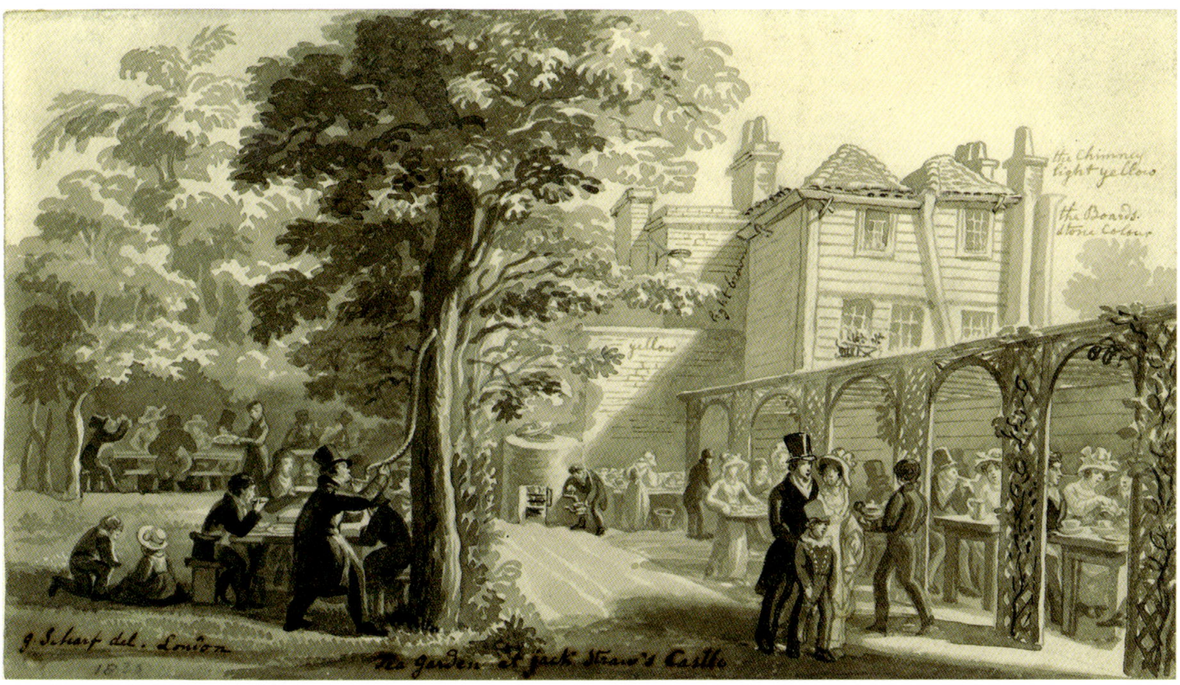

down the length of the water. A lighthouse is clearly visible in the centre of the nearest reservoir, whilst a fountain plays in the one shown at the far end of the tank. These boats were intended to be scale models of actual vessels whose design was meant to improve the stability of paddle steamers. However, as one observer commented in the press: 'We apprehend, however, that the comparison is hardly fair between little boats slowly revolving in a tub of still water, and a great vessel running at a rate of twelve miles an hour on a rapid river.'[76] Towards the right of the drawing, in the foreground, Scharf has included one of the most popular and noisy of the exhibits. This was the steam powered machine gun invented in 1825 by the American Jacob Perkins. The gun could fire bullets along the length of the Adelaide Gallery at such a velocity, that when they hit the iron target, shown in the background towards the right, they would be '. . . flattened to the thickness of a shilling piece'.[77] One visitor recalled the experience of seeing the gun fire, which would be let off every hour with a concussive explosion: 'The man who showed it gave a kind of lecture upon it; assured the audience that the Duke of Wellington came to see it the day before yesterday, and told the speaker that if he could have had the benefit of the steam-gun at the Battle of Waterloo, that engagement would have been over "in about half an hour, instead of lasting all day". He also said that all the regiments in our present army would be furnished with steam-guns, and it was expected in consequence that there would be no more fighting.'[78] In spite of the Duke of Wellington's supposed 'endorsement' of the gun this last sentiment proved ill-founded. Above the main hall can be seen the viewing gallery, which also served for the display of paintings. The collections of the National Gallery of Practical Science were frequently visited by Scharf and his journals record his many excursions there.[79] On one occasion he records having painted in seven colours a circular plate that was used for the 'steel cutting engine' that formed part of the displays at the Adelaide Street Gallery.[80] His fascination with new technology is also evidenced in his journals and in several other drawings, apart from this one (see cat. 32).

London on the move

39. *Coach in Piccadilly (see p. 50)*

1829
Pencil, (138 x 221)
1862,0614.883

Set in Piccadilly, Scharf captures the moment just before the London to Plymouth stage-coach is due to set off, heading west down Piccadilly and out on to the Bath Road. One final passenger is shown putting on a great coat to protect him from the elements before he climbs up onto the rear seating. In the foreground goods from the countryside have been delivered, including a dead hare. Transport of both goods and people in early nineteenth-century London, as in the rest of Britain, was still predominately undertaken using horse-drawn vehicles, such as the one so vividly described here. However, things were about to change radically through the advent of industrialisation and the development of locomotive technology.

40. *Mr Gurney's steam carriage (see p. 51)*

1827
Pencil, (140 x 225)
1862,0614.881

The period before the development of the railways, particularly the 1820s, saw the development of many forms of experimental locomotion that did not rely upon the horse. One of these was the 'steam carriage' invented by the Cornishman Sir Goldsworthy Gurney (1793–1875) and which Scharf has depicted in this drawing dating to 1827, the year that the vehicle made its first appearance on the London streets. The Gurney Steam Carriage Company, whose manufactory works were located in Regent's Park, was the first commercial steam-carriage company to go into operation. His vehicles, which could reach speeds of up to 20 miles per hour, initially ran from central London to the suburbs of Hampstead, Highgate, Edgware, Stanmore and Barnet. However, in 1829 one of his carriages made the round trip between London and Bath in a day, averaging 14 miles per hour.[81] By 1831 a regular service between Gloucester and Cheltenham using Gurney's carriages, running four times a day, was attempted.[82] Although the design of the steam carriage owes a great deal to the conventional horse-drawn coach it was intended to supersede, Scharf, ever interested in new scientific and technological developments, has clearly shown the complicated piston-based mechanism of the undercarriage (contrasting with the rather simple tiller for steering), as well as the two chimneys located to the rear of the vehicle with seating above the rear-mounted boiler. Gurney's Steam Carriage was itself superseded by the opening of the first railways in the 1830s and by 1832 he stopped building them.[83]

41. *Constructing the Birmingham Railroad, near Chalk Farm, London (see pp. 43 and 51)*

1836
Pencil, with grey wash, (231 x 239)
1862,0614.418

In 1834, Robert Stephenson started work on the first railway linking London and Birmingham, cutting through north London and terminating at Euston. The opening up of this first railway linking the capital with the centre of industrial production in the Midlands would profoundly change the way both people and goods could be moved over long distances and around the country. The cutting of the tracks through the hitherto middle-class suburbs of north London also altered the face of the metropolis. Investors and the major railway companies, such as the London and Birmingham Company, eagerly bought up land in order to pull down whole swathes of housing to build tracks, bridges, viaducts, tunnels and the new termini – such as Euston Station. Charles Dickens, in his novel *Dombey and Son*, vividly described the way in which London was being changed by the railways, particularly the Birmingham railway:

> The first shock of a great earthquake had, just at that period, rent the whole neighbourhood to its centre. Traces of its course were visible on every side. Houses were knocked down; streets broken through and stopped; deep pits and trenches dug in the ground; enormous heaps of earth and clay thrown up; buildings that were undermined and shaking, propped by great beams of wood. Here, a chaos of carts, overthrown and jumbled together, lay topsy-turvy at the bottom of a steep unnatural hill; there, confused treasures of iron soaked and rusted in something that had accidentally become a pond. Everywhere were bridges that led nowhere; thoroughfares that were wholly impassable; Babel towers of chimneys, wanting half their height; temporary wooden houses and enclosures, in the most unlikely situations; carcases of ragged tenements, and fragments of unfinished walls and arches, and piles of scaffolding, and wildernesses of bricks, and giant forms of cranes, and tripods straddling above nothing. There were a hundred thousand shapes and substances of incompleteness, wildly mingled out of their places, upside down, burrowing in the earth, aspiring in the air, mouldering in the water, and unintelligible as any dream. Hot springs and fiery eruptions, the usual attendants upon earthquakes, lent their contributions of confusion to the scene. Boiling water hissed and heaved within dilapidated walls; whence, also, the glare and roar of flames came issuing forth; and mounds of ashes blocked up rights of way, and wholly changed the law and custom of the neighbourhood. In short, the yet unfinished and unopened Railroad was in progress; and, from the very core of all this dire disorder, trailed smoothly away, upon its mighty course of civilisation and improvement.[84]

42. *Terminus of the North-West Railway, Euston Square*

1843
Pencil, (91 x 164)
1862,0614.419

The novelty of the railway provided an inspiration for many artists in the 1830s and 1840s – Scharf included – as 'railway mania' swept the country.[85] He mentions in his journal his first glimpse of an engine: 'Me and Henry went on the Birmingham Railroad near the tunnel through which we looked for the first time and saw a steam engine enter it, which was a very interesting sight, they were beginning a handsome stone arch at the entrance near Chalk Farm, near which I took a sketch the summer before.'[86] Passenger carriage design for the new railways was slow to develop and in this small, loosely handled sketch, Scharf has shown the open carriages that were in common use for third class passengers up until the 1840s when an Act of Parliament

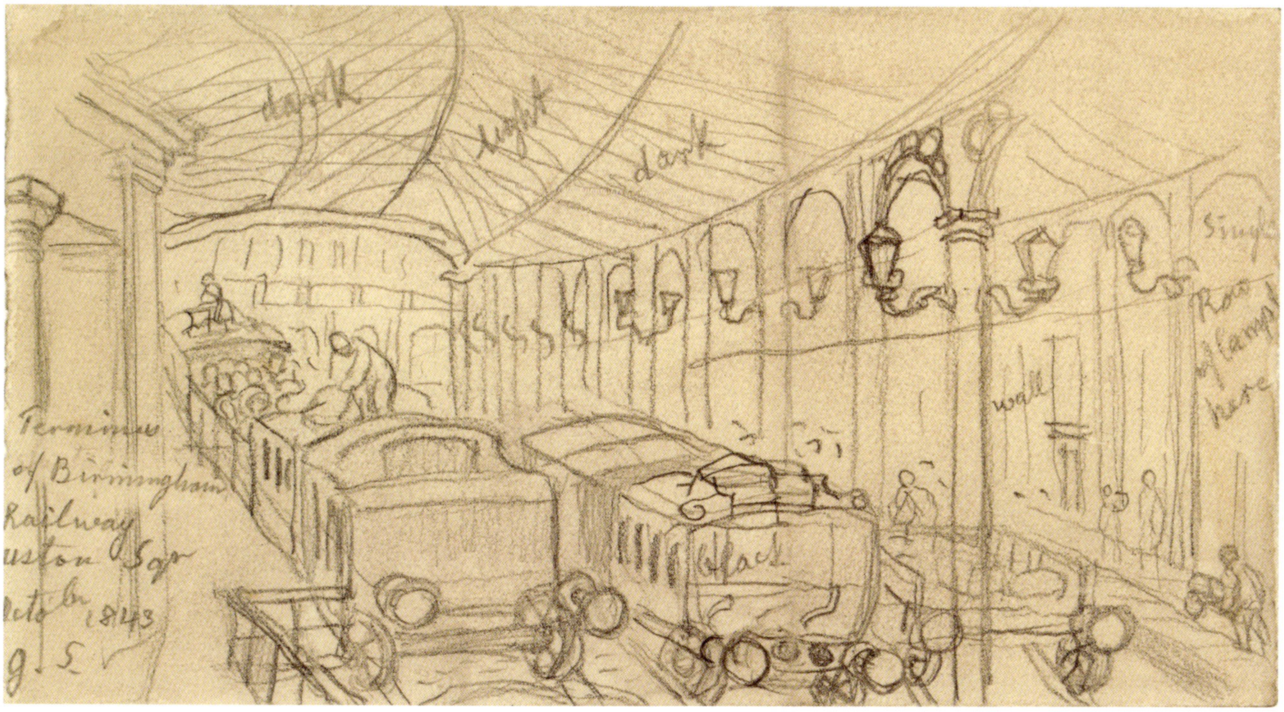

was passed in 1844 requiring all carriages to be enclosed.[87] In the carriage, towards the left, the heads of the passengers are clearly shown. A trunk is being loaded into the carriage in front. Euston Station was opened in 1837 with one platform for arrivals and one for departures. The arch that Scharf mentions in his journal entry refers to the monumental Doric screen that was built in front of the entrance in 1838, designed by Philip Hardwick (1792–1870). Scharf also drew this monument (BM 1862,0614.769). The screen was demolished in 1963 when London's oldest main-line terminal was redeveloped.[88]

43. *Lime kiln on the canal near Kingsland, London (see p. 44)*

1824
Watercolour over pencil, (141 x 237)
1862,0614.546

This view shows a section of the Regent's Canal as it crossed eastwards across Kingsland towards Hackney. The canal, which transported goods and raw materials, linked the Grand Junction Canal at Paddington Basin with the Thames at Stepney. Started in 1812 it was built by the engineer and architect James Morgan (*c.*1773–1856).[89] With the opening of the Birmingham Railway in 1838 the Regent's Canal saw a marked increase in the amount of goods being transported using it, particularly coal for the railways. The changing face of London demanded the transportation of huge quantities of building material; between 1823 and 1832 the tonnage of material being supplied by the canal for London's booming building trade doubled. The lime kiln that Scharf has shown in this view would have supplied the raw materials for the production of mortar for bricklaying and was ideally located in order to receive the limestone used in making quicklime from quarries outside London and then transporting quicklime to the suburbs of west London then under construction.[90]

Commercial London

44. *A Cowkeeper's shop in Golden Lane (see p. 53)*

1825
Watercolour, (140 x 225)
1862,0614.120

45. *The Westminster Dairy in the Quadrant, Regent Street, near Piccadilly Circus*

1825
Watercolour, (228 x 138)
1862,0614.122

From the mid-eighteenth century London, as the capital of the largest maritime trading empire that had yet arisen, was probably the greatest shopping emporium of the globe. It was certainly the largest city in the world and its inhabitants became fashionable consumers and in cat. 44 and cat. 45, Scharf examines the change in taste amongst Londoners. The two drawings were purposefully paired as Scharf explained on a note written on cat. 44: 'This I drew in Golden Lane in order to compare it with an elegant milk shop in the Quadrant, Piccadilly.' Golden Lane, in the East End, was located in one of the less salubrious areas of the city and was a well known hideout for thieves.[91] Scharf has shown the old milk shop front; a plaster cow advertising the shop's trade, recalls the old fashioned eighteenth-century shop signs that by the 1820s had been removed from the landscape of the street in more fashionable areas.[92] Milk and eggs are being sold fresh from the animals from the counter to the left – at the back of the shop Scharf has clearly shown the cows waiting to be milked in their stalls. In marked contrast, the fashionable Westminster Dairy presents an elegant frontage behind the Doric portico, which ran the length of the Quadrant, the curved section of the street between Piccadilly and Oxford Street. It sheltered the elegant pedestrians of Regent Street, as depicted by Scharf on the right, from the elements. Regent Street was laid out by Nash, building work finally being completed in 1820, as a thoroughfare that would connect Carlton House with Regent's Park. Named after the Prince Regent, it soon became a fashionable shopping street which specialised in imported and luxury goods and even saw the development of the precursors of today's department stores. Redeveloped between 1916 and 1920, Nash's Quadrant still remains one of London's prime shopping areas.[93]

46. *Old Covent Garden Market (see p. 54)*

1825
Watercolour, (248 x 379)
1862,0614.31

The name Covent Garden derives from the fields that formerly belonged to Wesminster Abbey or 'convent'. In the 1630s, Francis Russell, Fourth Duke of Bedford, commissioned Inigo Jones to design a magnificent new Italianate *piazza* on the land that would be the equivalent of the Place des Vosges in Paris. This would be the first of London's great squares. By 1656, though, it was also the location of a temporary market that traded from the gardens of Bedford House.[94] In 1670, this temporary market was granted a new licence allowing it to be held every day apart from Sundays and Christmas Day. This allowed Covent Garden Market to grow and develop, becoming one of London's busiest, crowded and chaotic markets. Scharf has shown the ramshackle wooden structures of the stalls, their lead roofs clearly visible, in this the north side of the market, which was probably one of the busiest areas. As there was no provision for storage in the open-sided stalls, goods and empty baskets were sometimes kept on the lead roofs. The lively Market also attracted many street entertainers (as it still does today). In his journal entry

45

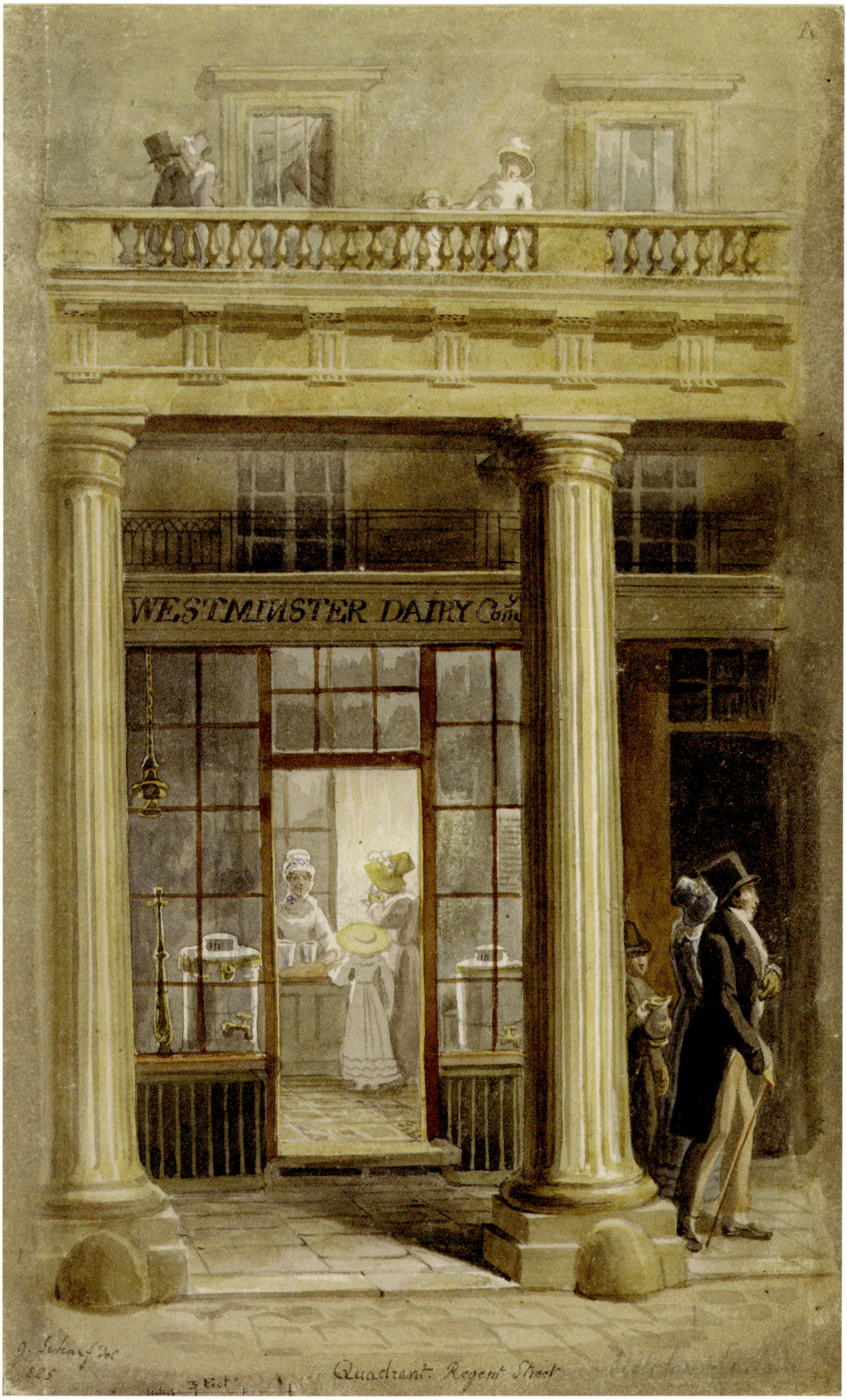
WESTMINSTER DAIRY Comp
G. Scharf Del
1825
Quadrant Regent Street

for 14 January 1837, Scharf describes: '... in going through Covent Garden Market I saw a stuffed shark, exhibited by a man, on a little wagon drawn by two dogs; it was very curious and about 12 feet long'.[95] By the 1820s it was clear that the facilities of the old market were inadequate and in 1828 a new act was passed for the regulation of trade. As part of this the old stalls, which Scharf had drawn, were to be replaced with the new market buildings, built by Charles Fowler (1792–1867), which stand to this day.

47. *Allen's shop in St Martin's Lane, near St Martin's Court*

1829
Watercolour, (138 x 227)
1862,0614.119

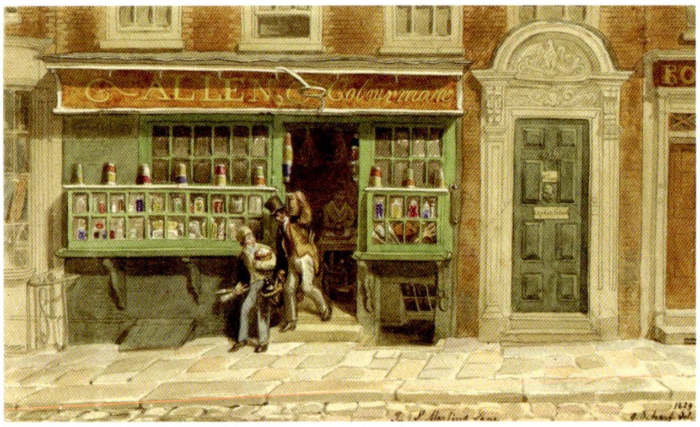

St Martin's Lane, where Scharf lived from 1817 to 1830, was associated with artists and fashionable artisans from the seventeenth century onwards. Amongst the residents of the area were Sir James Thornhill (1675/6–1734), Sir Joshua Reynolds (1723–1792) and Henry Fuseli (1741–1825). In 1735, William Hogarth (1697–1764) instigated the founding of the St Martin's Lane Academy, where artists could draw from the male and female nude and where sculpture and painting were also taught.[96] In addition, Thomas Chippendale (bap.1718, d.1779) lived at and ran his business from Nos 60–61.[97] Allen's Colourman, situated a few doors away from Scharf's house at No. 96, was run by one Edward Prascey Allen. The shop, which is recorded as an artists' supply shop from the 1790s at least, was located in the converted ground floor of one of the fashionable residences that had developed along St Martin's Lane in the late 1600s. Originally it had been the residence of the notorious French doctor John Misaubin (1673–1734) who made his living selling a quack cure for venereal disease.[98] The ornate doorcase to the right in all probability dates to the period of residence by Misaubin, who had employed the French painter Andien de Clermont (active 1716–1783) to decorate the interiors of the impressive townhouse. When Scharf painted this view, a late eighteenth-century shop front had been inserted into the façade of the once fashionable residence with jars of colours and brushes clearly displayed in the window. A sign on the door of the house announces that the rest of the house has been taken over by a school for ladies, run by one Sarah Watts. It has been suggested that the figures of the adult man and boy might be Scharf and his son George.[99]

48. *A sheet of flyposters*

1815–1860
Watercolour over pencil, pen and black and brown ink, on two conjoined sheets, (225 x 131)
1862,0614.1190

49. *A sheet of flyposters*

1815–1860
Pen and black ink and watercolour, (126 x 142)
1862,0614.1191

The rise of mass consumer culture, and with it a visually aware public in London, also resulted in the development of early advertising. London's streets were full of placard holders whose aim was to attract consumers to the various services, goods or amusements that were on offer to the everyday Londoner in the 1820s to 1830s. In addition the walls of buildings were plastered with flyposters, such as the ones

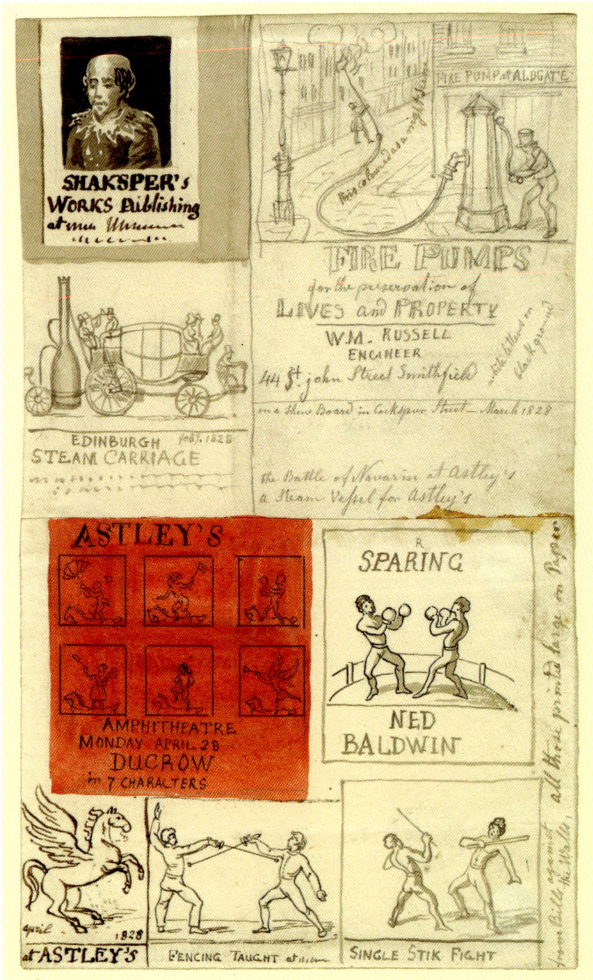

48

49

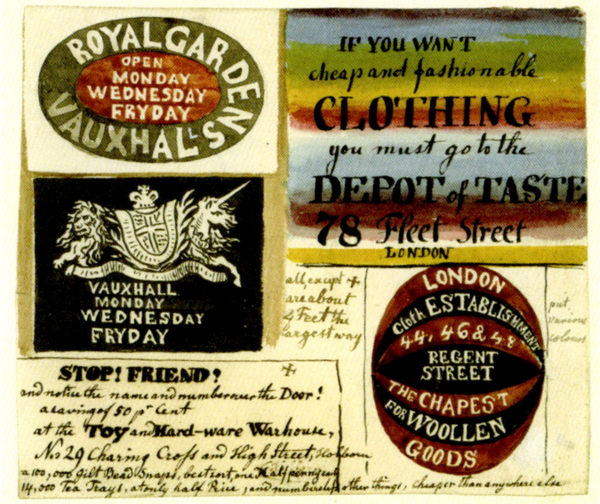

advertising the steam carriage to Edinburgh (see cat. 40) or the elaborate advert for fire pumps, whose composition recalls Scharf's drawing of a similar scene (see cat. 21). On the same sheet is an advert for Astley's Amphitheatre. This was located near Westminster Bridge and named after its powerfully-built owner, Philip Astley. It was a venue for various entertainments, such as equestrian, acrobatic, conjuring and other such displays. The well known clown, Grimaldi, performed there.[100] Often, these flyposters could be garishly coloured, such as the one ironically advertising the 'Depot of Taste', a clothing retailer in Fleet Street, in order to catch the eye of the passer by, or by addressing the reader directly as in the flyposter for a toy and hardware warehouse at No. 29 Charing Cross and High Street, Holborn, which instructs the passer to 'Stop friend!' and read the range of goods on offer. Scharf notes the size of these flyposters and records that they were 4 feet across at the widest extent. On the same sheet we see an advert for Royal Gardens, Vauxhall. The Royal Gardens, or simply Vauxhall Gardens, had, since the eighteenth century, been one of the most fashionable recreation areas of London. It continued so into the first quarter of the nineteenth century with many diversions organised for the entertainment of the London public. In 1827 a re-enactment of the Battle of Waterloo, which Scharf had participated in as a British officer, was held there.[101] Scharf's interest in brightly coloured mass cultural imagery and consumer advertising sets a very early precedent for the far later interest in this field by modernist artists such as Pablo Picasso, Georges Braque or by later Pop artists like Andy Warhol and Richard Hamilton.

Soane and Scharf

50. *Part of Mansion House Street, and corner of the Bank of England*

1833
Pencil on three conjoined sheets, (372 x 228)
1862,0614.448-450

Scharf was aware of Sir John Soane's work as an architect who had shaped the face of Regency London. In fact he had attended a lecture composed by Soane, but read by Henry Howard, on 6 February 1834 at the Royal Academy.[102] As an avid museum goer he also visited No. 13 Lincoln's Inn Fields.[103] However, by about the 1830s, when Scharf started drawing the Bank of England, the octogenarian Soane's career as an architect was in decline. This is one of several studies that Scharf produced of the Bank of England (seen on the far right), and which would eventually lead to a lithographic print commission (see below). The Bank was

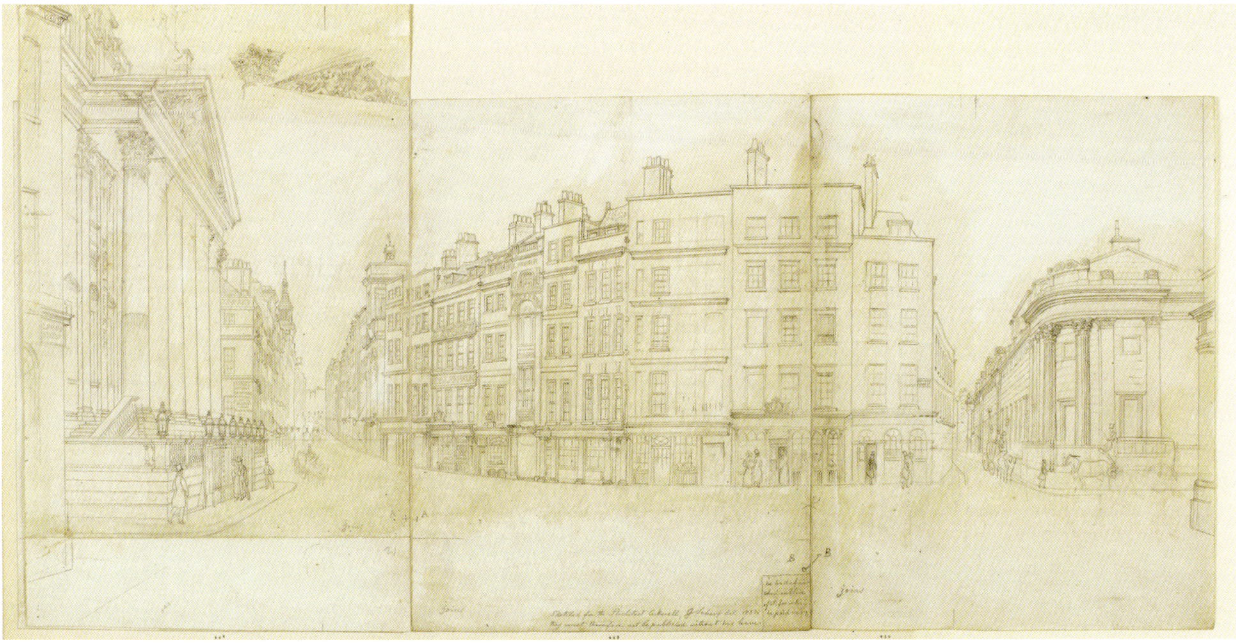

Soane's most famous building and when completed it became a notable landmark in London.[104] Here, Scharf has shown the corner of the Bank at the intersection of Mansion House Street and Princes Street. The corner is articulated by two Corinthian columns in the grand order and flanked by pilasters (see cat. 52). He has also shown the blank exterior screen walls, which formed a 'curtain wall' around the perimeter of the building. The 'windows' that can be seen in the attic storey and that recede into the distance along the St Bartholomew's Lane façade of the Bank are in fact blank and were used by Soane to relieve the plain curtain walls. In fact, he purposefully limited the number of actual windows or openings to the exterior of the Bank in order to express the '... strength and security ...' of the Bank in a manner reminiscent of a fortress.[105] His use of monumental Corinthian columns, derived from those of the Temple of Vesta at Tivoli and which can be clearly seen here expressed '... opulence ... masculine energy and luxuriant richness ...'.[106] To the right, Scharf has shown the portico of the Mansion House, with its richly carved tympanum (a separate study of its sculptural programme, along with a capital, can be seen just above this towards the left). The sculpture, by Sir Robert Taylor (1710–1788), shows a personification of London trampling *Envy* whilst Father Thames looks on.[107] The Mansion House was built from 1739 by George Dance the Elder. At the bottom of the three conjoined sheets that make up this view, Scharf has made a note stating that this sketch was produced for Charles Robert Cockerell, who became Architect of the Bank of England, following Soane's retirement in 1833. He has also noted how the three separate sheets should align correctly.

51. *The New Dividend Warrant and Pay Office, at the Bank of England 1835* *(see p. 21)*

Pencil, on two conjoined sheets, (237 x 374)
1862,0614.519

Following his 1833 sketch of the Bank, Scharf was engaged by Cockerell to sketch the New Dividend Warrant and Pay Office of the Bank of England for a lithograph of the same subject.[108] This drawing was a preparatory sketch for this print but does not reflect the final version of the lithograph, which showed the long perspective of the Office. Cockerell succeeded Sir John Soane as the Architect to the Bank of England in 1833 and extensively remodelled Soane's earlier structure.[109] The New Dividend Office was one of the rooms that Cockerell reconstructed. Cockerell's new rooms were situated in the south-west wing of the Bank and formed an open 'L'-shaped space that was subdivided into a three-aisled hall through the use of paired Corinthian columns, as seen in this view towards the right. Formerly, this space had been occupied by Soane's Dividend Warrant, Cheque and Bill Offices. Scharf has shown the western end of the Office, as he would in the lithograph, but here he has used a much narrower view than in the final print. The large, elaborate and rectangular prism-like structure in the centre of the room is a heating stove. Its florid form does not accord with the more sombre neo-classical stoves that Soane installed in the Bank. He notes that he has not drawn the stove to scale. Scharf records in his journals that the final lithograph, pulled from the stone by Hullmandel,[110] proved a success, with thirty employees of the Bank subscribing to it on the first day the finished print was shown there.[111]

52. *Capitals to pillars and pilasters at the Bank of England*

1833
Pencil, (71 x 136)
1862,0614.451

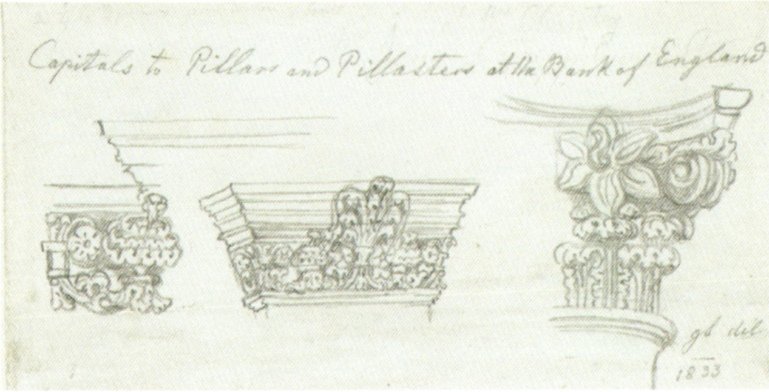

This small study of details of the Bank's architecture shows the opulence of Soane's architectural vision. Having seen the magnificent public buildings and spaces of Rome as a student, and being familiar with Paris, which he saw on his way to Rome and on two much later visits, he was aware that London lacked a really monumental urban architecture to rival that of the 'eternal city' or Napoleon's achievements. 'It is humiliating indeed, to see how much more numerous, more extensive, and more magnificent the public buildings are in all the great cities on the continent than in London' as he complained.[112] Soane's response to this perceived lack of urban monumentality was his Bank of England building which both in its grand conception and in its detailing, such as these capitals, addressed this lack of urban grandeur. Soane has used a particularly opulent form of the Corinthian order for the capitals of the pillars based on those seen at the Temple of Vesta, Tivoli, and has also used unusually decorative capitals on the antae pilasters along the Bank's façades, which are richly carved with floral motifs. These distinctive antae capitals were also used by Soane in the Lothbury and Governor's Courts of the Bank as well as his Privy Council Chamber, at the former Board of Trade Building, Whitehall (now the Cabinet Office). A plaster model of this distinctive capital hangs in the Upper Drawing Office of Sir John Soane's Museum. Such small-scale preparatory sketches, focusing upon one small detail or fragment of a composition, would have helped Scharf to create the type of highly resolved drawings of buildings, such as his drawing of the Mansion House and Bank of England or his accurate prints of buildings such as the lithograph of The New Dividend Warrant and Pay Office at the Bank of England (see cats 50 and 51).

The changing face of London

53. *View from the New River, Islington, London* (*see p. 14*)

1816
Watercolour, (243 x 372)
1862,0614.557

Scharf produced this drawing in 1816 and it is the earliest work that we know from his London period. It was the opening of the Regent's Canal in 1820 (see cat. 42) and also the cutting through of the London to Birmingham railway (see cat. 41) that would change the face of Islington, as industrial and slum tenement areas began to appear around York Way and the population increased rapidly. When Scharf drew this view, although these developments were in the not distant future, the Islington he has depicted still shows its rural character. In the early nineteenth century it was a fashionable place to take recreation in the fresh air along the banks of the New River, visible in the foreground of this drawing, which was an artificial canal cut through in 1613 to allow clean water from the River Lee to enter the capital. In the middle distance Scharf has shown the steeple of St Mary's, on Upper Street, of which only this steeple now survives following an air raid during World War II. On the distant horizon, to the left, the dome of St Paul's Cathedral is clearly visible.[113]

54. *A view in Brompton* (*see p. 46*)

1822
Watercolour, (246 x 363)
1900,0725.10

Originally a small village, to the west of Kensington, known as Broom Farm, Brompton only began to develop in the nineteenth century. When Scharf drew this view, along what is now the Fulham Road, the area was still characterised by its semi-rural nature with low-density housing; on the left a man is sitting on a stile with fields in the background. In fact, in 1820 it is recorded that some 520 acres of Brompton were used as farm land, including the famous Brompton Park Nursery, which now lies under the Victoria and Albert Museum. However, in this view modernity is beginning to creep in. Scharf has shown oil-burning street lights lining the road on the left, whilst in the far distance the terraces of Knightsbridge can be glimpsed.[114]

55. *Part of the ruins of St Stephen's Chapel, Palace of Westminster, after the fire*

1834
Watercolour over pencil, on two conjoined sheets, (496 x 271)
1862,0614.669

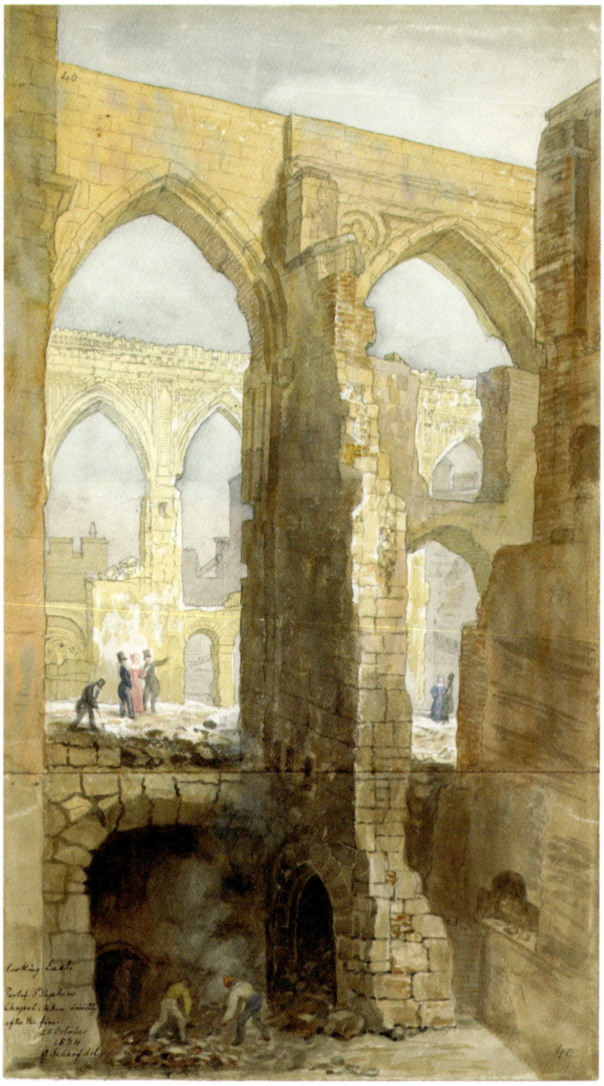

On the evening of 16 October 1834, at around six thirty, a stove in the old Palace of Westminster, which had become overheated due to too many tallies being forced into it for burning, set alight the old Medieval Palace of the Kings of England, including the famous Painted Chamber as well as St Stephen's Chapel, which dated to the reign of Henry III. The fire, burning through the night, was witnessed by large crowds of Londoners who had gathered by the Thames near Westminster Bridge.[115] Scharf went to the burnt- out site of the Palace the next morning, when the ruins were still smouldering, having received permission to sketch there from Sir Robert Smirke.[116] These various studies of the ruins were intended for three specific finished works or projects including a painting showing 'The Ruins of St Stephen's Chapel'; a large panorama, 'The Ruins of the Late Houses of

Parliament' and a lithograph of the same subject.[117] This drawing, and other studies in the British Museum, probably relate to the former.[118] The drawing is inscribed with both colour and descriptive notes that would have helped Scharf in the final composition although he mistakenly states that the view is taken looking east rather than north. He also notes that the drawing was made '... directly after the fire 25 October 1834 ...'. Scharf exhibited the finished painting at the Royal Academy, where he records it was given '... a good place ...'.[119] It was then hung in the King's entrance to the Houses of Parliament (see cat. 57), before finally going on display at Adelaide Street.[120] On 31 July and then again on 22 August 1835 Scharf called on Sir John Soane at 13 Lincoln's Inn Fields in order to try and sell the painting to him (see also cat. 56).[121] On both occasions Soane was out.[122] Scharf's poverty forced him to sell the painting at Christie's a few months before his death. The present location of this work is unknown.

56. *Panoramic View of the Ruins of the Late Houses of Parliament, 1834*

1834–1845
Pencil, watercolour (?) and oil on paper on canvas, (815 x 1415)
Collection of the Palace of Westminster
3793

This painting is probably Scharf's most significant work and he certainly accorded it great importance. The panorama can be understood to encapsulate his interest in architecture, historical monuments and the desire to be accorded the status of a recognised 'gentleman' artist rather than an artisan printmaker or mere watercolourist. It is also a highly idiosyncratic painting in part explained by its complex history. The work is painted using a mixed-media technique.[123] The underdrawing is in pencil, visible most clearly in the background section showing Westminster Bridge. Scharf then probably applied watercolour in a conventional manner, before re-working the composition in oil (see below). The broad, monumental sweep of the panorama, from the west wall of St Stephen's Chapel on the right to the distant Somerset House on the left, is seemingly an accurate and highly detailed depiction of the view.[124] Scharf has used a very high vantage point, positioning himself on the roof of Westminster Hall, from which the view is taken. He recorded in his journal how, whilst making preparatory sketches, '... it being dangerous to go into the ruins of St. Steven's Chapel [sic], I went upon the lead of Westminster Hall ... but staying until it was dark, and going to the door through which I came up and found it locked, after knocking and waiting for sometime, I called out to somebody in a court below who went to tell them of it at the Exchequer Office'.[125] The exaggerated foreshortening of the wall of St Stephen's Chapel, to the right and of Westminster Hall, to the left can be explained by Scharf's original intention to 'hinge' the painting along the far right edge. This second wing, which would have shown the view up to Westminster Abbey, is now missing but would originally have balanced the perspective of the surviving left-hand wing. This complex perspectival system seems to have given Scharf a number of compositional problems. This is most clearly evident in the radically foreshortened east wall

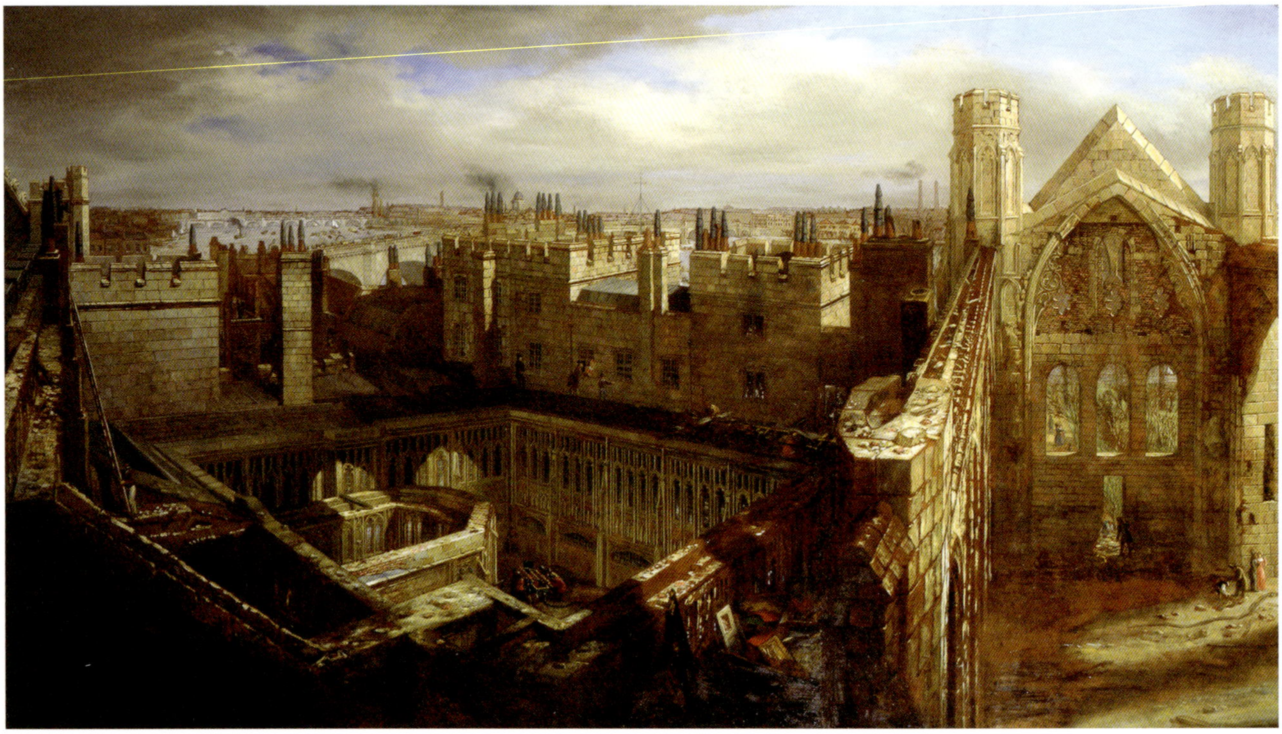

of the aforementioned Chapel. This section has been painted on a separate piece of paper that has been cut out and pasted on to the surface of the painting. Scharf has also reduced the number of bays of the cloister that surrounds the private Chapel of Henry VII, left, perhaps in an attempt to fit the architecture into the complex composition. He has similarly shortened the length of Westminster Hall on the left. Scharf's panorama was shown at the New Watercolour Society's Exhibition where it received an enthusiastic response and was then displayed in the Committee Room of the House of Lords. Probably because of this, Scharf undertook to publish a lithograph based on his sketches of the same subject. Scharf had already showed his drawings to Hullmandel who liked them.[126] On 27 November he decided to use these sketches of Westminster as the basis of the large-scale lithograph, 4 feet and 8 inches long by 18 inches wide.[127] It seems the project did not come to fruition, in spite of the fact that the Duke of Wellington and Charles Barry expressed interest and although an explanatory print of the proposed lithographic panorama was produced.[128] Following the display of the panorama at the New Watercolour Society, Scharf tried to sell it to Smirke without luck. He then offered it to the Trustees of the British Museum, again without success, then to the Queen and later the Board of Works.[129] Scharf returned to this painting once more on 12 August 1845, when in an attempt to make the painting more attractive to prospective buyers he records in his journal that he painted a fresh sky in oil over the original watercolour(?) one. At some other stage he reworked further sections in oil.[130] Scharf was forced to sell the panorama at auction shortly before his death. It raised the small sum of £2 10s, together with the painting of St Stephen's Chapel, at Christie's sale room. Thought lost since 1860, the panorama reappeared in 1993 in South Africa. It is likely that at some point after 1860 the right-hand side of the panorama was lost.

57. *Sketches of part of an iron gate at the entrance to the House of Lords*

1851
Pencil, on two conjoined sheets, (210 x 174)
1862,0614.670

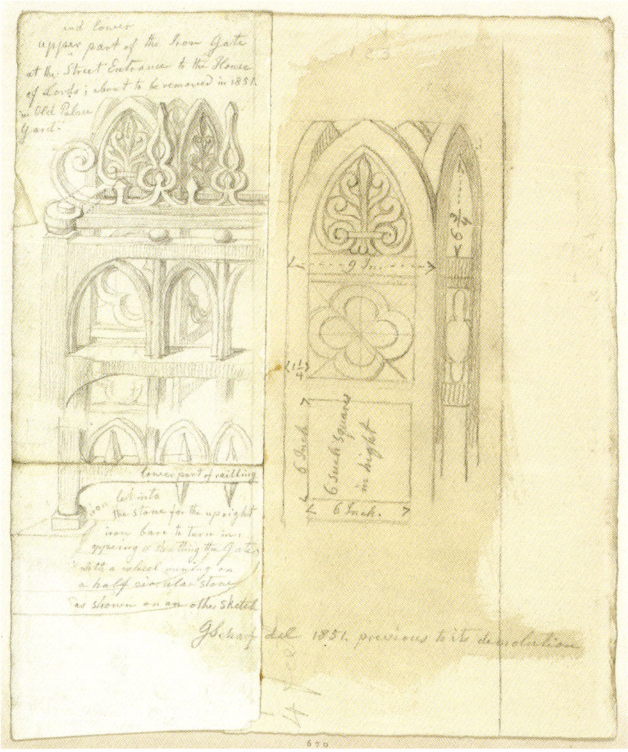

This drawing, inscribed in Scharf's hand, shows a gatepost and part of the gates at the entrance to the House of Lords.[131] The entrance to the Lords, leading to the *Scala Regia*, a monumental staircase, in neo-classical style, for use by the King when entering Parliament in procession, had been built by Sir John Soane from 1822 to 1823. The entrance included a curved cloister with an iron gateway, which Soane had designed in a neo-Gothic style in order to harmonise with an earlier range of buildings in that style by James Wyatt (1746–1813) (see cat. 58). In order to effect the transition between the Gothic forms of the cloister, Wyatt's range and the classical ones of the *Scala Regia*, Soane created a lobby, which, in keeping with the late phase of his architectural style, combined neo-classical and Gothic forms. The small fragment of decorative iron work in this sketch reflects this stylistic synthesis. The lancet-window form of the gate post is crowned by a Greek *anthemion* motif taken directly from the repertoire of Classical architecture. Below this is a Gothic *quatrefoil*. Soane's *Scala Regia* and his entrance to the House of Lords survived the fire of 1834; however, in the rebuilding of the Palace of Westminster they were pulled down in 1851. Scharf's small sketch is possibly the only record of the ironwork of the entrance to the House of Lords made just before Sir John Soane's additions to it were removed to make way for the present building. The purpose of this small study is unclear. Scharf records that by the beginning of March 1836, the final vestiges St Stephen's Chapel and parts of the old Palace of Westminster had been demolished before he had a chance to record all its details fully. He had to rely on sketches specially produced for him of the entrance of St Stephen's Chapel by another hand. On 22 March 1836, he began a small drawing the 'Ruins of the Entrance to the Late Houses of Parliament'. This drawing does not seem to be related to this work.

58. *Part of the Old Houses of Parliament and the New in progress, including the Victoria Tower (see p. 49)*

1851
Pencil, (235 x 314)
1862,0614.678

The competition for the rebuilding of the Palace of Westminster, following the fire of 1834, sparked a vigorous debate regarding the appropriate style to use between exponents of the neo-classical style and those who favoured a more 'national' style of architecture, such as the Elizabethan or Gothic.[132] In the end a compromise was reached. Charles Barry (1795–1860), an architect trained in the Classical tradition, was awarded the commission in 1836. However, as he had little experience in working in a historicist manner, Augustus Welby Northmore Pugin (1812–52) was chosen to clothe Barry's building in neo-Gothic ornament.

This highly detailed view shows three different building phases of the Houses of Parliament including a very recognisable part of the iconic building that we know today. Although dated to 1851 it still clearly shows Sir John Soane's neo-Gothic entrance to the House of Lords on the left (see cat. no. 57) which would finally be demolished in September of that year. The building with two superimposed thermal windows and a square castellated tower just to the right of this entrance belongs to James Wyatt's earlier range of buildings that housed the House of Lords. Between them, Scharf has shown the series of temporary, wooden structures that were built to house the various Parliamentary offices that had been displaced by the fire. However, the most important accent in the drawing is provided by the massive bulk of the Victoria Tower on the right-hand side. This tower would have a dual function in the newly rebuilt Palace. It would serve as a monumental entrance for the sovereign to replace Soane's old one and would also act as a repository for parliamentary records.[133] Though incomplete, it already looms over the lower and older surviving elements of the Palace. Pugin's Royal Beasts, flanking the lancet-shaped entrance portal can clearly be seen as can the slender clustered columns that articulate the façade of the Tower. When completed in 1855, the Victoria Tower would be the tallest and largest secular tower in the world standing at some 395 feet high, including the flagstaff.

59. *The Townley Gallery and the erecting of the New Gallery, the British Museum*

1828
Watercolour, (192 x 248)
1862,0614.626

The Townley Gallery of the British Museum, seen towards the left of this view, had been built in order to house the collection of classical sculpture amassed by Charles Townley (1737–1805), Trustee of the British Museum, and which entered its collections in 1805. Amongst these works was the

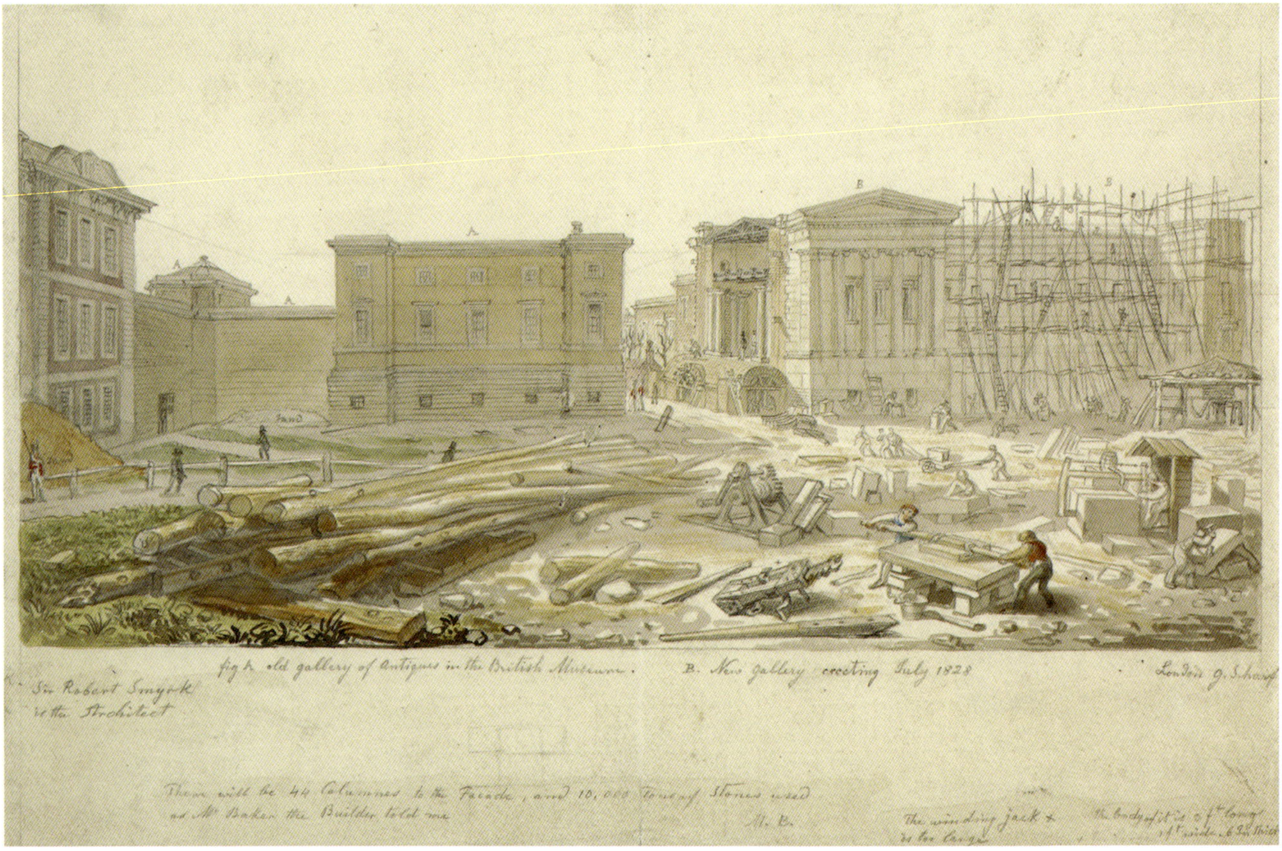

Roman copy of the famous Greek statue of the *Discobolus* and the *Townley Vase*, which inspired Keats to write 'Ode on a Grecian Urn', in 1819. Scharf produced a drawing showing part of the interior of this gallery with Townley's sculptures on display (BM 1862,0614.632). The building of the Gallery was located near the north-west corner of the old Montagu House (see cat. 34). This old seventeenth-century building can be seen on the far left of the drawing. As the collections of the British Museum expanded rapidly, in some part caused by the Napoleonic Wars through the acquisition of objects that were formerly in French collections, such as the renowned Rosetta Stone, Old Montagu House and the various structures that had grown around it, such as the Townley Gallery, proved too small for the Museum. In 1823, Smirke began work on creating a totally new building to house the Museum's collections. The new British Museum would become the most imposing example of Greek Revival architecture in London. Scharf notes the scale of the undertaking on the recto of this drawing: 'There will be 44 columns to the facade and 10,000 tons of stone used as Mr. Baker the builder told me.' The work was accomplished in stages, with the King's Library built first from 1823 to 1826, followed by the West Wing, which we see in this view. However, the West Wing was not fully completed until the Townley Gallery was pulled down in 1846. The large open space in the foreground of this view, formerly part of the garden of Montagu House and used as a builders' yard as work on Smirke's building progressed, would later become the site of the British Museum's Reading Room designed by Sydney Smirke, (1798–1877), the brother and pupil of Sir Robert Smirke who had started the rebuilding of the Museum.

60. *Group of men fitting and laying gas pipes (see p. 35)*

1834
Pencil, (230 x 138)
1862,0614.304.*

It was not just the building of London's great public monuments that drew Scharf's attention. He was also interested in the more mundane changes that were taking place in the city's streets, which would nevertheless change the way Londoners lived in their metropolis. He notes seeing the first asphalt pavements being laid near Oxford Street[134] and sketches sewers being laid in Fleet Street and gas mains in Tottenham Court Road (see figs 7, 10, 12 and cat. 28). Another improvement to the city's infrastructure is shown in this sketch of workmen laying a gas main. The cobbles of the road have been lifted, allowing the surprisingly shallow trench to be dug, into which the gas main is being laid. Scharf has clearly shown the connectors, spaced at regular intervals along the gas main, which would have piped the gas up to the lights, mounted on posts, at street level. Gas street lighting was first demonstrated in an experimental scheme for lighting Pall Mall in 1807. By 1823, there were four companies which supplied gas in London: the London Gas, Light and Coke Company; the City of London Gas Light Company; the South London Gas Light and Coke Company; and the Imperial Gas Light and Coke Company. With these four companies supplying London's needs, gas lighting soon replaced the old oil lamps in most of central London by about 1827.[135] In 1834, when Scharf sketched this view, the familiar network of underground gas and water mains beneath London's main streets was already in place although it took a little longer for gas lighting to be used in the domestic context. The perceived safety risk and the cost of the new lighting source acted as disincentives.

61. *View of the east side of the College showing demolition work and the roof lanterns of the old museum*

Grey wash, (255 x 300)
RCSSC/ P301

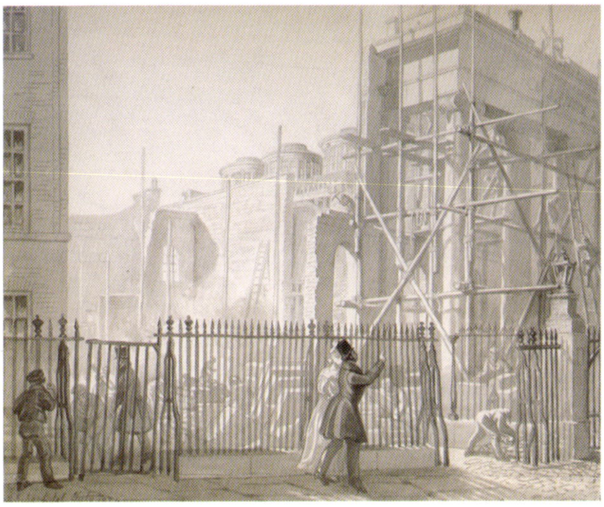

In 1800 the former Company of Surgeons received their royal charter and became the Royal College of Surgeons. To mark this change in status they undertook to rebuild and extend the two houses they had previously purchased on Lincoln's Inn Fields (Nos 41 and 42). This also allowed them to house the collections of John Hunter FRS (1728–93) whose collection of some 14,000 anatomical specimens had been purchased by the Government and entrusted to the care of the Company of Surgeons. This would become known as the Hunterian Collection and its range and scope matched those of European scientific and medical institutions. As one observer commented on the College and the Hunterian: 'The whole earth has been ransacked to enrich its stores.'[136] The architect commissioned to rebuild the Royal College of Surgeons was George Dance the Younger, (1741–1825), the teacher of Sir John Soane, and although the new building, completed in 1813, was not an imposing structure it did have a very fine Ionic portico of six plain columns. However, by the 1830s it became clear that Dance the Younger's building was no longer big enough to house the Royal College of Surgeons and in 1834 Charles Barry was called in to design a new building which entailed the demolition of the former College. In this view, Scharf has shown the demolition work in progress. The eastern end of the College has already been pulled down up to the entrance portico, which has been covered in protective scaffolding. Of the remaining structure, the most notable and visible features are the series of circular lantern-like skylights that lit the hall used to house the College's museum. Barry's building, including a new museum and library was opened in 1838.[137] Scharf was a regular visitor to the Royal College of Surgeons. He was employed by them to draw anatomical and fossil specimens, as well as produce lithographs of these subjects. He also attended many lectures that were held in the College and that were open to interested members of the public.

62. *View taken from the south-east, with five columns of the portico (see also p. 56)*

Watercolour, (710 x 560)
RCSSC/ P408

As part of Barry's rebuilding and extension work another adjoining house – No. 40 – was purchased by the Royal College of Surgeons. However, his plans for extending the College eastwards along the south side of Lincoln's Inn Fields were hampered by the College's insistence that Dance's portico should be respected and incorporated into the new building. This would have made the new façade asymmetrical. In order to overcome this aesthetic, as well as structural, problem Barry opted to dismantle the outermost western column of the portico and re-erect it on the eastern end.[138] In this view, Scharf has shown the portico, looking north, as free-standing, following the demolition of the main body of the building. The westernmost column, which has already been dismantled, is still to be moved into its new position as evidenced by the rebate of the portico's architrave on the right. The western side of Lincoln's Inn Fields can clearly be seen in the background, as can one of the new gas lamps on the gate post to the square on the right-hand side. These were installed from 1819 to 1823 and replaced the old oil lighting in the square. Some of the obelisk bases for these older oil lamps were saved by Sir John Soane and can be seen in the Monk's Yard and at the western end of the Crypt in his Museum.

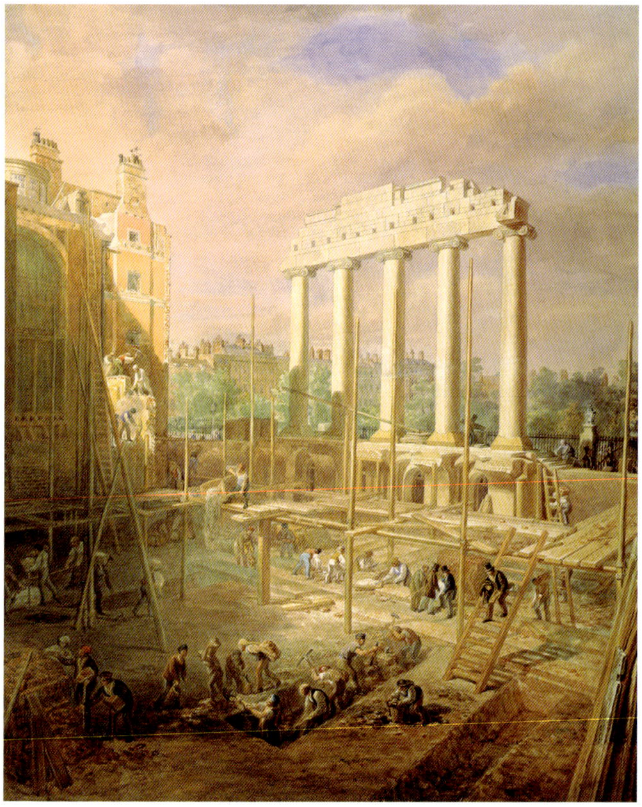

1 In 1815 the annual Nuremberg Albrecht Dürer Day was inaugurated, which would be celebrated up until the end of the nineteenth century. In 1840, the world's first public monument to an artist – a bronze statue of Dürer – was erected on the Milk Market in Nuremberg. It is likely that Scharf would have seen this statue. For an account of the 'Dürer cult' see Koener, Joseph, *The Moment of Self-Portraiture in German Renaissance Art*, The University of Chicago Press: Chicago, 1993, pp. 188–189
2 Journal entry dated 15 June 1839
3 *Regulations for the Dress of General, Staff and Regimental Officers of the Army*, the Adjutant-General's Office, Horse Guards: London, 1831
4 See also footnote 29 p. 24
5 Jackson, Peter, *George Scharf's London: Sketches and Watercolours of a Changing City. 1820–50*, John Murray: London, 1987, p. 31
6 Journal entry 17 March 1847
7 Peter Jackson, 'Scharf, George Johann (1788–1860)', *Oxford Dictionary of National Biography*, Oxford University Press, 2004 [http://www.oxforddnb.com/view/article/24795, accessed 18 Nov 2008]
8 Francisca de Haan, 'Fry , Elizabeth (1780–1845)', *Oxford Dictionary of National Biography*, Oxford University Press, Sept 2004; online edn, May 2007 [http://www.oxforddnb.com/view/article/10208, accessed 18 Nov 2008]
9 Fry also notably advocated the need for female prisoners to be '. . . under the care of women . . .' and in separate prisons. She published her views in 1827 under the title *Observations on the Visiting, Superintendence, and Government, of Female Prisoners*, followed, in 1840 by *Hints on the Advantages and Duties of Ladies Committees who Visit Prisons*
10 Journal entry 16 January 1838
11 Journal entry Monday 31 December 1838
12 Journal entry 17 October 1838. This entry states that his son '. . . did it [the portrait] very well'
13 George Scharf the Younger was conceived before his parents married. The late Scharf scholar, Peter Jackson, in unpublished research, suggests that the social stigma this may have caused the future Sir George Scharf the Younger may have been the cause of the later rift between father and son. I am grateful to Mrs Valerie Jackson Harris for providing this information
14 Tellingly, in 1839, he drew a self-portrait and a portrait of George the Younger, which he intended to send to his brother in Bavaria. The journal entry recording this does not mention whether a portrait of Henry was also made at the same time
15 Later regulations for court dress prohibited lace and specified cambric instead. I am indebted to Lucetta Johnson, the Courtauld Institute of Art, and Meg Dorman, Kensington Palace, for this information
16 Journal entry 16 January 1838
17 His father would also work on Layard's books. See journal entry end October 1850 where Scharf the Elder states that he sketched a 'middle-sized' Assyrian Bull for the second edition of Layard's book on Nineveh
18 Peter Jackson, 'Scharf, Sir George (1820–1895)', *Oxford Dictionary of National Biography*, Oxford University Press, Sept 2004; online edn, Jan 2008 [http://www.oxforddnb.com/view/article/24796, accessed 19 Nov 2008]
19 In particular he mentions 'Mr Doggett the iron-monger's house', which is not shown in this view of Bishopsgate Street
20 In this respect, he follows a quite traditional pattern for the use of sketchbooks filled with 'stock' figure studies set by artists from at least the fifteenth century onwards. Notable examples include the albums of sketches by Jacopo Bellini in the British Museum and in the Louvre
21 Journal entry 14 April 1836, Scharf mentions 'outlining' once more, a sketch of a woman receiving alms on Maundy Thursday, that he had originally drawn in 1830
22 Romilly tragically committed suicide following the death of his wife shortly after being elected
23 Sir John Soane, as one of the architects engaged by the Office of Works, was responsible for Westminster Hall. However, he declined the responsibility of arranging the Hall for the Coronation Banquet as he felt he would 'sink [under the] frightful responsibility of the task'. See Colvin, H., Ed., *History of the Kings Works*, Vol. VI, 1782–1851, Her Majesty's Stationery Office: London, 1979, p. 649
24 The significance of this choice of costume was used to mark visually the explicit difference between the 'revolutionary' origin of Napoleon's regime and that of the British monarchy. Napoleon's coronation robes, in part inspired by 'classical' prototypes, had been designed by Jean-Baptiste Isabey. See Cumming, Valerie, 'Pantomine and Pageantry: The Coronation of George IV' in *London: World City 1800–1840*, Fox, Celina Ed., Exh. Cat., The Museum of London, London, 1992, pp. 45–46
25 Prince Pükler Muskau in Cumming, Valerie, 1992, op. cit., p. 39
26 Ibid., p. 47
27 *The Sun*, 28 June 1838, p.4
28 Cumming, Valerie, 1992, op. cit., p. 47
29 Schwarzbach, F S, 'George Scharf and Early Victorian London', in *Victorian Artist and the city: A Collection of Critical Essays*, Nadel, Ira Bruce and Schwarzbach, F S, Eds, Pergamon Press: Elmford, New York, 1979, p.95
30 *The London Encyclopedia*, Weinreb, Ben and Hibbert, Christopher, Eds, Papermac: London, 1993, p. 498
31 O'Connell, Shelia et al., *London 1753*, Exh. Cat., The British Museum, London, 2003, p. 64
32 Journal entry 9 November 1833
33 Weinreb, Ben and Hibbert, Christopher, Eds, 1993, op. cit., p. 496
34 Kelly, William, 'The Great Mace and other Corporation Insignia of the Borough of Leicester', *The Royal Historical Society*, 1874, p. 20
35 Weinreb, Ben and Hibbert, Christopher, Eds, 1993, op. cit., p. 496
36 Ibid.
37 Ibid., pp. 353–54
38 Ibid., p. 354
39 It has been suggested that Sir Christopher Wren (1632–1732) designed the reconstruction. The present form of the Hall dates to 1862 when a new roof, more in keeping with the Gothic architecture of the Hall, was added. See ibid.
40 Journal entry 9 February 1835
41 In his journal entry for 1 October 1836, Scharf states that he sent this print, along with his lithograph of the Bank of England (see cats 18 and 51), to his former classmate Gaetner, who was now a professor at the Royal Academy in Munich, as a present
42 Journal entry 1 June 1834
43 These included an exhibition of a wax anatomical study by 'Signior Seratoni of Florence', a model of St Peter's in Rome by 'C.Vai of Brescia', a collection of armour '. . . used at the Egyptian tournament . . .', as well as an exhibition of North American 'curiosities' and an exhibition of painting and sculpture at the British Institution in Pall Mall. For a discussion of nineteenth-century exhibitions see Altick, Richard D, *The Shows of London: A Panoramic History of Exhibitions, 1600–1862*, Harvard University Press: London and Cambridge, Massachusetts, 1978
44 See Pearce, S, 'Giovanni Battista Belzoni Discovers the Tomb of Seti I in the Valley of the Kings' in *The Collectors Voice: Critical Readings in the Practice of Collecting*, Pearce, S, and Bounia, A, Eds, Ashgate Publishing Ltd: Farnham, 2002, pp. 98–105
45 Schwarzbach, F S, op. cit., p. 95. The present location of this sketch is unknown
46 This uniform is similar to that worn by the 'Beefeaters' or Yeomen Warders although the Yeomen of the Guard are distinguished by their crossed belts
47 See Weinreb, Ben and Hibbert, Christopher Eds, 1993, op. cit., pp. 904–906 and Jackson, P, 1987, op. cit., pp. 20–21
48 Journal entry 3 July 1835
49 Journal entry 4 July 1835
50 Jackson, P, 1987,op. cit., p. 34
51 Ibid.
52 Journal entry 8 March 1846
53 O'Connell, Shelia et al., 2003, op. cit., pp. 77–81
54 Barringer, T, *Men at Work: Art and Labour in Victorian Britain*, Yale University Press: London and New Haven, 2005, p. 1
55 Ibid., p. 2
56 The Chartists, of whom Scharf was aware, presented petitions to Parliament in 1839, 1842 and 1848 which called for workers' rights and the first trade unions began to form, including the Grand National Consolidated Trades Union, which operated from 1833 to 1834
57 This Act was primarily concerned with the regulation of the textile industry. It was followed by the Factory Act of 1842 (or Ten-Hour Act) which restricted working hours for women and children to ten hours per day
58 The Architectural Publishing Society, *The Dictionary of Architecture*, Whiting and Co.: London, 1892, Vol. VIII, p. 83
59 See: Priestly, J B, *The Prince of Pleasure and His Regency 1811-20*, Sphere Books Ltd: London, 1971, pp. 113–137
60 In order to gain access to the collections of the British Museum, visitors were required to apply for tickets by leaving their name, rank and address at the door in person. The request for admission would then be processed, although it could take some time. Visits to the collections were by guided tour only. It is recorded that in 1776 visitors who had applied for admission for April of that year were still waiting in August for their tickets. This state continued into the early nineteenth century. In 1808 some 2,500 visitors were admitted. One of these, Benjamin Silliman, complained: 'It is really distressing to be summoned by a host of things which are full of information, and then be hurried away from them just as one is beginning to single out particular objects.' See: Altick, Richard D, 1978, op. cit., pp. 30 and 440–42
61 In 1807 the requirement for tickets was dropped by the British Museum, allowing free admittance to 'any person of decent appearance', although limiting numbers to 120 visitors per day. Ibid., p.440
62 Journal entry 19 May 1845
63 In fact, Scharf erroneously believed that Montagu House had been built by the French King Louis XIV. See journal entry 14 August 1845
64 Jackson, P, 1987, op. cit., p. 98
65 Journal entry 27 September 1845
66 See journal entry 23 November 1833
67 Journal entry 25 April 1837

68 Brookes, Joshua, *A Prodromus of a Synopsis Animalium compromising a Catalogue Raisonné of the Zootomical Collection of Joshua Brookes, Esq. FRS etc.*, Gold and Walton: London, 1828

69 Knox, Tim, 'Joshua Brookes' Vivarium: An Anatomist's Garden In Blenheim Street, W1', in: *The London Gardener*, vol. III, 1997–1998, p. 33

70 Ibid., p. 34

71 Ibid., p. 30. See also correspondence from Sir Joshua Brookes to Sir John Soane dated 30 April 1830, Sir John Soane's Museum, Priv. Corr. I-B-18-1. I am grateful to Helen Dorey for drawing my attention to this letter

72 Correspondence from Sir Joshua Brookes to Sir John Soane dated 30 April 1830, Sir John Soane's Museum, Priv. Corr. I-B-18-1

73 Ibid. Soane also possessed a copy of the 1827 catalogue of the Brookesian's collections (Sir John Soane's Museum, PC47.1)

74 In a note sent to his friend and biographer John Forster, Dickens proposed an excursion to the 'Castle' by extolling the merits of its food and drink: 'You don't feel disposed, do you, to muffle yourself up, and start off with me for a good brisk walk over Hampstead Heath? I know a good 'ous there where we can have a red-hot chop for dinner, and a glass of good wine'

75 See Jackson, P, 1987, op. cit., p. 144 and Weinreb, Ben and Hibbert, Christopher Eds., 1993, op. cit., p. 427

76 Fox, Celina Ed., 1992, op. cit. p. 379

77 Ibid., p. 377

78 The gun was said to be able to fire at a rate of seventy bullets per four seconds, although it is probable that the actual figure was lower. Ibid., p. 378

79 See journal entry 22 November 1833

80 Journal entry 14 August 1833

81 It did break down on the way however. See Fox, Celina Ed., 1992, op. cit., p. 325

82 Ibid.

83 Ibid.

84 Dickens, Charles, *Dombey and Son*, Bradbury and Evans: London, 1848, p. 46

85 Turner's 'Rain, Steam and Speed', the National Gallery, London, before 1844, is the most celebrated example of an artist's response to 'railway mania'

86 Journal entry 22 April 1837

87 Harter, Jim, *World Railways of the Nineteenth Century: A Political History in Victorian Engravings*, Johns Hopkins University: Baltimore, 2005, pp. 247–248

88 Weinreb, Ben and Hibbert, Christopher Eds, 1993, op. cit., p. 273

89 Ibid., p. 662

90 Baker, T F T, et al., 'Islington Communications', in *A History of Middlesex: Islington and Stoke Newington Parishes*, Vol. 8, Victoria County History, 1985, pp. 3–8

91 Charles Dickens used it for inspiration. See Jackson, P, 1987, op. cit., p. 45

92 For a description of the disappearance of shop-signs see: O'Connell, Shelia et al., 2003, op. cit., pp. 52–55

93 Weinreb, Ben and Hibbert, Christopher Eds, 1993, op. cit., pp. 660–662

94 O'Connell, Shelia et al., 2003, op. cit., p. 131

95 Journal entry 14 January 1837

96 O' Connell, Shelia et al., 2003, op. cit., pp. 161–163

97 Weinreb, Ben and Hibbert, Christopher Eds, 1993, op. cit., p. 756

98 Misaubin's notoriety was so great that Hogarth based the figure of the Doctor in the third plate of his 'Marriage à la Mode' – 'The Inspection', c.1743, on the Frenchman. See Hallett, M, and Riding, C, *Hogarth*, Exh. Cat., Tate Britain: London, 2006

99 Jackson, P, 1987, op. cit., p. 32

100 Weinreb, Ben and Hibbert, Christopher, Eds, 1993, op. cit., pp. 29–30

101 Ibid., pp. 936–38

102 This was originally given by Soane in 1819, and was Lecture No.V in his course of lectures as Professor of Architecture at the Royal Academy. In it Soane explained the origins of Gothic architecture, which he praises, by way of describing the demolition of the old pagan monuments of Rome. He then goes on to lament the loss of many fine houses in London, especially those located on the Strand. Scharf recorded the Strand prior to its redevelopment (see cat. 21), documenting the very houses which replaced the mansions Soane talked of. Scharf may also have been inspired to record the ruins of the Old Palace of Westminster having heard this lecture (see cats 55, 56, 57 and 58)

103 In his journal entry for 14 June 1844 we read: 'I. Mrs. [Scharf], Miss Hicks and Henry went out to see the late Mr. Soane's collections of Antiquities – pictures and models in Lincoln's Inn Fields, which is very interesting'

104 Amongst the more illustrious visitors was the Russian Tsar Alexander I who visited the Bank in 1814 where he met Sir John Soane

105 Britton, John, *The Original Picture of London*, London, 1826, p.124 reprinted in *John Soane Architect: master of Space and Light*, Richardson, M, and Stevenson, M, Eds, Exh. Cat. Royal Academy of Arts, London, 1999, p. 210

106 Ibid.

107 Weinreb, Ben and Hibbert, Christopher, Eds, 1993, op. cit., p. 509

108 Journal entry 9 May 1835

109 Sir John Soane became Architect to the Bank of England in 1788, a post he held until 1833 when he was succeeded by Cockerell. Apart from the New Dividend Office, Cockerell reconstructed the Warrant, and Cheque and Accounting Offices in 1834–5 and subsequently remodelled them from 1848 to 1850 as an enlarged Private Drawing Office. Following the Chartist Riots of 1848, Cockrell reconstructed the attic storey of Soane's Bank to include a fortified parapet walk. Both Soane and Cockerell's interiors were lost when the Bank of England was gutted in the 1920s reconstruction of the building. For a full discussion of Soane and Cockerell's work on the Bank see: Abramson, Daniel M, *Building the Bank of England: Money, Architecture, Society 1694–1942*, Yale University Press: London and New Haven, 2005 and *John Soane: Master of Space and Light*, Richardson, M, and Stevenson, M, Eds, 1999, op. cit., pp. 208–251

110 Journal entry 12 April 1836

111 Journal entry 5 October 1836

112 Sir John Soane, Lecture No. XI, reprinted in Watkin, David, *Sir John Soane: Enlightenment Thought and the Royal Academy Lectures*, Cambridge University Press: Cambridge, 1996, p. 637

113 See Jackson, P, 1987, op. cit., pp.142–143, Weinreb, Ben and Hibbert, Christopher, Eds, 1993, op. cit., pp. 424–425, 758 and 953–959 and Ward, Robert, *London's New River*, Phillimore and Co. Ltd: London, 2003

114 See Jackson, P, 1987, op. cit., p. 145 and Weinreb, Ben and Hibbert, Christopher, Eds, 1993, op. cit., p. 99

115 Amongst them was Turner who famously recorded the destruction of the old Palace in a series of paintings

116 Journal entry 17 October 1834

117 Scharf also records in his journal entry for 10 April 1838 that: 'I made a model in pasteboard of a cosmoramic view of my picture of the Ruins of St Stephens, to be exhibited at the Gallery of Science Regent St'. This refers possibly to the smaller painting rather than the larger panorama. See: Jackson, P, 1987, op. cit. pp. 11–12 and 18. See also Anonymous 'Parliament fire picture comes to light after 100 years', *The Daily Telegraph*, London, 30 December 1993

118 BM 1862,0614.656*; 1862,0614.656; 664; 1862,0614.660; 1900,0725.15; 1900,0725.14 and 1900,0725.13

119 Journal entry 6 April 1836

120 Journal entry August 1836

121 Soane, as an Attached Architect to the Office of Works, had worked on the old Palace of Westminster (see cat. 57) and architectural fragments of the Gothic fabric of the Palace were incorporated into the Monk's Parlour and Monk's Yard at 13 Lincoln's Inn Fields. It is probable that Scharf approached Soane because of his work on the Palace. Smirke was also an Attached Architect to the Office of Works

122 Soane's diary records that from 24 July to 25 August 1835 he was staying in Worthing

123 The use of canvas backed paper, though unusual, was used by other artists in the eighteenth and nineteenth centuries, such as Thomas Jones, Frederick Leighton, William Holman Hunt and Ford Maddox Brown. See also Carlyle, L, *A Critical Analysis of Artist's handbooks, Manuals and Treatises on Oil Painting Published in Britain Between 1800–1900: With Reference to Selected Eighteenth Century Sources*, PhD thesis, the Courtauld Institute of Art, 1991

124 Scharf wanted also to produce a panorama of London, having been inspired by a panorama of ancient Rome that he had seen. See journal entry 15 February 1840

125 Journal entry 27 October 1834

126 Journal entry for 17 October 1834

127 Journal entry 22 August 1835

128 Journal entry 16 June 1836

129 Ibid.

130 In order to make the work seem more like a conventional oil painting the paper support was glued on to a canvas backing

131 St Stephen's Chapel was used as the House of Commons until the fire of 1834

132 For an account of this debate see Fredericksen, Andrea, 'Parliament's Genius Loci: The Politics of Place after the 1834 Fire', in *The Houses of Parliament: History, Art, Architecture*, Riding, Christine and Riding, Jacqueline, Eds, Merrell Publishers Ltd: London, 2000, pp. 99–111

133 For an account of the influence of Soane's Royal Entrance on the designs of the new Sovereign's Entrance to Parliament see Sawyer, Sean, 'Sir John Soane and the Late Georgian Origins of the Royal Entrance', in Riding, Christine and Riding, Jacqueline, Eds, 2000, op. cit., pp. 136–147

134 Journal entry 6 November 1838

135 A lecture drawing showing examples of gas street lamps, dated 1819, was prepared for Sir John Soane, although it was never used. See also Fox, Celina Ed, 1992, op. cit., pp. 291–93

136 Ibid., p.134

137 Ibid., p.133

138 Jackson, P, 1987, op. cit., p. 136